FUNDAMENTALS OF RESEARCH

ANUBHAA M WALIA
MANPREET UPPAL

Notion Press

No.8, 3rd Cross Street, CIT Colony,
Mylapore, Chennai,
Tamil Nadu-600004

First Published by Notion Press 2020
Copyright © Anubhaa M Walia & Manpreet Uppal 2020
All Rights Reserved.

ISBN

Paperback: 978-1-64892-644-0
Hardcase: 978-1-64892-649-5

This book has been published with all efforts taken to make the material error-free after the consent of the authors. However, the authors and the publisher do not assume and hereby disclaim any liability to any party for any loss, damage, or disruption caused by errors or omissions, whether such errors or omissions result from negligence, accident, or any other cause.

While every effort has been made to avoid any mistake or omission, this publication is being sold on the condition and understanding that neither the authors nor the publishers or printers would be liable in any manner to any person by reason of any mistake or omission in this publication or for any action taken or omitted to be taken or advice rendered or accepted on the basis of this work. For any defect in printing or binding the publishers will be liable only to replace the defective copy by another copy of this work then available.

To the epitomized men in our lives, our guardian angels in heaven,

Sh. Trilok Chand Maurya

&

S. Harmandar Singh Uppal

……can never thank you enough !

Preface

Academicians & industry professionals have always felt the need to study & incorporate 'Research' in their respective domains. The subject matter under the purview of research, therefore, though perplexing, finds huge relevance. Much work as such, has been done already in this subject and compiled in the form of far-ranging books touching a variety of concepts & sub-concepts.

As researchers in our own limited capacity, we read through a plethora of texts available over a stretched time frame in order to understand it all. And this brought us to the gap that existed, the soft spot which highlighted the need for our book, as presented here.

'Fundamentals of Research,' attempts to answer elementary queries and is primarily based on our first-hand experience as students of research, practitioners, teachers, and corporate professionals. In interactions spanning well over two decades, all of what we came across, from multiple rudimentary to advanced questions that perplexed, have found in this book, a compiled record.

This book, therefore, becomes our platform to put forth what we thought had always intrigued us. We have attempted to explain concepts from the grass-root level to their applicability in real-world situations. Bridging the academia-industry divide in thought processing & bringing congruence in intellectual disposition is the core ideology of this book. We have, as we move along with the discourse of the book, tried to explain & illustrate critical dimensions about research in its fundamental yet multidisciplinary applicability.

This book addresses students with an understanding of the research concepts and techniques, report writing, sampling, data collection, etc. with simple examples, caselets, and check your knowledge series. It forms an ideal text for readers with minimal knowledge of research as well as for those with intermediate knowledge who need a quick refresher regarding particular aspects of research design and methodology.

What made us write this book?

While the vague concept of this compilation was something we had always been brooding upon, ground reality started seeping in as we proceeded with our Doctoral researches. The urgency of finding answers, using the right instruments, measurements, left us struck by the expanse of this subject. They predominately existed an opportunity to explore & understand, and to keep up this thought, we started our journey in the winter months of 2019. Setting before us a clear timeline of a year, we moved ahead with our milestones prescribed in terms of the chapter and unit by unit advancement. The precise and clear objectives were: developing a clear understanding of appropriate methodology irrespective of discipline and explaining the usage of different research methods and techniques with realistic scenarios for a relatable context.

Continuing with our engagements at hand and balancing the work on the book, we treaded upon the path taken until we came to a stage the world noticed a jolt, COVID-19 Struck!. Panic attacks, depressive thoughts, anxiety, and insecurity were just some of the feelings we all went through, and amidst all, it became imperative to look upon the silver lining of positivity to pull through the dark days.

March 19th, 2020, outbreak, lockdown, and Janta curfew because of the COVID-19 pandemic aggravated the realization of extreme uncertainty on personal, professional & social fronts. None could predict how long and how much more damage it may bring to all. We had to be positive and wait for things to get better, and that is when what prevailed was a thought to utilize the gloom of quarantine to bring forth a new set of perspectives to the readers and utilize the six weeks of nationwide lockdown. To contribute our bit by way of compiling & presenting to our audience what remained pending as a brainstormed and a yet to synchronize project. As our efforts see the morning light, and we are finally ready to present our book, we are highly indebted to our students, corporate professionals from the analytics team, academicians, and learned colleagues for providing the necessary stimulus/inputs/details for writing this book. Our gratitude also to the reviewer of the manuscript of this book. At this point, we also would like to extend due credit to multiple existing texts on the subject that have been looked at and form the supporting ideology along with the subject. The book finds, besides the author's perspective, thoughts inspired by well-written pre-existing texts in the domain which guided us through. We present here a compilation of many along with our added dimension to the context.

We extend our heartfelt appreciation to all our near and dear ones in helping us write and prepare for this book. Being a woman and so realizing fully well the work-life balance dilemma of the lovely ladies around us, it becomes imperative here to thank: Chaanan, Ajooni, Kiran, Ashu, Zeri, Ellnaaz & our precious Tanvir forever encouraging us.

In the end, the most vital of all, our parents for there relentless motivation & constant push, and endearing support by our loving partners.

We look forward to suggestions from all our readers for further improving the subject content as well as the presentation of this book!

– Anubhaa & Manpreet

COVID-19 LOCKDOWN.......Yet the Positivity Prevailed!

"If you're trying to achieve, there will be roadblocks. I've had them; everybody has had them. But obstacles don't have to stop you. If you run into a wall, don't turn around and give up. Figure out how to climb it, go through it, or work around it."

– Michael Jordan

Having done some professional writing in our individual capacities, we as authors thought we could anticipate what it took to structure, plan, and align our thoughts in the form of a sequential array of topics. However, what we could not anticipate was the challenge the COVID-19 lockdown would throw onto us. The announcement of 'staying-in', 'no movement', coming to terms with the hard-hitting reality that while we were at a stage requiring working together uninterrupted for hours & days, we could not even for now possibly meet.

What seemed an obstacle, however reshaped into a resolve as we took on the Herculean task of a true 'work from home' on our book, working in pace, while at our own place.

What followed was a series of phone calls, Google meets & Skype sessions, spaced in-between by running tasks around the house devoid of any helps. The true picture of the work-life balance emerging as we juggled to and fro from 'Kitchen to Laptop' & from things around the house, to chapters around the book.

The final stages of the text at hand, the Q&A, and most importantly, the multiple rounds of proof-reading, all accomplished with no physical interface & in totality using the multiple modes of virtual communication.

Multiple mornings of, 'not possible' saw by the end of the day, 'Yes! we can', and emerged, 'The Fundamentals of Research' as you see it today.

The belief ***"If you hear a voice within you say 'you cannot paint', then by all means paint, and that voice will be silenced."*** **– Vincent van Gogh**

Presenting our first book & many more to follow!!

– The 'socially distanced' authors!

About the Authors

Dr. Anubhaa Maurya Walia

Human Process Interventionist, Trainer, Researcher & OD Consultant

Anubhaa completed her bachelor degree in commerce from Lady Shri Ram College and received a Ph.D. from School of Management, Indira Gandhi National Open University for her research project on "Followership styles and Leadership styles in selected Manufacturing and Servicing sectors'.

In a distinguished career spanning for over 20 years of rich experience, she has worked with Honeywell, ICICI Bank, Moody ICL Certification were she was heading L&D & Quality verticals, carries International certification of Facilitation by DDI (USA), Certified Coach by Mind Gym (UK), Certified Change Agent & People Management facilitator by Australian Institute of Management (Australia), and Six Sigma-Change Agent by ISI & QAI (India). She is a recipient of Emerging HRD thinker award (Gold Medalist) consecutive three times by Indian Society of Training & Development (Ministry of HRD).

She is founder of PRISM™ Philosophy (www.prismphilosophy.com), is a leading Training and OD consultancy firm, where training and learning is based on PRISM™ stand for Prepare, Respect, Implement, Share and Maintain.

She is a highly sought-after trainer/facilitator, speaker, and consultant at National & International level. Her active engagement in research work on Organisation Development, Leadership & Followership has been acknowledged and well received by a host of industry and academic publications.

You may reach her at anubhawalia@gmail.com and social media @anubhawalia.

Manpreet Uppal

Academician, Researcher, Trainer & Consultant

Manpreet Uppal is a University medal awardee in Hons. in Economics from Punjabi University, Patiala, followed by a Masters Degree in Marketing. Currently, she is pursuing her doctoral research with Aligarh Muslim University on understanding Customer relationship resources & trying to establish their impact on the Omni-channel retailer in the Indian retail scenario.

In an enriching career journey spanning over 20 years, the author has been proudly entrusted with pivotal roles in esteemed Universities, in core areas involving not only academic delivery but also developing and enhancing the course curricula. Curriculum development, redesigning & revamping the redundant with the contemporary, thereby working towards enhancing the student employability quotient continue being her forte.

Being a marketer and understanding the need to move beyond the classroom has led Manpreet to deep dive into assignments much larger. She has been deeply immersed in marketing platforms ranging from both offline & online, social networks being her ace up. Keen interest in maintaining the marketing interface of premier B-schools as also Universities, has enabled her understanding of the factual customer expectation and backing it by relevant deliverables spiced up with just the right amount of promotions.

With her current engagements, Manpreet is deeply involved in marketing development skills & productivity enhancement. She is best known for her engagement workshops through a series of factual correlations. Driving contents at prestigious online portals, authoring research publications across marketing & research, and striking an academic and industry blend by way of teaching at B-schools & Universities in the National Capital Region along with partnering in a series of corporate training & research consultancies are some of her accomplishments.

An augmenting experience of over two decades of teaching, training & consulting endow Manpreet with credentials that offer a unique combination of perspective and skills.

You may reach her at manpreetuppal0703@gmail.com and social media @manpreetuppal

Foreword

The first edition of this book 'Fundamentals of Research', provides an updated, comprehensive, and stepwise understanding of the research processes. Each chapter equips the audience with a balanced blend of theory, techniques, and illustrations from a broad perspective of industry situations to make the learning simplistic, entertaining, yet more systematic. The relevance of mapping the theoretical concepts touched to their application in industry & academia is never overlooked. The present book provides the necessary level discussion enabling researchers and students with familiarisation to the use of research methods and techniques. This book does not rely on presumptions and can be used equally at par by both students and industry professionals. The conceptual base has been put forth in a comprehensive yet simplistic way, addressing even the minutest explanations required by the reader. The book moves along an underlying path of sequential steps as it appears in research implementation. Each topic & subtopic dwelled upon, follows a series of chronological succession. The last chapter brushes on the persistent surge for analytics inclusion in business research. While analytics and it's in-depth coverage & applicability moves beyond the scope of this text, the author's intent is clearly to give the reader an overview into the next dimension of analysis & interpretations.

Upon completion of a preceding chapter and quick recaps by way of CYK's and progress test questions, the antecedent chapters and document fall into a logical progression. Besides self-checks & progress assessments, an exciting element of the book is the multiple caselets and exhibits for better and more practical understanding of concepts as fitted into scenario-based applicability. Diagrammatic representation of multiple concepts has been incorporated for easier recall and grasp. The inclusion of published research papers in established templates adds to the authenticity & verifiability of text.

Keywords included at the beginning of each chapter facilitate a quick close look at inclusions within each chapter, thereby enabling faster probe & discovery of interest areas along with the text.

The encapsulating touch comes in the form of a closing case that encompasses all domains & relevant research inputs touching upon all along with the discourse into a holistic application leading to realistic conclusions as per the reader's introspect.

All along the course of developing the text, the fundamental belief was to understand and offers solutions to student & researcher's queries as put to and accumulated by the authors over a time period of two decades of interactions with a similar audience. The text has been written in a language easily comprehensible, relatable, yet all-inclusive. The authors have tried to incorporate accumulated experiences spanning across industry & real-word experience of research application in training & academia into the book in a language and flow as should be comprehended by students, amateurs & professionals alike.

The book intends to serve as a textbook for students at the graduate and postgraduate level, along with being a quick reckoner for instant reference to research professionals.

As we present, 'Fundamentals of research,' we wish & hope it is well recieved and organized fundamental guide for researchers in social science and other areas.

Contents

Introduction to Research

> **Keywords:** *Research, Basic Research, Applied Research, Research types, Validity, Reliability, Suitability, Research problem, Dependent variable, Independent variable, Control variable, Intervening variable, Moderator variable, Research process, Research Proposal, Timelines.*

The word research comes from the now obsolete French word 'recherché' which means to search in-depth and to 'to investigate thoroughly'. In a very generic perspective, the study aims at discovering. Research comprises of intellectual investigation of human efforts aimed at discovering, interpreting, and updating knowledge on different aspects. It is an organized and systematic way of finding solutions to problems.

Definition

The term "Research" seeks to gather & assimilate information on a particular topic. Alternatively, research is a systematic investigation. The methods of research include all the techniques used for conducting research. Research methodology is an approach in which research problems find solutions in a detailed manner. It is a science involving the study of how research progresses sequentially. The researcher also tries to find solutions to an identified problem by using different steps. Hence, the scientific approach, which adopted for conducting research, is called methodology.

Zora Neale Hurston said, "Research is formalized curiosity. It is poking and prying with a purpose with an intent to contribute to the existing body of knowledge."

L.V.Redman and A.V.H Mory, in their book on 'The romance of research', define it as "a systematic effort to gain new knowledge."

C.R.Kothari, in his book 'Research Methodology – Methods and Techniques', defined "research is a scientific and systematic search for relevant information on a specific topic."

The Oxford dictionary defines research as "the systematic investigation into the study of materials and sources to establish facts and reach new conclusions."

We would, at this point, define research as "Research is to understand facts by using observation and experimentation." This process helps in a better understanding of situations & events, individuals' behavior or theories, and offers practical insights. It aims to describe an inexplicable phenomenon or series of events that have been mysterious and to which no definite conclusions have been at arrived. E.g., to study the traffic on the highway from Chandigarh to Delhi on Sundays might be a study as it may only include reporting data. However, if the research investigator were to delve into the reasons as to why the traffic built up the way it did by speaking to a sample population of the car owners, he might be able to develop some insights. These could be useful for traffic inspectors for the development of new strategies and solutions.

Research therefore, broadly focuses on the objective of arriving at the most suitable decision from within a set of various choices, which apparently might offer limited solutions.

Importance of Research

Research facilitates effective management, and for effective decision making, we need to generate accurate information. The information should be gathered systematically, and decision-makers should empathize with an objective investigation rather than being intuitive.

Features of Research

1. Research starts with a problem, presented in the question.
2. Research attempts to identify a problem, stated in clear, unambiguous terms.
3. Research requires a plan. It categorizes, aims, objectives & key questions.
4. Research deals with the primary problem through appropriate sub-problems.
5. Research seeks direction through appropriate hypotheses and draws upon apparent assumptions.
6. Research deals with facts and their meaning.

Research Aim

The primary aim of any type of research is to find out the reality and facts which are unknown. The **research aim** expresses the intention or aspiration of the research study. It summarises in a single sentence what you hope & wish to achieve at the end of the research. The aim should be specific and phrased by using SMART concept specific, measurable, achievable, realistic, and time-bound. Although each research aim has its reason for providing an answer to the research question, the aim of the research is:

1. To achieve skilfulness or to get different opinions by investigating a problem which is not clearly defined (study with these objectives are known as exploratory or formulative).
2. To establish the relationship with something which occurs or is related i.e., study concerning whether certain variables are associated (this is called diagnostic research).

3. To test the hypothesis of a reasonable liaison between different variables and assessing the plausibility by using sample data (this type of research falls into hypothesis-testing research).

Research Objectives

Stating research objectives is the starting point of research. **Research objectives** divide research aim into several parts. The main objectives of research not only determine the scope & depth of the task at hand but also provide an overall direction to the research. To simplify, the research aim specifies WHAT needs to be studied, and research objectives comprise of a number of steps that address HOW research aim will be achieved.

Objectives may range from general to specific. The general objective underline tasks aimed at in a generic & overall perspective, whereas the specific objectives split up the general objective into smaller specific sequential questions addressing the various aspects of the problem. Specific objectives specify precisely what you will do in each phase of your study, how, where, when, and for what purpose.

Generic research objectives:

- To explore a new idea.
- To gain insights into the occurrence of a phenomenon.
- To understand the characteristics of an individual, situation, or event correctly & with accuracy.
- To identify the frequencies of occurrence of events.
- To establish a cause and effect relationship.
- To test the relationship between two variables.

Specific Research objectives:

> *Example:*
> *Research title:* Effects of organizational culture on business profitability: a case study of XYZ Co.
> *Research aim:* To assess the effects of XYZ organizational culture on business profitability.
> *Research objectives:* it would facilitate the achievement of this aim:
> - *Analyzing the nature of organizational culture at XYZ by 31ˢᵗ March, 2021.*
> - *Identifying factors impacting XYZ organizational culture by 31ˢᵗ December, 2020.*
> - *Analyzing impacts of XYZ organizational culture on employee yearly and monthly performances by 31ˢᵗ March, 2021.*

Specific research objectives essentially focus on answering the 3W1H questions by understanding problem constraints. These 3W1H are What, Why, When, and How.

What - This element talks about 'what' are the problems and around what critical areas the research shall focus. Clarity at this level involves thorough insight into aims, objectives, and the problem overview.

Why - This element involves an assessment of the current scenario and 'why' it has led to this choice of problem. It could hint at possible lacunas in information and decision making which research intends to answer. This step would involve a review of available literature to understand the problem scenario and identify and describe variables connected to it.

When - This element every research is prone to be impacted with the time frame constraints, this step talks about the inquiry set up and its efficacy as linked up to specific scenarios.

How - This element is one of the most critical elements since the blueprint or the research design starts here. Based on the problem, its aims and objectives, we would establish the data sources, the research instruments, quantitative statistical measures to be deployed, the evaluation techniques & the presentation techniques.

Types of Research

All types of research can be classified into two major divisions, basic and applied.

Basic Research – Basic research is fundamental research driven by a scientist's curiosity. The motivational drive to the researcher here is to expand knowledge, not to invent. The purpose and objective of this category of research is to present assimilated knowledge in an organized form, which may be eventually shared and put to use by others.

Applied research – Applied research, on the other hand, is designed to solve practical problems, rather than to gain knowledge. Applied research aims to prove a specific hypothesis of value to clients paying for the research. The orientation of applied research is on testing out facts and associations vis-à-vis presenting data, which was the focus of primary research. E.g., a management institute is trying to arrive at associations between low student involvement in classes and increasing degree of absenteeism to a plethora of reasons like abstract course design, faulty layout, outdated teaching pedagogy, to name a few. The attempt is to understand causes in order to find correctives or to eliminate the negating elements.

While the purpose of the research is to check and establish facts to enable decision making, the process of research may be open to severe flaws of human error like biasing and halo effect. Overcoming the errors might be achieved by a repeated reassessment of research findings while some primary criterion prevails, which is classified into various categories described below.

	BASIC RESEARCH	**APPLIED RESEARCH**
INTENTION	To expand general knowledge of processes	To improve the understanding of a particular problem
RESULT	Universal principles	Solution to a particular problem

A detailed classification of research categories would include:

(i) Descriptive vs. Analytical: Descriptive research includes surveys and fact-finding studies, whereas analytical research uses real facts or information for analysis to make a critical evaluation. Descriptive research consists of inquiries or investigations of different kinds. The primary purpose of descriptive research is an explanation of the set of circumstances as given. Ex post facto research is also used to elaborate on this type of research in different areas. The ex post facto research is a kind of research in which the researcher predicts the possible causes behind an effect that has already occurred.

(ii) Applied vs. Fundamental: Applied research refers to finding a solution for a specific, practical problem. The problem is often associated with various fields faced by an individual, society, industries, or sectors like economics, politics, health, business, etc. Whereas fundamental research, also called basic research or pure research, is mainly concerned with the formulation of a theory and improvement of scientific knowledge. The primary aim of applied research is to find out a solution to some critical practical problems. In contrast, fundamental research is handling towards finding information that has an overall sense of application to already existing knowledge.

(iii) Quantitative vs. Qualitative: In natural sciences and social sciences, quantitative research is related to an object that is expressed in terms of quantity or something that can be counted. Such type of research involves a systematic experimental analysis of observable phenomenon via statistical, mathematical, or computational techniques in numerical form such as statistics, percentages, and more. In contrast, Qualitative research is a concern relating to quality or variety. Such type of research is typically descriptive and more laborious to analyze than quantitative data. Qualitative research involves looking in-depth at non-numerical data. To simplify, Quantitative research is a variable-based measurement of the phenomenon under study, whereas qualitative research is an attribute-based study on subjective assessments like desires, opinions, behaviors, preferences.

(iv) Conceptual vs. Empirical: Conceptual research relates to some abstract idea. It focuses on the concept and theory that explain the concerned problem under study. Logicians, philosophers, and theorists use it to develop new concepts or to again understand the existing ones. On the contrary, empirical research relies on experience or observation alone. It is a way of gaining knowledge, utilizing direct and indirect observation or experience. We can also refer to it as an experimental type of research.

Researches with various designs & methodology, adapted for different purposes, maybe tested upon their degree of efficacy & quality in processes of conduct and the subsequent results furnished. For researches to be acceptable and incorporated into business processes, every research must satisfy the given parameters:

Reliability: Every research has to be free from individual biasing. There is no scope of allowing room to suggested alternatives on account of researchers individual preferences.

Objectivity: As far as possible, the elements of research should be objective. The objectivity in process and design facilitate testing, which reduces the chances of arriving at individually preferred or biased options.

Validity: Research must have applicability of results stretching to various time frames and in similar constraints. Unless specified as a specific limitation to specific research, results arrived at must hold for similar conditions at multiple time frames and across geographical boundaries.

Suitability: The findings of the research must match with the problems and objectives suggested at the beginning. If any deviations from the objectives are noticed, the results would be misleading; the process and efforts on gathering data would become futile.

Research Variables

A component, element, or anything that can change or vary, is defined as a variable. The varying factor could be noticed in an individual, a situation or event, or even in a business or organization. The use of variables in research talks about classifying them into the causative variables and then noticing the impact on factors to be studied or the resulting outputs. Commonly identifiable variables in research include:

1. Dependent Variable: The dependent variable is the variable being tested and measured in an experiment, and is 'dependent' on the independent variable. This variable measures the impact of introducing or altering the independent variables. For example, if the independent variable is a new type of teaching pedagogy introduced, the resulting dependent variable will be student's performance in a test designed to check the content taught using the pedagogy. As such, the change in the dependent variable depends on the change in the independent variable.

2. Independent Variables: These variables are controlled, introduced or manipulated by the researcher. They are the 'cause' factors to which the 'effect' is the dependent variable. In an experiment, the researcher is looking for a possible effect on the dependent variable that might be caused by changing the independent variable. For example, in the case, as mentioned earlier, the independent variable is the new teaching pedagogy, the impact of which is being measured by the test on content understanding.

3. Intervening variables: These variables impact the relationship between an independent and a dependent variable. The intervening variables are usually caused by the independent variable and becomes the cause of the dependent variable. These are also known as the mediating variables. E.g., understanding the association between income & longevity. Having money does not make one live longer. The variables that intervene are better quality of life, access to more comforts & better health care, which in turn increase longevity.

4. Moderator variables: These affect the independent and dependent association or relation by modifying or altering the effect of the intervening variables. Typical moderator variables in students' understanding of course delivery include gender, age, and IQ levels.

5. Control Variables: These variables have no direct impact on the result, and their presence may actually add biasing or otherwise negate the impact of the independent variable; as such, they should be brought under control. It is an excellent thought to maintain a control group of respondents in experimental studies that operate in the same circumstances as the experimental group.

6. Extraneous variables: The extraneous variables refer to factors in the environment, which may have an effect on the dependent variables but cannot be controlled by the researcher. Extraneous variables can be harmful & dangerous. They may challenge the validity of research, making it impossible to know whether the independent variables or extraneous factors caused the effects. As they are beyond control, it becomes imperative to state that they may have a possible impact when reporting the research findings.

Research Process

The research process consists of a sequence of actions or steps necessary to carry out research and the desired progression effectively. The following order relating to various steps provides a useful procedural instruction regarding the research process:

I-Identification of the Research Problem

There are two types of research problems like those which **relate to states of nature** meaning, they denote the hypothetical conditions of what the lives of people might have been like before societies came into existence and those which **relate to relationships between different variables.**

Initially, the researcher must recognize the problem he/she wants to study i.e., he/she must decide the general area of interest or part of the subject-matter that requires inquire. At the onset, the problem may be discussed broadly and then the doubts, if any, relating to the problem resolved. Then, the probability of a particular clarification must be considered before working on the formulation of the problem.

Two steps are involved in formulating the research problem, viz., understanding the problem systematically, and reshaping the same into significant terms from an analytical point of view. One of the best approaches to understand the problem is to discuss it with contemporaries or with those having some knowledge in the related matter.

In an academic institution, the researcher can take assistance from a mentor who is usually experienced and has several research problems in his mind. In private business units or governmental organizations, the problem is usually resorted to by allocating it to the administrative agencies with whom the researcher can discuss the problem initially, understand how it comes about, and what reflections are involved in its possible clarification.

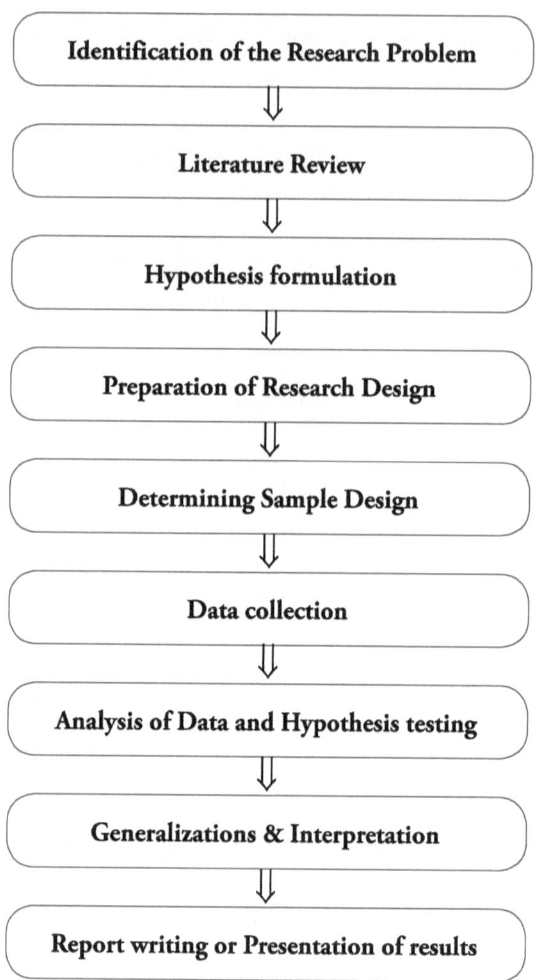

A. Classifying the problem stages

All researches aimed at decision making go through a series of stages for problem identification:

Stage I

Problem understanding stage: At this stage, it is crucial to lay down the initially proposed objectives, outcomes, and issues. This stage would aid in the choice of research designs adapted as a later part. Understanding stage involves:

- Establishing the objectives of the research
- Determining potential

Stage II

Problem selection stage: This stage outlines the various set of alternatives or options which might be suggested or seem relevant. The research process would further move into a comparative assessment of these to arrive at decision making.

- Selection of opportunity to pursue
- Develop the best-suited alternatives

Stage III

Problem Redefining Stage: In the final stage, the researcher lays down specific problems based on comparative assessments as per criterion laid down in the previous stages. This involves:

- Evaluating the research problem statements
- Selection of the best research problem statement

B. Identifying the problem

All accomplished researches start with the first primary task of identifying a suitable topic. The topic of research is a question, an unresolved controversy, or a gap in knowledge. This search requires an awareness of current issues in the subject and an inquisitive and questioning mind. It is of great interest to the researcher as the process of research would be long and tedious. A choice of a lively and involving topic would cut monotony and keep offering incentives to high morale. The selected problem should be significant enough. Replicated topics or trivial and insignificant issues must be screened out and avoided. It should be matching up with the scope of the study and measured up against the time and cost-efficacy limitations. The research problem, if not absorbed right at the very beginning, may, later hamper the process. The data inputs required for the topic must be feasibly available. Lack of substantial data or inappropriate data would demean the results. Also, it is important to skip topics involving debatable or controversial issues as these would lead to later, 'Do not know' or 'No comments' type of responses, making it difficult to arrive at conclusions. The problem, once clearly stated, is understood, and questions may be drawn. It can later be split into sub-problems and made actionable thereon.

The problem once identified and emphatically stated, the next step would be to finalize the steps in the research plan.

C. Developing the research plan (Setting up the scope of the problem)

- **Specify the Research Objectives**

Specify the precise objectives of the research. The objective must be manageable & achievable. Also, it is a good idea to stick to 2-3 clear goals only. The multiplicity of objectives and goals would lead to clutter, which leads to deviation from the path and confused and ambiguous results.

- **Review the problem context**

Understand the environment in terms of available resources, constraints & feasibility of the research. A literature review would facilitate in-depth analysis.

- **Examine the nature of the problem**

Research problems vary from simple to complex, depending on the number of variables and the nature of their relationship. Understanding the nature of the problems will reveal the variables affecting and the data inputs required.

- **Define Variable Relationships**

This step would involve identification, classification & establishment of associations between various variables impacting research. The sequence of steps under this stage would fall as –

❖ Determining the variables that affect the solution to the problem.
❖ Determining the degree to which each variable is brought under control.
❖ Determining the functional relationships between the variables and identify variables that are critical to the solution of the problem.

- **Evaluating the alternate courses of action**

Trying to anticipate the possible outcomes of the alternative courses of action hastens up the choice of the potentially suitable one.

II-Literature Review

Once the research problem is identified, the researcher must study all the available literature to get her/himself familiar with the selected problem. She/he may review two types of literature, first is the conceptual literature, which is related to the concepts and theories, and second, the empirical literature, which consists of previous studies similar to the proposed research problem.

The researcher should undertake a vast literature survey concerned with the problem. For this, the abstracting and indexing journals and published or unpublished bibliographies are the first place where the researcher can get the information or knowledge. Academic journals or conference proceedings or government reports & books are the other sources the researcher can refer to, for study. After this, the researcher revises the problem into analytical or operational terms i.e., putting the problem in as specific terms as possible. This assignment of formulating or defining a research problem is an essential step in the entire research process.

The primary reason for conducting research is to produce new knowledge and to disseminate, to make it available to everyone. When approaching a research project, it is imperative to understand the current state of knowledge in the chosen subject as it is a waste of time spending months producing knowledge that is already available. Therefore, the first step in planning a research project is a literature review. That is, to go through all the available information sources in order to track the latest knowledge and to assess it for relevance, quality, and gaps. This will indicate where additional research is required. This section explains where to find the necessary information, how to analyze it, and present it so that it is used to devise a solid basis for the research project.

The oft-repeated instruction to, '**do a literature review**' enhances some of the complexities of the task. Nevertheless, why should it be done? The review that forms part of the research proposal, paper, thesis, or dissertation is an essential introduction to the research project and underpins the argument about why the project is worth doing. It forms a distinctly recognizable section near the beginning and leads on to the more specific and practical description of the research activities. In the dissertation or thesis, usually, one of the first chapters consists of a critical appraisal of the research literature relevant to the research subject under consideration. The review forms a more extended version of what falls under a proposal.

To understand the present 'state of the art', the researcher needs to read thoughts of other people who have written about research in the subject and make some kind of an assessment of where the research will fit into that body of work. The need to establish, what is being proposed and has not been done in the same way before. The 'how' is essential, because the way previous research was conducted will provide a useful source of experience in using appropriate research methods for collecting and analyzing data. The review may be used to show sources of inspiration in developing ideas – and that does not just have to be only from academic sources as it should also demonstrate a good understanding of the contemporary conceptual frameworks both in academia and industry.

Literature review tends to reveal a lot on attitudes of the researcher and the seriousness of his/her intentions, along with the level of organization and clarity of thought achieved.

(Reference: Research paper by Anubhaa M Walia. Here she looks at the literature about an essential aspect of her study – Relationship between followership styles and leadership styles. Visit section: *Paper Based on Primary Research pg no 261*

III-Hypothesis formulation

After the literature survey, the researcher should make a 'hypothesis' or a working hypothesis. A hypothesis assists in converting the research problem and objective into a comprehensive explanation or prediction of the expected results of the study. It follows from the research problem, literature review, and conceptual framework.

A working hypothesis, however, is a guess made to test the logical or empirical outcome of the research.

Since the hypothesis is open to testing, therefore, it should be specific and limited to the scope of the research. It sharpens the researcher's thinking and focuses on the essential facts of the problem.

Hypothesis formulation could involve the following approaches:

(a) Discussions with colleagues and experts about the research problem, its source, cause, and the objectives in search of a solution;

(b) Assessment of data and records;

(c) Evaluation of similar previous studies and

(d) The personal investigation involves the original field survey.

Thus, any hypothesis formulated as a result of prior thinking about the subject, assessment of the available data, and material, including related previous studies. The formulation of a working hypothesis is an essential step in any research process.

IV-Preparation of Research Design

Numerous types of research designs are available & the researcher has to select the one most appropriate for the specific project at hand. The choice of design depends upon the nature of the problems posed by the research. Each type of research design involves multiple research methods used to collect and analyze the type of data generated by investigations. Here is a list of common research designs, with a short explanation of the characteristics of each.

Historical

Historical designs aim at a systematic and objective evaluation. The synthesis of evidence in order to establish facts and draw conclusions about events that occurred in the past mean historical design. It includes historical inputs, such as archaeological remains as well as documented sources of the past. It is often necessary to carry out tests in order to cross-check the authenticity of this data. Apart from informing about previous times and re-evaluating beliefs about the past, historical research is in use to find contemporary solutions based on the past. It stresses the importance of interactions and effects.

Descriptive

This design relies on observation for collecting data. It attempts to explain situations in order to establish the norm i.e., Prediction on what can happen again under the same circumstances. 'Observation' can take many forms. Depending on the type of information sought, interviews are conducted, questionnaires distributed, visual records made, even sounds and smells

Descriptive – DESCRIBE

"....attempt to explore and explain while providing additional information about the topic"

– Builds an exploratory research

– Usually requires lot of data

recorded. Noteworthy is that the observations are written down or recorded in some way, in order that they can be subsequently analyzed.

The scale of research is under the influence of two major factors: the level of complexity of the survey and the scope or extent of the survey.

Exploratory

Exploratory research is defined as research used to investigate a problem that is not clearly defined. It is conducted to have a better understanding of the existing problem, but will not provide conclusive results. Hence study is conducted to know more about it. This research will help in formulating the problem and procedure of the study.

> ***Exploratory - EXPLORE***
> *"...the initial research into a hypothetical or theoretical idea"*
> - *Taking well defined theories and applying them in your area*
> - *Developing your own theory from a scratch*

Explanatory

This is conducted for a problem that was not well researched before, demands priorities, generates operational definitions. It provides a better-researched model and with the primary purpose of trying to explain why events occur, build, elaborate, extend, or test the theory. It focuses on explaining the aspects under-study in a detailed manner.

> ***Explanatory - EXPLAIN***
> *"...tries to explain relationships between variables"*
> - *Builds on both exploratory and descriptive research*
> - *Finally explains WHY things happen.*

Correlation

This design is used to examine a relationship between two variables, where there is some kind of influence of one on the other, also called a causal relationship. Causal statements describe what may be a 'cause and effect' relationship, where one causes changes in the other. The dependent variable is the variable to be explained (the 'effect'), and the independent variable is the variable expected to account for (the 'cause' of) the dependent variable. The cause being the 'independent variable,' and the variable that is affected is 'dependent variable.' The correlation between two variables can either be none (no correlation); positive (where an increase in one results in the increase in the other, or decrease results in a decrease); or negative (where the increase in one results in the decrease in the other or vice versa). The degree of association is often measurable.

Comparative

This design uses comparisons of past and present or different parallel situations. It can look at situations under different scales, macro (international, national) or micro (community, individual). The analogy is applicable to identify similarities in order to predict results – assuming that if two events are similar in specific characteristics, they could well be similar in others too. In this way, the comparative design implies to explore and test what conditions were involved in causing certain events, so that it is possible, to understand the likely effects of making individual decisions.

Experimental

Experimental research tries to isolate and control every relevant condition which determines the events investigated and then observes the effects when the manipulation of conditions occur. At its simplest, making changes to an independent variable and the effects observed on a dependent variable under controlled condition. Although experiments involve exploring a particular event, they usually require a hypothesis (prediction) to be formulated first in order to determine what are the variables under testing and how can they can be controlled and measured. There are several classes of an experiment – **pre, true, quasi,** et al., that are characterized by the amount of checking, including control involved in the methods.

Simulation

Simulation is a process of representing the properties or behavior of a system by means of another system. Often **simulation** is carried out through the use of a computer program. It involves devising a representation in a small and simplified form (model) of a system, creating prototypes of a real-world experiment. It is a model in which experiments can be conducted, creating a higher level of completeness than a normal experiment. Simulation models can assist in both complex and simple experiments, and they can be used with almost any social process. It is similar to experimental design, but it provides a more artificial environment. In an artificial environment, it works with original materials on the same scale. Simulation models can be mathematical (number-crunching in a computer) or physical, working with two or three – dimensional materials. The performance of the model must be assessed and calibrated against the real system to check that the results are reliable. Simulation enables ideal situations under testing 'what if'?

Evaluation

Evaluation research can be defined as "the use of scientific methods to measure the implementation and outcomes of programs for decision-making purposes" (Rutman 1984, p. 10). This descriptive type of research, also known as program evaluation refers to research purpose instead of a specific method. It is a design to deal with complex social issues. It is the systematic assessment of the worth or merit of time, money, effort, and resources spent in order to achieve a goal.

A common purpose of evaluation research is to examine:

- the level of awareness,
- costs and benefits,
- cost-effectiveness,

- attainment of objectives, and
- quality assurance.

Action

Action research may also be called a 'cycle of action' or 'cycle of inquiry', since it typically follows a predefined process that is repeated over time. It is a methodology of research generally applied in the social sciences. It seeks transformative change through the simultaneous process of taking action of conducting research, which is linked together by critical reflection. It starts with identifying a problem, collecting data, filled by organizing, analyzing, and interpreting the data leading to developing a plan to address the problem, implementing the plan, and evaluating the results of the actions taken, finally identifying a new problem, and repeat the process.

Basically, this is an 'on the spot' procedure, designed to deal with a specific problem in a particular situation. There is no attempt made to separate the problem from its context in order to study it in isolation. What appears to be useful changes incorporated, and then constant monitoring and evaluation are carried out to see the effects of the changes. The conclusions from the findings are applied immediately and further monitored to gauge their effectiveness. Action research depends mainly on observation and behavioral data. Because it is so bound up in a particular situation, it is difficult to generalize the results i.e., to be confident that the action will be successful in another context.

Ethnological

Ethnological research focuses on people. In this approach, the researcher is interested in how subjects under study, interpret behavior rather than imposing external theories. It takes place in the undisturbed natural settings of the subjects' environment. It regards the context to be as equally important as the actions it studies and attempts to represent the totality of the social, cultural, and economic situation. The cultural background and assumptions of the researcher may unduly influence the interpretations and descriptions. Moreover, there can be confusion over the use of language and different meanings given to words by the respondents and researcher.

Depending upon the method of research, the designs are also known as survey design, case study design, observation design, and experiment design.

In a brief summarization, the research design is a plan of action. Once the problem gets selected for research, there is a need to constitute a plan of study and should focus on the following components.

- Need for study
- Review of the previous study
- Problem statement
- Hypothesis formulation
- Operational definition

- Scope of the study
- Source of data
- Method of collection
- Tools & techniques (Survey, observation, interviews, questionnaire)
- Sample design
- Data analysis
- Presentation of the result of the study
- Time estimates
- Financial budget
- Administration of query

V-Determining Sample Design

Every object that involves any type of inquiry constitutes a 'universe' or 'population.' Complete detail of any object in the 'population' is known as a census inquiry. It can be supposed that in such type of inquiry, all the items are under coverage and not a single element is left, and the highest accuracy obtainable. However, realistically this may not be true because a single element of bias in such inquiry will get more substantial as the number of observations increases.

Moreover, there is no way to scrutinize elements of bias or its level except through a survey or use of sample checks. Besides, such type of inquiry comprises a lot of time, money, and energy. Apart from this, census inquiry is not possible practically under many conditions. For example, blood sugar testing is done only on a sample basis. Hence, quite often, we select only a few items from the population for our study purposes. The selection of items in such type of manner is technically called a sample. The researcher must decide the way of selecting a sample or choose a sample design for his study. In other words, a sample design is an exact sketch determined before any type of data collection for obtaining a sample from a given universe.

There are two types of sampling: non-probability and probability sampling. Non-probability sampling uses a subjective method of selecting units from a universe and is generally easy, quick, and economical. Therefore, it is useful to perform preliminary studies, focus groups, or follow-up studies. Non-probability samples are those based on straightforward sampling, judgment sampling, and quota sampling techniques. Probability sampling uses an objective method allowing each element in the population and an equal chance of being selected in the sample. This sampling techniques find its basis on simple random sampling, stratified sampling, systematic sampling, cluster/area sampling.

VI-Data collection

Data collection involves the systematized approach to collecting and collating data from a variety of sources to arrive at a meaningful conclusion or an accurate picture. It helps in generating relatable answers to research questions, evaluate outcomes and make predictions. Multiple methods of data collection, both quantitative and qualitative can be used for research. Surveys, interviews, and focus groups are primary instruments for collecting information and case study, scenario building are commonly used secondary source. Contemporary data collection tools include mobile devices, website traffic, server activity, and other relevant sources, depending on the project.

VII-Analysis of Data and Hypothesis testing

Data analysis is an essential part of the project. The information gained from the analysis of the preliminary data collection leads to a better understanding of the situation and helps to determine what further data collection is required. This process is repeated in order to build up an increasingly sophisticated understanding of the subject under study. The quantitative analysis deals with data in the form of numbers and uses mathematical operations to investigate their properties. The levels of measurement used in the collection of the data, i.e., nominal, ordinal, interval, and ratio, are an essential factor in choosing the type of analysis that is applicable, as are the numbers of cases involved. Some of the primary purposes of quantitative analysis are to:

- measure
- make comparisons
- examine relationships
- make forecasts
- test hypotheses
- construct concepts and theories
- explore
- control
- explain.

VIII-Generalisations and Interpretation

A hypothesis, once tested and upheld several times, might be possibly adapted by the researcher as a generalization, i.e.,foundations for a theory. Typically, the basic essence of research rests on its capability to draw generalizations. In a situation where a researcher has no clear hypothesis to test upon, he may bank upon investigations on existing researches. This may be termed as interpretation. This process of investigation may sometimes set grounds for newer line of queries and may lead to the future direction of research.

Interpretations, on the contrary would mean drawing meaningful results of findings in order to find applicability to research problems.

IX-Report writing or Presentation of the results

The research report comprises of a compilation of what has been done along the process. Writing of reports must be executed with great care and must follow a specified layout.

The layout of the report should be as follows:

- the preliminary pages
- the main text
- the end matter.

The **preliminary pages** of the report include title and date, acknowledgments & a foreword. This should be followed by a table of contents, a list of tables & a list of graphs and charts if used in the report.

The **main text** comprises of the following sub-sections:

Introduction: It is a clear statement of the research objectives and an overview of the suggested methodology to be adopted in the research. The introduction should also talk about the scope of the study as well as possible limitations the researcher might face.

Report Body: This begins with secondary sources consulted, the entire research process description as executed, sorted logically in specific sections as per their occurrence.

Summary of findings: The introduction should be followed by a statement of findings and recommendations. Findings may be elaborated & discussed at length.

Conclusion: This is a final summing up of the report drawn as the last part of the report.

Appendices in respect of all technical data should be listed at the **end of the report**. Bibliography i.e., list of books, journals, reports, etc., all secondary sources of data used must be included. Index forms the concluding element of the report.

Researcher Guide

To conduct a student research project, it is a good idea to follow a schematic and sequential approach. Some guidelines which might seem relevant would be broadly categorized into two Parallel division:

A – Research Blueprint

I Understanding the problem in totality: This should start with identifying a suitable topic by way of a literature review to study previous researches conducted on similar topics. Understanding the problem would help in acquiring more clarity over the question, variables, and constraints affecting the scenario. Also, it would give a fair idea about where did the research concludes and even establish the conclusions drawn as the take-off point for the research at hand.

II Try to create an action plan: The action plan would cover the suggested methodology to match up with problem questions and objectives. Also, it would be equally important at this stage to understand and establish deadlines, to know the data sources available & start work on getting ethical approvals. Finally, one of the most important steps here would be to understand the examination and evaluation criteria to enable report delivery and presentation as per the said specifications.

III Work on communication and research skills: This would be in continuation of establishing the resources. While communication would play an extremely critical role in accumulating primary data, its relevance would further be highlighted in the presentation of the completed study. At this stage, the researcher should draw up the communication and research skills as also start lining up proficiencies in terms of physical resources like a work station/computer and also soft skills like language command and delivery.

IV Implement the plan: Practising what has been thought up and planned would most certainly be the most integral element. Self-monitoring and working on targets and maintaining a time scale here would be extremely useful. Setting up time goals enables both sticking on to the path and also avoiding wastage and time lags in deviators and crises, which might be witnessed anywhere along the process.

Research Proposal

A research proposal is a succinct summary of the research report. It is an initial draft which talks of the suggested components as the research progresses. It will be beneficial to clarify the aims of the research and what is needed to do to achieve the desired outcome. It will also be useful as a way to inform others of their intentions. The presentation of a research proposal is always required by courses that contain research exercises, such as writing dissertations or a thesis. In professional life, for all research projects that need funding, a detailed research proposal will be required as a part of the funding application. Academic research proposals are usually composed of the following elements:

- *the title;*
- *aims of the research;*
- *the background to the research – context and previous research;*
- *a definition of the research problem;*
- *outline of methods of data collection and analysis;*
- *possible outcomes;*
- *a timetable of the project and description of any resources required;*
- *list of references.*

B – Framing Timescales

Drawing a timescale very effectively helps to manage time as milestones are laid down for self-assessment. The choice of timescale varies across various researches, primarily depending on the type of research undertaken & the time availability within any given contract or planned semester.

Plotting a timeline on the research progress stages:

The main stages of research are identified and listed below in actual practice. The transition between one stage, and another is not always

---

Time-bound sequence of research stages

Two months: Reading, exploring, taking notes, planning, setting up systems, writing introduction

Two months: Writing a literature review

One month: Refining, editing writing up research methods

One month: Collecting & recording data

One month: Analyzing the data

One month: Concluding and compiling bibliography and appendices

One month: Proofreading, correcting & binding

so well defined. For example, during the research, it maybe required to keep going back to steps already covered, say literature review referred to the current stage of questioning. As such, sometimes, some stages may take much longer than expected due to unanticipated deviations or distracters. It is, therefore, essential for the students to carefully plan out a timetable and establish deadlines on completion of each stage. A crucial step for research would be working out a practicable timetable that connects the main stages of research.

While assessment schedules will vary across various universities, some joint assessment stages are identifiable. It is advisable to keep track of the assessment stages so that the report timeline progress and presentation match up.

The critical stages identified here are:

1. Development stage

The initial stages of ongoing discussions during which a series of changes are made in the report. This stage involves formative feedback, reviews, and suggestions by the supervising researcher or project guide. This stage will go on until the final submission of the research report.

2. Assessment stage

The research report at this stage would be formally measured or evaluated against the specified criteria. Criteria have been specified well in advance. This stage does not involve the researcher's involvement and is primarily at the disposal of the supervisor or guide.

3. Internal Moderation

Review by a guide in the researcher's presence. The guides will meet to share their comments and grades given. The agenda of this meet-up is to highlight flaws in the report, which are then subject to rectifications.

4. External Moderation

Samples of the research report will be moderated & edited by an external moderator so as to ensure fair, unbiased & reliable assessment at all centres. Post the suggested stages; the final draft is now ready for reference

Researcher might follow the suggested template to map up the milestone to research timelines.

Exhibit 1: Research Timeline Template

STAGE	MILESTONE TARGETED	PROGRESS MONITORED	TARGET DATE
	RESEARCH START DATE:		
I	Establish a general area of interest	YES/ NO	Proposed target date:
I	Include preliminary brainstorming	YES/ NO	Proposed target date:
II	Conduct preliminary research	YES/ NO	Proposed target date:
II	Literature Review	YES/ NO	Proposed target date:
III	Develop researchable framework/research proposal	YES/ NO	Proposed target date:
III	Select appropriate title	YES/ NO	
IV	Select the most suitable methods for data collection	YES/ NO	Proposed target date:
IV	Initiate data gathering.	YES/ NO	
V	Collating, analyzing, presenting, and interpreting data	YES/ NO	Proposed target date:
V	Ongoing Literature Review	YES/ NO	
VI	Writing the research project/report	YES/ NO	Proposed target date:
VI	Proof-Reading	YES/ NO	
VII	Repeat, review and re-writing	YES/ NO	Proposed target date:
VII	Project submitting post printing & binding	YES/ NO	
	PROPOSED RESEARCH COMPLETION DATE :		

Recap & Review Section

SUMMARY Chapter 1

Research is a part of systematic knowledge and an investigation to discover answer to problems. The research aims to provide the answer to the research questions raised. It covers the research process involving several stages included in the business research process. These are the selection of a researchable problem, review of previous research/work, formulating a hypothesis, identifying the source of data, construction of data collection instruments, collection of data, processing and analyzing of data, and finally interpretation and report writing.

Exhibit 2: "Samsung Goes Solomo"

Samsung Goes SoLoMo for Smart Television Product Launch – Mobile ad and mobile game, writ large, helped woo consumers to check out smart TV

From early October through mid-November 2012, Samsung, through its agency Starcom Worldwide, ran a social-mobile advertising campaign that targeted shoppers based on location. Using location-based advertising technology from JiWire, the brand and agency sought to get consumers out of their homes and into physical retail stores to experience the Samsung TV.

With the Smart TV launch in fall 2012, Samsung introduced motion control and voice control features. The challenge was not only to create consumer demand for an entirely new TV category but also to get consumers to experience the TV in person. Based on Samsung's consumer research, 86% of people who bought a Samsung Smart TV first experienced the product at retailers.

The brand's research also indicated that online reviews and word of mouth slowly drove smart TV purchases, so the goal became to drive consumer awareness of Samsung's new product by getting people to experience it in stores. Then the hope was to compel them to share their experience with friends and family.

An idea to wrap the campaign around the Angry Birds mobile game led Samsung to the campaign strategy it decided to pursue. Samsung partnered with Angry Birds to demonstrate how motion and voice control work on the Samsung Smart TV. The campaign goal was to get consumers in stores and playing Angry Birds on big TVs to experience firsthand the motion and voice control.

"We [decided] to leverage a SoLoMo [social, local, mobile] experience, especially since smartphone users so commonly leverage social networks on their mobile devices," said Erica Chen, global associate director at Starcom Worldwide.

Mobile technology platform JiWire delivered location-specific ads to consumers' mobile phones—only when they were within particular stores or a 5-mile radius of a store. The ads included the name and address of the closest store so shoppers could access directions from their current location with one click.

"We know people are more likely to be active and spontaneous when they are already on the go," Chen said. "Or even better, when they are already near the retail destination."

The ad encouraged users to visit local retail stores to experience Angry Birds on the Samsung Smart TV. The ads also incorporated check-in buttons so that consumers could share, with their friends and followers, their location, and the experience of being in the store playing Angry Birds on the smart TV. By checking in, users could enter a sweepstake to win a Samsung Smart TV.

Samsung hoped these calls to action would motivate consumers to share their experience.

Measuring consumer engagement—engagement with the ad, clickthroughs, the number of consumer actions, as well as retail store traffic—Starcom reported that the campaign results outperformed their expectations. Starcom and Samsung also measured social engagement through Facebook check-ins, social sharing, sweepstakes entries, and in-store experience surveys.

"By leveraging hyper-location targeting, we were able to talk to consumers while they were already close to the stores," Chen said. "This hugely increased the likelihood of them taking action while in the store.

Metrics for Samsung's Angry Birds Integrated Smart TV Product Launch, Nov 2012
44 Seconds average engagement time
1.03% Clickthrough rate
An engagement rate of 1.7X industry average
58% of consumers who viewed the in-ad retailer location list took the next action to view a specific retail location, which ultimately drove foot traffic to the store and lead generation
58% of customers became more positive about the Samsung Smart TV after the in-store experience (Based on in-store reports)
Note: Campaign ran from Oct through mid-Nov 2012   *Source:Starcom Worldwide, March 29, 2013*

Read more at *http://www.emarketer.com/Article/Case-Study-Samsung-Goes-SoLoMo-Smart-TV-Product-Launch/1009935.*

Check Your Knowledge

CYK 1 Identify the correct sequential order recommended in the development of a research idea?

a. Research topic, research problem, research purpose, research question, hypothesis.

b. Research topic, research purpose, research problem, research question, hypothesis.

c. Research topic, research problem, research purpose, research question, hypothesis.

d. Research topic, hypothesis, research problem, research question, research purpose.

Answer (b)

CYK 2 Maintaining a 'to do' list could be a good idea to avoid time wasters. Which of these are included in this list:

a. Minutes of the previous meeting

b. Data findings

c. Targeted milestones

d. Reference list

Answer (b)

CYK 3 Which of these would not be right while working on a research project deadline:

a. Progress on goals should be matching up with submission requirements

b. You can keep going back to literature anytime and in whatever depth even when it delays your progress to milestones

c. Split up work into smaller units for better focus

d. Do not allow distracters to slow down your progress.

Answer (b)

CYK 4 Which of the following is the most appropriate example of 'Basic research'?

a. Checking the impact of job satisfaction on the productivity of a group of workers

b. Exploring the different elements of a research design

c. Trying to study the factors which lead to increased employee morale

d. Measuring the impact of a newly released advertisement campaign on the sales of a brand

Answer (b)

CYK 5 What should be the first stage of research adopted by a management college set to open its campus in a new, unfamiliar area?

a. Exploring the potential of management education in this area

b. Deciding on the promotion mix for the college

c. Establishing the criterion & procedure for admissions

d. Debating on what all management programs seem relevant to the college

Answer (a)

CYK 6 A management college has been witnessing an increasing trend of student absenteeism in early morning classes. The authorities are interested in assigning reasons so correctives could be under offer. Some possible issues could be:

The early morning classes comprise of elementary courses, which may not be of interest to a majority of students.

Morning traffic rush

Monotonous teaching pedagogy

Which of these is the research problem in the given scenario?

a. Discovering causatives to students lack student interest

b. Discovering reasons for increasing absenteeism

c. Clearing the monotony in-class pedagogy

d. Identifying the more important subject to draw student's interest

Answer (b)

CYK 7 "Morale of workers in an organization is strongly influenced by monetary incentives when given on time and in the right approximation."

Identify the dependent variable in research intended to check the same

a. Worker performance level

b. Increase in salary

c. Company orientation policy

d. Worker morale levels

Answer (d)

CYK 8 An excellent qualitative problem statement:

a. Defines the independent and dependent variables;

b. Conveys a sense of emerging design;

c. Specifies a research hypothesis to be tested;

d. Specifies the relationship between variables that the researcher expects to find.

Answer (d)

Questions

1. Define business research. What constitutes a good research plan? Illustrate.

2. Does exploratory research always lead to conclusive study? Give reasons to support the answer.

3. The research process involves a series of intricate sequential steps. Does this apply necessarily to all types of researches & why?

4. What are the essential components of a business research proposal?

5. Write short notes on
   a) Causal research
   b Methods of research
   c) Experimental research
   d) Research Report

Research Plan

> **Keywords:** *Research aim, Research objectives, Research question, Quantitative & Qualitative research, Qualitative & Quantitative data*

Research, as elaborated in the previous chapter, talks about discovering things we do not know. Research is something that people undertake in order to find out things in a systematic way, thereby increasing knowledge. We attempt to find answers to questions yet unanswered and unexplained. All researches aim at gathering an in-depth understanding of the problem.

The aim of the research is to reflect upon the problem, which forms the starting point of all researches. The preliminary steps in the research process are formulating the research & its hypothesis. The problem specifies questions to which answers would later be sought. Eventually, the methodology to follow would depend on the choice and understanding of the identified problem.

Research Problems

A research problem refers to the 'difficulty which a researcher faces in the context of a theoretical or practical situation and wants to find a solution for the same'. A research problem, as such, is one that requires a researcher to identify the best solution for a problem.

Multiple factors may complicate the problem. For instance, the environmental changes affecting the efficiencies of the chosen courses of action. The number of alternative courses

Sources of Research Problems
The following sources can help you to identify problems:
- *Business Problems*
- *Day to day problems*
- *Technological changes*
- *Unexplored areas*
- *Theory of one's own interest*
- *Books, Thesis, Abstract, Articles*
- *Policy Problems*
- *Discussion with subject matter experts*

of action may be extensive and similar to other factors. All such elements should be thought of in the context of a research problem.

The research problem taken up for the study must be carefully selected. The task is tough, while it may not appear to be so. Every researcher must find his path to original and exclusive problems.

The following points guide a researcher in selecting a research problem:

i.   The subject which has already been extensively researched must be avoided, as gathering new insights could be challenging.

ii.   The choice of controversial subjects should be avoided.

iii. Too narrow or too vast a problem should be avoided.

iv.   The subject selected should be familiar.

v.   The relevance of the subject, the qualifications, and expertise of a researcher, costs & time factor involved must be considered in the selection of a problem.

vi.   The preliminary study must precede the selection of a problem. This may not be crucial when the problem involves the conduct of research very similar to something that is already done. However, when the field of inquiry is new and does not have an existing set of well-developed techniques, it is advisable to use a brief feasibility study. Alternatively, before the final choice of a problem is made, a researcher must answer the following questions:

(a)   Is she/he trained enough to carry out the research?

(b)   Does the research fall within the budget she/he can afford?

(c)   Will she/he get cooperation from those who will be participating in the research as subjects?

Typically a research problem is said to exist if the following conditions prevail:

❖ There has to be an individual involved.

❖ There should be at least two possible alternatives or courses of action.

❖ There should be at least two possible outcomes or end results of the process.

❖ The alternative courses of action must provide some chance or probability of obtaining the objective, but the chances by the two cannot be the same, else the choice would be immaterial.

❖ In the end, results by the two alternatives must differ.

As such, the components of the research problem are:

❖ An individual or group with some difficulty or problem must be identified.

❖ An objective to be attained must be specified.

❖ There should be an alternative means for achieving the desired objective. This suggests that there must be at least two courses available to the researcher.

❖ The ambiguity that might persist around the selection of alternatives must be answered by the relative efficiency of possible alternatives.

❖ Difficulties or limitation always prevails in a specific environment.

To conclude, a research problem requires a researcher to find out the best or the most optimum solution for the given problem, i.e., to choose the course of action by which the objective can be attained most suitably in the context of the given environment.

A problem may be written in:

Declarative form: A problem written in the form of a declaration or disclaimer open to testing and acceptance, e.g., Motivation levels of workers have a direct association to their IQ.

Interrogative form: A problem written in a question format, e.g., Is the motivation levels of workers impacted by their IQ? In both cases, the next step would be to specify objectives and place them in a hierarchical arrangement. A thorough understanding of each would follow.

Steps in defining a problem

I-Stating the problem in a general way

This involves selecting a topic sourced from the researcher's experience, insight, or even literature review e.g., 'Leadership styles in Indian organizations'.

Stating a clear research problem clarifies the purpose of the study both to the researcher as well as the audience. A well-defined problem statement is an effective tool for the research process & accomplishment.

Stating the problem in a general way

⇓

Resolving the ambiguities

⇓

Evaluating a research problem

II-Resolving the ambiguities

The research problem, once stated, can be examined to understand its research objectives, its context or environment, its nature, variable relationships & anticipating the possible consequences of alternative approaches. Based on the same, the scope of the problem may be enhanced; if it is too specific, or narrowed or if too vast already.

A good Research problem statement should be:
- *Specific*
- *Interesting*
- *Measurable*
- *Achievable*
- *Relevant*
- *Relatable*
- *Researchable*

Further, at this stage, subtopics may be defined for establishing the scope of the study e.g., subtopics for the problem here at hand could be:

- Studying current leadership styles
- Categorizing organizations
- Matching management with competency

III-Evaluating a research problem

This involves an in-depth study about processes results leading to a more specific formulation of the problem and trying to see the feasibility of the study with regard to the existing constraints operating in the scenario where the research is to be conducted. E.g., Understanding access to data sources, time availability, legal & ethical issues.

This stage helps to get feedback from teachers, students, and coworkers for the revision of the research question. Some considerations that help revise & redefine the problem are:

- Thought consensus on the research problem not achieved.
- The clarity in understanding of the chosen matter.
- Adding subtopics to the context of the study.

The evaluation makes the problem more realistic in terms of data availability, leads to the formulation of a well-defined research problem that is not only meaningful operationally but, at the same time, capable of providing a working hypothesis and for means of solving the problem itself.

Research Questions

This is an alternative to research objectives where the key issue to be focused on in a research project is stated in the form of questions. Given below are the objectives rephrased as research questions.

Research Question 1

Is the consumer's behavior affected by sales promotional tactics like free T-shirts, shopping baskets, and discount coupons?

Research Question 2

Is the buying behavior of a young adult consumer affected by sales promotion?

Research Aims

It is a statement indicating the general aim or purpose of the Research Project and is an essential task in any research project. If enough time and thought are not devoted at the start to accurately define this, precious resources may be spent and wasted on collecting

---

1. Research question

- *It is a starting point which formulates a research problem that you want to investigate*
- *Clearly framed*
- *Justifiable (important, original, answerable)*

2. Aim

- *It is to answer the research question and is a summary statement*
- *Aims are statements of intent. They are usually written in broad terms*

3. Objectives

- *Translate aim into operationalized study components*
- *Some may be formative. Otherwise, primary and secondary objectives translate directly into primary and secondary hypothesis, and outcome measures*
- *Prioritise objectives*
- *Present them in active language, e.g., 'to quantify', 'to determine', collect, construct, classify, develop, devise, measure, produce, revise, select, synthesise.*

irrelevant or unnecessary research data. Therefore the sentences stating the aim of the research project are very brief and should be to the point.

For e.g., 'To investigate the effect of sales promotions on buyer behavior'.

Research aims are comprehensive and introductory rather than specific and focused.

Research Objectives

It is a specific statement indicating key issues to be focused upon in a research project. It may be possible to have several research objectives under the same research aim. For e.g.,

Objective 1

Could be to examine the relationship between different promo mechanisms (e.g., free T-shirts, shopping baskets, discount coupons for future shopping, etc.)

Objective 2

Could be to examine the relationship between sales promotion and consumer behavior of young adults

Matching problem questions with objectives

A well-defined statement of the problem serves as a guide to the researcher in designing further the course of the study. The statement of the research should identify the major variables involved in the study. Also, it is essential to specify the nature of the population under study and accordingly suggest the possibility & suitability of empirical testing.

EXAMPLE

Research Question	*Research Aim*	*Research Objectives*
What is the impact of COVID-19 on Mobile Sale?	*Evaluate the impact of COVID-19 on Mobile Sale?*	*1. To explore the underlying factors that causes the emergence of the COVID-19* *2. To assess effect of COVID-19 on Mobile sale*
Research Ques-tion *How online marketing affects consumer behaviour among Delhi University students?*	*Research Aim* *Analyse the effect of social media on consumer behaviour among students of Delhi University*	*Research Objectives* *1. To assess the current level of popularity of social media among Delhi University students* *2. To identify main factors impacting the efficacy of online marketing among Delhi University students* *3. To forecast the implication of social media among Delhi University students*

Research Methodology

The term methodology refers to the method adopted as a holistic view of the research process with the sequential steps involved. It is concerned with the following main issues:

- Why did you collect certain data?
- What data did you collect?
- Where did you collect it?
- How was it collected?
- How would you analyze it?

Research methodology should meet the following criteria:

1. Identify the sampling methods and the target population involved. (Justifications to the choice of sampling methods must be offered.)
2. Describe the tools, techniques & instruments used for both qualitative and quantitative measures.
3. Planning a clear outline or experimental design of the research.
4. Identification of protocols to be used in data collection and recording.
5. Clarifying & describing the data analysis procedures.
6. Furnish a plan of action to specify milestones, important points, and any other contingency developments.

Data may be categorized depending upon whether it can be reduced to numbers or presented only in words. This affects the way it is collected, recorded, and analyzed.

Data comprising of numerical variables will always be **quantitative,** and data comprising of categorical variables will certainly be **qualitative**. As such, the type of data can be identified before its collection, depending on whether the variables involved are numerical or categorical.

Based on the problems posed, the objectives projected, and the methodologies suggested, all researches can be classified under four main approaches.

1. **Quantitative research**
2. **Qualitative research**
3. **Pragmatic research**
4. **Participatory research**

1. Quantitative research

The focus of Quantitative research is on accumulating, analyzing & interpreting numerical data; it emphasizes measuring the scale, range, frequency, etc. of variables under study. This data is highly detailed and can be presented and analyzed statistically. Also, since data is reflected numerically, quantitative information facilitates specific comparative analysis. Quantitative data is data about numeric variables (e.g., how many; how much; or how frequently). Objectivity is an integral component of quantitative research. Researchers would leave no stone unturned to ensure that the research is really measuring what is being claimed to be measured. For example, if the study concerns the environmental impact on students grasping the subject, it is imperative to understand all environmental variables like classroom size, number of classmates and associations among them, teaching pedagogies etc.

Quantitative data, although relatively challenging to gather, is more logical and offers a platform for statistical and numerical analysis.

For example, you measure the effectiveness of a newly released promotion by taking a count of the number of new users or market share.

Researchers have one or many hypotheses. These refer to the questions they wish to address. These include predictions about possible associations amongst the things & variables they seek to investigate. In order to find these answers, the researchers maintain and involve multiple instruments, inventories (e.g., paper or computer tests, observation checklists, etc.) backed up with a clear plan of action. Data here is collected by various procedures and prepared and sorted for statistical analysis. Computer-aided packages could be used for the same. The analysis allows the researchers to determine the extent of the relationship between two or more variables.

2. Qualitative research

Qualitative research, on the contrary, is more subjective in nature compared to Quantitative research. It involves examining and reflecting on the less tangible aspects of a research subject, e.g., values, attitudes, perceptions. It is based primarily on soft skills assessment. Although this type of research can be easier to start, it can often be challenging to interpret and present the findings as it is open to a lot of communication gaps and perceptual biasing. Unlike quantitative research, which relies on numbers and data, qualitative research is more focused on how people feel, think, and why they make certain choices.

For example, qualitative research would measure perceptions, feelings, and emotions generated as a result of a new tag line or a new logo. In a more experimental sense, projective techniques like story completion test or TAT (Thematic Apperception Test) tend to be more qualitative in their approach.

Qualitative researchers apply an inductive approach, which involves developing a theory or inferences based on the data collected. This involves moving from the specific to general and is, as such, called a bottom-up approach. It involves recording, analyzing, and trying to understand the meaning and relevance of human behavior, actions, and experience, which includes conflicting beliefs, and emotions. People's judgments, feelings of comfort, emotions, ideas, beliefs, etc. can only be described in words. These record qualities rather than quantities, hence they are called qualitative data. Words cannot be manipulated mathematically, so require different analytical techniques.

The process of data collection and analysis, although methodical, allows much more flexibility than in quantitative research. Observation and interaction are methods used for data collection based on the subjects or participants, e.g., (i) through participant observation, (ii) in-depth interviews, and (iii)focus groups. (The proceeding sections talk about a detailed and elaborate study of qualitative & quantitative techniques and procedures). There is no conversion into the numerical form and no subsequent statistical analysis.

Qualitative data typically measures 'types' (subjective orientation) and is represented by a name, symbol, or a numeric code. It talks about categorical variables (e.g., what type).

Importance of quantitative and qualitative data

Both quantitative and qualitative data provide different perspectives & results and are often used in combination to ascertain findings on a population in totality. For example, if data are collected on monthly or annual income, the number of dependents, asset evaluations in terms of financial worth are quantifiable in nature, whereas the nature of the occupation, residing city, etc.are more subjective and qualitative.

We can collect Quantitative and Qualitative data from the same data unit. The choice basis is whether the variable under study is numerical or categorical. For example:

Data unit	Numeric variable	Quantitative data	Categorical variable	Qualitative data
An individual	Number of people in the family	4	Hobbies	Painting
	Income (monthly or annual)	20 Lakhs pa	Occupation	Business
A house	Dimensions of the house you own	200 square meters	Location of the house	Countryside
A business	Number of employees	112	Nature of the industry	Retail

Difference between Quantitative and Qualitative Research

QUANTITATIVE RESEARCH	QUALITATIVE RESEARCH
Quantitative = Quantity	Qualitative = Quality
Structured methodology	Unstructured methodology
The purpose is to quantify the extent of variation in a situation	The purpose is to describe the extent of variation in a situation
Emphasis on a larger sample size	Smaller sample size can be considered
Emphasis on measurement of variables	Emphasis on the description of variables
Assembles required information from a large number of the respondent but has a narrow focus in terms of the extent of inquiry	Assembles required information from a few numbers of the respondent but covers multiple issues

Deductive Analysis; articulated in the context of "justification"	Inductive Analysis; articulated in the context of "discovery"
Focusses on testing theories, prediction and hypothesis	Focusses on exploring and understading ideas and provide meaning
Key terms are: testing, measurement, objectivity, replicability	Key terms are: understanding, context, complexity, subjectivity
Closed ended questions	Open ended questions
Mainly expressed in numbers, tables, graphs, statistics, analysis and comparison with data obtained over past years and with estimates.	Presentation of data is expressed in Quotes, narrative-style extracts to allow reality as it has been experienced during the study.Mainly expressed in words
Type of respondent is a variable individual	Type of respondent is a unique individual

3. Pragmatic approach to research (mixed approach)

This approach involves using or devising the method which apparently best suits the research problem. Pragmatic researchers, as such, use any of the methods, techniques, instruments, and procedures which may be typically associated with quantitative or qualitative research. They believe and adapt in the research every method, understand the limitations of each, and also the fact that alternative research approaches can be complementary.

This research may involve the use of different techniques simultaneously or one after the other. For example, face-to-face interviews or focus groups can be followed up with a questionnaire using the interview findings to measure attitudes in a large scale sample with the objective of conducting statistical analysis.

Depending on the measures used, the collected data is analyzed in the most appropriate manner. Also, it is sometimes possible to convert qualitative data into quantitative data, and vice versa.

4. Participatory approach to research

This approach aims at trying to bring positive changes in the lives of the respondents. The researchers are likely to have an agenda and try to give the groups they are studying a consensus or voice. They focus on their research to directly or indirectly result in some kind of reform. It is essential that they involve the group being studied in the research, preferably at all stages, so as to avoid further marginalizing them.

The researcher adopts a relatively neutral position than the typical scientific researcher. This may involve informal interaction or otherwise striking a connection with the research participants. The findings of the research may be reported in informal terms, often using the specific words of the research participants.

Recap & Review Section

> **SUMMARY Chapter 2**
>
> *This chapter covers an overview of the research plan, focussing on identifying problems and usage of research methodology. Without a problem, we cannot proceed with research. Problem is some set of difficulty experienced by the researcher, and solving this difficulty is the task of research. The researcher should be interrogative to search for a problem. The problem must be defined and specified. Based on the problems posed, the objectives projected, and the methodologies suggested, research is classified under four main approaches: Quantitative, Qualitative, Pragmatic, and Participatory.*

Caselet 1 – Online Booking

Presently, Indian travelers can criss-cross the globe with just a few clicks by using various online portals for booking airline tickets, hotel reservations, etc. Online booking involves pursuing of available information on travel websites and then making a reservation. You can check out various travel sites, which collate the flight details of all airlines. These sites are the apt place to book or bid for air tickets. Travel portals, such as makemytrip.com, travelguru.com, arzoo.com, yatra.com, indiatimes.com, rediff.com, or cleartrip.com, would provide you all details of flights along with their fares. The fares are reflected in ascending order by the lowest priced featuring first.

The number of customers who book travel tickets by the online method is growing day by day. However, a switch from the offline environment to the online environment creates certain doubts in the minds of consumers. Such doubts in literature are termed as perceived risks.

Also, the Internet revolution has helped in bringing significant changes in market transparency, defined as the availability and accessibility of information to market participants. For example, air travelers can use online travel agencies for hundreds of travel offers, compared to typically few offers from travel agents or airlines prior to the Internet era.

With the traditional queuing system, the advent of e-ticket booking over a decade has led to the mushrooming of online travel agencies offering a wide variety of services for a faster and more convenient mode of ticket booking of a train or flight ticket to something as exotic as a holiday. They offer various packages with holiday itineraries and a convenient pick-up and drop service.

Presented with the scenario analysis as put forth, Chaanan, CEO of Gheri.com, a travel portal that has been in existence since 2017, wondered whether she could now look at a bigger customer base.

Questions

1. What is the kind of research study that you can undertake for Ms.Chaanan?
2. Formulate the research problem and the objectives of your study.

Check Your Knowledge

CYK 1 Match the following

1. Research Aim	a. Is unemployment related to partner violence?
2. Research Objective	b. To investigate factors associated with partner violence
3. Research Questions	c. Examine the relationship between employment and partner violence

Answer

1-b, 2-c, 3-a

CYK 2 A good qualitative problem statement:

a. Defines the independent and dependent variables;

b. Conveys a sense of emerging design;

c. Specifies a research hypothesis to be tested;

d. Specifies the relationship between variables that the researcher expects to find.

Answer (d)

CYK 3 Which of the following quantitative research questions is superior?

a. "What is the effect of participation in various extra-curricular activities on academic performance?"

b. "What effect does playing high school football have on students' overall grade point average during the football season"?

Answer (b)

CYK 4 Match the following:

a. Studying job descriptions at Company– Infosys   i) Experimental research

b. Estimating the price of stocks in the next two years   ii) Applied research

c. Measuring impact of health drink on immunity   iii) Descriptive

d. Test marketing of a new phone   iv) Exploratory research

Answer

a-iii, b-iv, c-i, d-ii

CYK 5 Research data that explores the attitude and opinions of customers is known as

a. Qualitative

b. Quantitative

c. Opinion poll

d. Focus group data

Answer (a)

CYK 6 Which of the following variables cannot be expressed in quantitative terms?

a. Socio-economic status

b. Demographic customer segmentation

c. Numerical aptitude

d. Customer dissatisfaction

Answer (d)

Questions

1. What is meant by the research problem?
2. What are the criteria for the evaluation of the research problem?
3. What are the primary differences between qualitative and quantitative research techniques?
4. What is qualitative research, and how is it conducted?
5. How does pragmatic approach differ from a participatory approach to research?
6. Explain the various points to be considered while selecting a problem.

Application Questions

1. You are a research executive with five years of experience in a premier university. The university is offering a number of postgraduate courses. Though any kind of educational qualification enhances one's personality, you still believe that the two-year MBA program offered by the university has a slow and steady impact on personality development (especially in terms of 'Big 5' Personality) of the students. A research needs to be undertaken to establish your thoughts. Suggest the suitable research design.

   What would be the variables?

2. You are the HRD manager with the Treasuremoda (India), a leading design company specialising in women wear and home furnishing. Treasuremoda has recently taken over a significant unit in Bangalore. You are sent on an assignment there and are given the task of introducing a new operation scheme in the production line, which your parent organization feels will improve both effectiveness and efficiency. But you realize during your stay that there is an underlying dissatisfaction amongst the internal employees, and it is essential to gauge their view and opinion about the takeover and their expectations before introducing the scheme.

   What is the recommended research design? And why?

Literature Review, Hypothesis, and Research Design

Keywords: *Literature review, Evaluating literature, Research design, Exploratory research, Causal research, Descriptive research, Experimental Design, Hypothesis, Null hypothesis, Alternative hypothesis.*

A formal survey of professional literature is termed 'LITERATURE REVIEW' that is an integral component of research. It helps in understanding the progress done by others and sets the direction for further action. This process will help in framing and focus on the question and move closer to the hypothesis.

The literature review consists of a summative & evaluative report on studies probed related to the selected area. The review should be able to describe, summarize, assess, and clarify the literature. It should offer a theoretical basis for the research and also help determine the nature of the research at hand.

This review not only helps in deciding the general research question, but once the question is decided, the same sources of information that were consulted when coming up with the general question can now be used again to narrow the focus.

Basic purposes of the literature review

To provide a context to the research

To justify the need for the research.

Ensure the research is not replicated.

To substantiate where the research would fit into the prevailing body of knowledge.

To facilitate the researcher to draw conclusions from existing theory on the subject.

To illustrate the approach with which the subject has been previously dealt.

To highlight and put forth flaws in previous research.

To project gaps in previous research.

To illustrate the works added to the understanding of the field.

To help refine, refocus, or sometimes even change the topic.

A literature review goes much beyond the initial search for information and eventually includes even the identification and articulation of associations between the reviewed literature and the research field.

A good starting point for a literature review could be search engines, online books store, and dedicated websites. They would usually have publications on the subject in the libraries, fact sheets, articles, and bibliographies.

Relevance

Once the research topic has been decided, it is imperative to start exploring literature available to find out and search what is already known on the subject. An integral part of any project is to demonstrate how it fits and is useful to the context. A literature review can be resorted to for this purpose.

The review of literature enables core benefits to the research:

Generating ideas to be incorporated into the project

On identifying the topic, reading around it can help to see how other similar researches have been conducted. This helps to form new opinions around the problem area and also providing details of work done already so that it becomes the take-off point for fresh research.

Developing a framework for analysis

Data once gathered needs to be analyzed, and this analysis is facilitated by way of exploring concepts and their relations to each other. These integral concepts will be framed from a critical analysis of the reviewed literature.

Collecting secondary data

Reading related to the subject may also reveal relevant instances of other similar organizations or numerical data that may be useful for comparison with the research data. It is, therefore, absolutely essential to start reading as early as a project research idea has been framed.

> *How to approach the literature review (Compiling data to enable promptness and ease of referral)*
>
> - *Start at a generic level and, thereafter, outline the main features of the topic being researched.*
> - *Extend a brief overview of key ideas relevant to the topic.*
> - *Summarise, sort, compare and contrast the publications of key writers in the area*
> - *Narrow focus to highlight the most relevant reviews to the research*
> - *Highlight all areas where the research can offer fresh insights.*

Formatting Literature

Several steps may be undertaken in writing a strong literature review:

- Gathering, organizing and evaluating information
- Identifying the key ideas of the literature
- Highlighting the core arguments in the literature review

- Synchronize the main points of the literature review
- Eventually, write the literature review

> *Organizing the Literature Review*
>
> *The literature reviewed becomes easy to refer to, if it is organized in a schematic pattern. Different forms of organizing reviews could be:*
>
> - *Topical Order: Organize by main topics or issues; emphasize the relationship of the issues to the main problem.*
> - *Chronological Order: Organize the literature by the date the research was published*
> - *Problem-Cause-Solution Order: Organize the review so that it moves from the problem to the solution*
> - *General-to-Specific Order: (Also called the funnel approach) Examine broad-based research first and then focus on specific studies that relate to the topic*
> - *Specific-to-General Order: Try to discuss specific research studies so conclusions can be drawn.*

Gathering, organizing and evaluating information

Literature reviews are designed to provide an overview of sources that involves planning, reading, organizing, critical thinking, evaluating, and writing.

Involving strategies for reading (reference checklist, search options, speed reading & notes for reference) at the beginning of the review would enable clear categories evolving. These will later be used to develop an overall structure for the literature review. It would be a good idea to carefully register how other researchers classify their data and to see how they are structured.

Good literature reviews examine each individual work on their own and also in comparison to other works by firstly identifying and then analyzing them on a number of different research aspects and ideas. Some basis of comparison may be research topic, argument put forward, results presented and conclusions, methodology, theoretical approach, and keywords in use.

> *Good literature reviews:*
>
> - *Focused – The topic should be specific and narrow. It should be confine to presenting ideas and reports on studies that are already related to the topic.*
> - *Concise – Ideas should be presented in as much brief as possible.*
> - *Logical – The flow of text among paragraphs should be in a smooth and logical movement from one idea to the next*
> - *Developed – Never leave the story half told.*
> - *Integrative – The review text should stress how the ideas in the studies are collated, reviewed and contributed to the topic.*

Identifying the key ideas of the literature

Organizing the research starts with identifying & exploring the main ideas and trends that frequently appear in the topic or may pertain to the research question. These could be used as main ideas to classify the information and also sources that have been read. Eventually, these ideas can be put to use as the main topics of discussion.

Highlighting the core arguments in the literature review

The literature review should focus on a central theme about the texts that were consulted and need to be assimilated. This closely relates to the research question because it puts forth a situation in the literature compiled, which can be strongly motivating.

Synchronizing the main points of the literature review

Once the main ideas have been identified, they need to be now presented as a part of the literature review. They need to be organized in such a way so as to support the main argument. A well-thought over review presents all the relevant aspects of the topic in a very coherent order that could lead the readers to understand the context and the importance of the research question and project.

Writing the literature review

As and when all ideas of the literature review are understood and framed in order, writing can now flow much smoother. It is important to highlight some frequently occurring errors that need to be avoided:

- The review is not logically organized
- The review is not focused on the essential facets of the study
- Review does not relate literature to the study
- Too few references or outdated references cited
- The review is not written in the author's own words
- The review reads like a series of disjointed summaries
- Recent references are omitted

Hypothesis

The word **hypothesis** (plural is **hypotheses**) is derived from the Greek word 'hypothesis' meaning 'to put under' or 'to suppose'.

"A tentative explanation or clarification for an observation, phenomenon, causes, or scientific problem that can be tested by further study and investigation" is hypothesis said by The American Heritage Dictionary. A hypothesis is a specific statement of prediction and temporarily accepted as true in the light of what is, at the time, known about a phenomenon, and it is employed as a basis for action in search of new truth.

A hypothesis, as a probable hunch, offers an explanation to the situations under observation so as to enable designing the study to approve or disapprove it. What a researcher is trying to arrive at is a working and positive hypothesis. It is very tough, demanding, and more than that time consuming to attempt arriving at making adequate discriminations in the complexities of facts without hypothesis. It offers a specific course and direction to the study, eliminating blind search and relentless accumulation of data, and also goes a long way to delimit the scope of the problem at hand. The research hypothesis is a specific, clear, and testable proposition or predictive statement about the possible outcome of a research study.

The relevance of making a hypothesis:

- Hypothesis offers probable explanations to facts and phenomena, is open to testing and validation. It prepares the investigator for certain aspects of situations that may be relevant from the perspective of the questions posed in the problem.
- Hypothesis facilitate the researcher with rational & logical statements, comprising of elements expressed in sequential order of associations that attempt to describe conditions or events, which have not been confirmed by facts already. It is as such a guide to help plan the sequence of steps to follow.
- Hypothesis enables setting the direction to research. It specifies what may be relevant and what is irrelevant. The hypotheses convey to the researcher what he needs to be search out and why? Thus it eliminates unnecessary review of irrelevant literature and the accumulation and working on useless or excess data.
- A hypothesis provides a framework for arriving at conclusions. The researcher usually finds it very comfortable to test each hypothesis individually and state the conclusions relevant to each. It, as such, supports the preparation of the outline for setting conclusions in a sequential & meaningful way.

The hypothesis gets the research process started by laying down the guidelines or sequential steps to follow. The main advantage of stating a research hypothesis is that it requires the researcher to thoroughly think through what the research question implies, what measurements and variables are involved, and what statistical methods should be considered to analyze the data.

There are basic ten criteria in formulating hypotheses. A **hypothesis** should:

1. Stand a test;
2. Be expressed in clear language;
3. Be In accordance with the general theme of other hypotheses statements in the same field of study;
4. Be coordinated with the theory of science;
5. Be a tentative answer to the formulated problem;
6. Be logical and simplistic;
7. Consider available research techniques (to be able to analyze and interpret the results);
8. Be specific;
9. Be relevant to the collection of the empirical phenomenon and not merely conclude value judgments; and
10. In the case of exploratory research generally there exist no hypothesis.

Steps in formulating a hypothesis

Formulation of Hypothesis in research is an essential task and involves a five steps approach:

- Identify, select, and finalize the problem questions to be explored.
- Back it up with a list of your probable answers to the questions.
- The questions must be sentenced & sequenced in terms of the variables identified.
- Usually, one hypothesis for each question must be offered.
- At least one experiment must be conducted to test each hypothesis.

These are now hypotheses open to being objectively verified and tested. Thus, it may be concluded that a hypothesis emphatically states what we are looking for and is a suggested proposition or solution which can be tested for its validity & reliability.

Source of hypothesis

The hypothesis may be arrived at from the statement of the problem. They may sometimes be based on the review of compiled and studied research literature, or else they may even be drawn from data collection and analysis.

As such, the various sources of arriving at a hypothesis may be:

- Historical data assimilated on similar topics
- Brainstorming with co-researchers.
- Initial exploratory research in an attempt to arrive at possible outcomes.
- Prior empirical research findings.

To sum it up, the hypothesis put forward as a result of prior thinking & exploring the subject, review of the available data and literature which covers related studies and the opinions.

Types of hypothesis

Depending on the variable, testing technique, research elements covered, the hypothesis may be categories into the following main types:

- Simple Hypothesis
- Complex Hypothesis
- Logical Hypothesis
- Empirical Hypothesis
- Statistical Hypothesis
- Null Hypothesis (Denoted by "H0")
- Alternative Hypothesis (Denoted by "H1")

Simple hypothesis is a prediction of the relationship between two variables, i.e., the independent variable and the dependent variable. E.g., Drinking sugary drinks daily leads to obesity.

Complex hypothesis examines the relationship between two or more independent variables and two or more dependent variables. E.g., Overweight adults who 1) value longevity and 2) seek happiness are more likely than other adults to 1) lose their excess weight and 2) feel a more regular sense of joy.

Logical hypothesis is a proposed explanation and can be verified. It expresses the relationship whose inter-link can be joined on the basis of a logical explanation. E.g., Cacti experience more successful growth rates than lotus in a desert. (Until we're able to test lotus growth in the desert for an extended period of time, the evidence for this claim will be limited, and the hypothesis will only remain logical.)

Empirical hypothesis, or working hypothesis, comes to life when a theory is being put to test by using observation and experiment. It's no longer just an idea or notion. It's actually going through some trial and error, and perhaps changing around those independent variables. E.g., roses watered with liquid Vitamin B grow faster than roses watered with liquid Vitamin E. (Here, trial and error are leading to a series of findings.)

Statistical hypothesis is an examination of a portion of a population and stated in quantitative terms. Typically, they are statements about one or more parameters that provide measures of the populations under study. E.g., If you wanted to conduct a study on the IQ level of Teenagers, you would want to examine every single teenager. This is not practical. Therefore, you will conduct research using a statistical hypothesis or a sample of the teenage population.

Declarative hypothesis is a hypothesis where a researcher makes a positive statement or announcement or declaration about the outcome of the study. The researcher makes predictions based on his/her theoretical formulations of what would be the outcome if the explanations of the occurrences he/she has stated in his/her theory are proved correct. E.g., 'The academic performance of extroverts is visibly higher than that of the introverts', is a hypothesis in the declarative form.

Research hypothesis refers to a hypothesis depicting predictable associations between two variables and is open to testing. The research hypothesis typically comprises of an assumptive statement that attempts to relate an independent variable to a dependent one or simply a cause to an effect. More often than not, a research hypothesis must involve, at least, one independent and one dependent variable. It should always be stated in a form open to testing in order to check its appropriateness as a solution.

Research hypotheses are classified into a directional and non-directional hypothesis.

- **Directional hypothesis:** Those hypotheses which offer or suggest the direction of the expected associations or relationships are collectively prefixed as the directional hypotheses.E.g. Respondents with higher IQ's have lower anxiety levels as compared to respondents with low IQ.

- **Non-directional hypothesis:** Those research hypotheses, which, on the contrary, do not specify the direction of expected associations or relationships come under the jurisdiction of the non-directional research hypothesis. For example, anxiety levels of respondents differ with IQ.

Null hypothesis (H0) exists when a researcher believes there is no relationship between the two variables, or there is a lack of information to state a scientific hypothesis. This is something to attempt to disprove or discredit. Null hypothesis, H0: The world is flat.

This is where the **alternative hypothesis** (H1) enters the scene. In an attempt to disprove a null hypothesis, researchers will seek to discover an alternative hypothesis. Alternative hypothesis: The world is round.

The null hypothesis puts forward a statement that no relationship between variables exists. Since null hypotheses are open to testing statistically, they are sometimes also called the statistical hypothesis.

Let's imagine that you are investigating the effects of a new employee induction program and believe that one of the outcomes will be that there will be less employee absenteeism. Your two hypotheses might be stated something like this:

The null hypothesis for study is:

H0: As a result of the XYZ company induction training program, there will be no significant difference in employee absenteeism.

H1: As a result of the XYZ company employee training program, there will be a significant decrease in employee absenteeism.

The null hypothesis, H0, represents a theory that has been put forward. The theory is either because it is believed to be true or because it is to be used as a basis for argument, but has not been proved.

We give special consideration to the null hypothesis. This is because the null hypothesis relates to the statement being tested, whereas the alternative hypothesis relates to the statement to be accepted if the null hypothesis is rejected.

The alternative hypothesis, H1, is a statement of what a statistical hypothesis test is set up to establish. Since the null and alternative hypothesis are contradictory, the evidence must be used to examined and decide whether to reject the null hypothesis or not.

Alternative Hypothesis

First, a tentative assumption is made about the parameter or distribution. This assumption is called the null hypothesis and is denoted by H0. An alternative hypothesis (denoted by H1), which is the opposite of what is stated in the null hypothesis, is then defined. The hypothesis-testing procedure involves using sample data to determine whether or not

A Hypothesis Checklist

- *Does your hypothesis focus on something that you can actually test?*
- *Does your hypothesis include both an independent and dependent variable?*
- *Can you manipulate the variables?*
- *Can your hypothesis be tested without violating ethical standards?*

H0 can be rejected. If H0 is rejected, the statistical conclusion is that the alternative hypothesis H1 is true.

A hypothesis is a statement supposed to be true until it is proved false. It may be based on previous experience or maybe derived theoretically. First, a statistician or the investigator forms a research hypothesis to be tested. Then she/he derives a statement that is opposite to the research hypothesis (noting as H0). The approach here is to set up an assumption that there is no contradiction between the believed result and the sample result and that the difference, therefore, can be ascribed solely to chance. Such a hypothesis is called a null hypothesis (H0). It is the null hypothesis that is actually tested, not the research hypothesis. The object of the test is to see whether the null hypothesis should be rejected or accepted.

If the null hypothesis is rejected, that is taken as evidence in favor of the research hypothesis, which is called the alternative hypothesis (denoted by H1). For example, assume that a radio station selects the music it plays based on the assumption that the average age of its listening audience is 40 years. To determine whether this assumption is valid, a hypothesis test could be conducted with the null hypothesis as H0: $\mu = 40$ and the alternative hypothesis as H1 : $\mu \neq 40$. Based on a sample of individuals from the listening audience, the sample mean age, x, can be computed and used to determine whether there is sufficient statistical evidence to reject H0. Conceptually, a value of the sample mean that is close to 40 is consistent with the null hypothesis, while a value of the sample mean that is not close to 40 provides support for the alternative hypothesis.

> ***Characteristics of Good Hypothesis***
> - *It should be clear, precise & specific.*
> - *It should be open to testing.*
> - *It should clearly state or express the relationship between variables.*
> - *It should be stated in very simple terms*
> - *It should maintain consistency with known facts.*
> - *It should offer explanations to the facts that pave the way to the need for explanation.*
> - *It should be backed up with empirical research.*

Mathematical Symbols Used in H0 and H1:

NULL HYPOTHESIS: H_0	ALTERNATIVE HYPOTHESIS: H_1
equal (=)	not equal (≠) **or** greater than (>) **or** less than (<)
greater than or equal to (≥)	less than (<)
less than or equal to (≤)	more than (>)

Errors in Hypothesis testing

Ideally, the hypothesis-testing procedure leads to the acceptance of H0 when H0 is true and the rejection of H0 when H0 is false. Unfortunately, since hypothesis tests are based on sample information, the possibility of errors must be considered. A Type-I error corresponds to rejecting H0 when H0 is actually true, and a Type-II error corresponds to accepting H0 when H0 is false.

In testing any hypothesis, we get only two results: either we accept, or we reject it. We do not know whether it is true or false. Hence four possibilities may arise.

i.   The hypothesis is true, but the test rejects it (Type-I error).
ii. The hypothesis is false, but the test accepts it (Type-II error).
iii. The hypothesis is true, and the test accepts it (Correct decision).
iv. The hypothesis is false, and test rejects it (Correct decision).

Hypothesis formulation Guidelines

Hypotheses are assumptions or tentative generalized conclusions, based on stated facts and statements, and partly conceptual. Although there are no clear cut rules to hypothesis formulation, some conditions favoring the framing of a good hypothesis may be:

• **Extensive literature review and accumulation of relevant background knowledge**: A researcher may arrive at a hypothesis on making subsequent observations of behavior, occurrences & by noticing trends or probable associations. Involving observation for primary inputs and supporting with relevant secondary inputs enabling meaningful conclusions. E.g., Carefully observing the routine behavior of workers in a plant and relating it to secondary inputs about the organization to discover motivational factors and their impact.

• **Creativity & intellectual insight (Ability to read between the lines)**
Hypotheses are also drawn through deductive reasoning based on a theory. A researcher might initiate a study by choosing one of the theories in his own interest area. Consequent to selecting the theory, the researcher goes on to draw a hypothesis from this theory through logical probing. Creative imagination, which forms an integral component of stating the hypothesis, is based on adventures, attitude, sound, insight, and agile intellect.

Research Design

Research Design is an arrangement of conditions for the collection and analysis of data; also, it is the master plan that aims to combine relevance to the research purpose. It specifies the methods and procedures for collecting and analyzing the needed information and stands for advance planning. The methods to be adopted for collecting the relevant data and the techniques to be used in their analysis, keeping in view the plan, structure, and strategy of investigation conceived so as to obtain answers to research questions and control variance. In short, it is a blueprint on how a research study to be conducted.

After the research problem is established, i.e., **'what'** the next step is **'how'** of the study.

Research design Definition:

Sellitz et al. (1962) state that research design is the arrangement of conditions for the collection and analysis of data. It is conducted in a manner that aims to combine relevance to the research purpose with economy in procedure.

Important Concepts relating to research design

1. The dependent and independent variable

A variable which depends upon other known as dependent and antecedent is known as independent

E.g., Effect of study on marks. Study is independent variable and marks is dependent variable.

2. Extraneous variable

Independent variable that is not related to the purpose of study, but may affect the dependent variable is termed as an extraneous variable

E.g., Effect of work environment on performance.

3. Control

Control in research is designed to minimize the effects of variables other than the independent variable. This increases the reliability of the results.

4. Confounded relationship

When the dependent variable is not free from the influence of the extraneous variable, the relationship between the dependent and independent variables is said to be confounded by an extraneous variable.

5. Research hypothesis

A predictive statement that relates an independent variable to a dependent variable is the research hypothesis. It must contain at least one independent and one dependent variable.

ESSENTIALS OF GOOD RESEARCH DESIGN

- *A clear statement of the research problem*
- *It specifies the sources and types of information relevant to the research problem.*
- *Ensures the smallest experimental error*
- *Reliability of data collected and analyzed.*
- *Includes time and cost budgets.*
- *Flexible, Appropriate, Efficient, Economical*
- *Procedures and techniques to be used for gathering information on the population to be studied.*
- *Methods to be used in the processing and analyzing data.*

6. Experimental and non-experimental hypothesis-testing research.

Research in which the independent variable is manipulated is termed as experimental hypothesis-testing research, and research in which an independent variable is not manipulated is called non-experimental hypothesis-testing research. E.g., Training and Performance, or Price and Sales, or Advertisement expenses and Sales.

7. Experimental and control groups (in experimental hypothesis-testing research)

Both these groups are drawn randomly from the same population, the only difference between the two groups is that the independent variable is changed for the experimental group, but is held constant in the control group.

8. Treatments

The different stimuli inflicted upon experimental and control groups are referred as treatment.

E.g., if we want to determine through an experiment, the comparative impact of three varieties of fertilizers on the yield of pulses, in that the three varieties of fertilizers will be treated as three treatments.

9. Experiments

Experiment is testing the cause and effect relationship under control condition. It is the process of examining the truth of a statistical hypothesis, related to some research problems.

10. Experimental units

It refers to the predetermined plots or the blocks, where different treatments are used.

Types of Research Design

There are a number of research designs available for investigation of the research objectives. Research design is of two types i.e exploratory and conclusive research design. The choice of the most appropriate design depends largely on the problem and objectives of the research.

TWO TYPES OF RESEARCH DESIGN

EXPLORATORY RESEARCH	CONCLUSIVE RESEARCH
Is loosely structured in design	Is well structured and systematic in design
Is flexible and investigative in methodology	Is a formal and definitive methodology that needs to be followed and tested
Does not involve testing of hypothesis	Most conclusive researches are carried out to test the formulated hypothesis
Findlings might be topic-specific and might not have much relevance outside the researcher's domain	Findings are significant as they have a theoretical or applied implication

DESCRIPTIVE	CAUSAL
Types of data is qualitative	Types of data is quantitative
Secondary data, surveys, panels, and observation are preferred methods used	Experimental Methods is used
Somewhat defined problem	Clearly defines problems
Describes in detail problems, situations, markets and customers	Test Hypothesis about cause and effect relationship. Uncover causality

CROSS-SECTIONAL DESIGN	LONGITUDINAL DESIGN
Interview a fresh sample of people each time they are carried out	Follow the same sample of people over time

SINGLE CROSS SECTIONAL	MUTLIPLE-CROSS SECTIONAL
Only one sample respondents is drawn	There are two or more samples of respondents

Three traditional categories of research design which are mostly used are:

- **Exploratory**
- **Descriptive**
- **Causal**

Exploratory Research

Exploratory Research explores and identifies new problems. The main purpose is to formulate a problem for more specific deep diving and for developing the working hypotheses for future operation. It is commonly unstructured research that is employed to access background information pertaining to the general nature of the research problem. This type of research is usually involved in a situation where the researcher does not have much knowledge about the problem and requires additional information. It is usually conducted to have a better grasp of the existing problem but does not lead to a conclusive result.

> *Exploratory research finds application in a number of situations,*
> - *In order to gain background information.*
> - *Understanding & defining terminology.*
> - *Clarifying problems and hypotheses.*
> - *Ascertaining research priorities.*
> - *Creating meaningful questions to be answered.*

Features of Exploratory Research

- Exploratory research mostly involves qualitative data.
- This is inexpensive yet time-consuming research with no predefined structure.
- There is often no prior relevant information available.
- It is interactive and open-ended in nature. It attempts to answers questions like 'how and why'.
- It is usually flexible as there is no standard for carrying out exploratory research.
- Conclusions can not be based on exploratory research.

The process of exploratory research varies according to the phenomenon, data, or insight. Also named as interpretative research or grounded theory approach, the results of this research provide answers to questions like 'what, how and why'.

Methods of conducting Exploratory Research:

The methods applied in the context of research design for exploratory studies are:

I Survey of concerning Literature

- Reviewing & evaluating pre-existing work done by other researchers.

II Experience survey

- Understanding through gaining access to the practical experience of people through a survey.
- Derive and obtaining relationships between variables and new ideas relating to the research problem.

III Analysis of insight stimulating examples

- This consists of the intensive study of selected instances of the problem areas in which the researcher wants to dwell upon.
- Existing inputs may be examined, and could go further by way of unstructured interviews.

Descriptive research

Descriptive research describes a population or phenomenon under study. This is used as it is important to have an understanding of what a research problem is about before beginning to investigate. This research is classified into different types according to the kind of approach being used:

The different types are:

Descriptive-survey: is using surveys to gather data about varying subjects. This data targets knowing the extent to which different conditions can be ascertained among respondents. For example, a researcher wants to estimate the entry-level qualification at a B-School. A survey can be used, and each item on the survey asks qualifications related questions and is subjected to a Yes/No answer.

Descriptive-normative survey: is an addition to the descriptive-survey, where the researcher adds the normative element. In this survey, the results of the study must be compared with the norm. For example, B-School wishes to test the capabilities of its students to make task teams. The tests are the evaluation tool in this case, and the results of the test are compared to the norm prescribed for each team member.

Descriptive-status: is a quantitative description approach seeking to answer questions about real-life situations. For example, a researcher is trying to find payouts of employees & mapping it up with their level of satisfaction. **Descriptive classification:** is used in life sciences for the classification of species.

Descriptive-comparative: involves considering two variables that are not manipulated and trying to establish a formal procedure to conclude the better of the two. For example, attempting to determine the better method of teaching between online & offline.

Features of Descriptive Research

- It uses quantitative methods of collecting information to be used for further statistical analysis of the population sample.
- It may also involve qualitative data to describe the research problem. This is because of the more exploratory than the experimental approach of this research.
- The research variables remain uncontrolled in this type of research.
- The results of the research form the basis for further research and can be analyzed and used in other research methods. This is because it provides basic information about the research problem.

Descriptive research is a framework used for conclusive research and is further subdivided into two categories: cross-sectional studies and longitudinal studies. **A cross-sectional study** investigates a specific chunk of the population under study. It is scientific in its approach. A single sample of the identified population that is studied over a stretched period of time is termed as **longitudinal study design**.

Causal research

Causal research, also called Explanatory research, is a category conclusive research because it reveals a cause and effect relationship between two variables. Like descriptive research, this research tries to prove an idea or a finding. However, it differs in methodology & purpose. While descriptive research is broader in scope, focussing on defining an opinion, attitude, idea, or behavior, causal research has only two objectives:

1. Understanding the cause & effect variables: For example, determining whether a certain drug has an impact on the understanding of children.

2. Establishing the relationship between the causal variables and net effect predicted: For example, quantifying the impact of drugs on the understanding level and observing how the relationship works.

Research designs used under causal research:

Experimental Design: This design was propagated by Professor R.A. Fisher. Experimental methods apply to methods in which the researcher tests the hypothesis of a causal relationship between variables. Experimental design refers to the framework or structural of an experiment.

We can classify experimental designs into two broad categories, viz., informal experimental designs, and formal experimental designs. Informal experimental designs are those designs that normally use a less sophisticated form of analysis based on differences in magnitudes, whereas formal experimental designs offer relatively more control and use precise statistical procedures for analysis. Important experiment designs are as follows:

Informal experimental designs:

- Before-and-after without control design.
- After-only with control design.
- Before-and-after with control design.

Formal experimental designs:

- Completely randomized design (C.R. Design).
- Latin square design (L.S. Design).
- Randomized block design (R.B. Design).
- Factorial designs.

1. Before-and-after without control design: In such a design a single test group or area is selected and the dependent variable is measured before the introduction of the treatment. The treatment is then introduced and the dependent variable is measured again after the treatment has been introduced. The effect of the treatment would be equal to the level of the phenomenon after the treatment minus the level of the phenomenon before the treatment. The design can be represented thus:

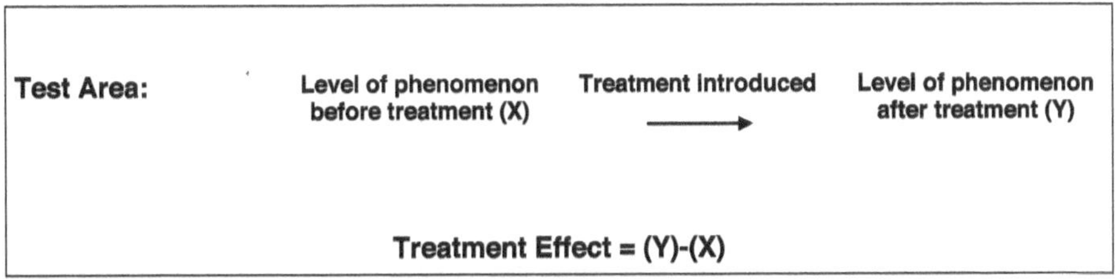

2. After-only with control design: In this design, two groups or areas (test area and control area) are selected and the treatment is introduced into the test area only. The dependent variable is then measured in both the areas at the same time. Treatment impact is assessed by subtracting the value of the dependent variable in the control area from its value in the test area. This can be Exhibited in the following form: The basic assumption in such a design is that the two areas are identical with respect to their behaviour towards the phenomenon considered. If this assumption is not true, there is the possibility of extraneous variation entering into the treatment effect. This design is superior to before-and-after without control design.

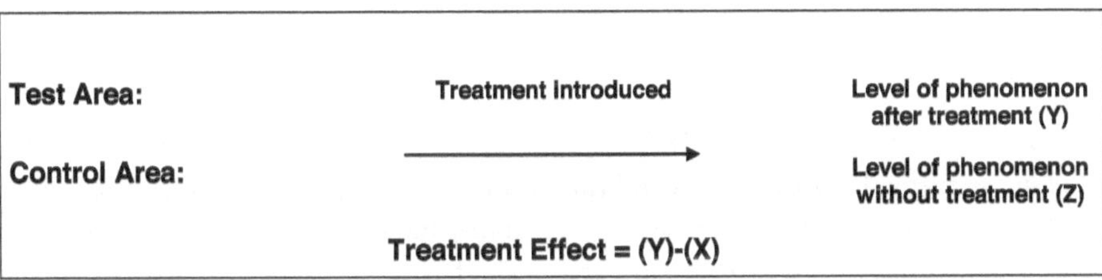

3. Before-and-after with control design: In this design, two areas are selected and the dependent variable is measured in both the areas for an identical time-period before the treatment. The treatment is then introduced into the test area only, and the dependent variable is measured in both for an identical time-period after the introduction of the treatment. The treatment effect is determined by subtracting the change in the dependent variable in the control area from the change in the dependent variable in test area. This design is superior to the above two designs for the simple reason that it avoids extraneous variation resulting both from the passage of time and from non-comparability of the test and control areas. But at times, the first two informal designs should be considered to overcome data, time, or a comparable control area.

Test Area:	Level of phenomenon before treatment (X)	Treatment introduced ⟶	Level of phenomenon after treatment (Y)
Control Area:	Level of phenomenon before treatment (A)		Level of phenomenon without treatment (Z)

Treatment Effect = (Y-X) - (Z-A)

4. Completely randomized design (C.R. design): Involves only two principles viz., the principle of replication, and the principle of randomization of experimental designs. It is the simplest possible design and its procedure of analysis is also easy. The essential characteristic of the design is that subjects are randomly assigned experimental treatments (or vice-versa). For instance, if we have 10 subjects and if we wish to test 5 under treatment A and 5 under treatment B, the randomization process gives every possible group of 5 subjects selected from a set of 10 an equal opportunity of being assigned to treatment A and treatment B. One-way analysis of variance (or one-way ANOVA) is used to analyse such a design. Unequal replications can also work in this design. Such a design is generally used when experimental areas happen to be homogeneous. Technically, when all the variations due to uncontrolled extraneous factors are included under the heading of chance variation, we refer to the design of experiment as C.R. design. We can present a brief description of the two forms of such a design as given in the figure.

Population	⟶	Randomly Selected	Sample	⟶	Randomly Assigned	⟶	Experimental Group	⟵	Treatment A	Independent variable
						⟶	Control Group	⟵	Treatment B	

5. Latin square design (L.S. design): It is an experimental design very frequently used in agricultural research. The conditions under which agricultural investigations are carried out are different from those in other studies because nature plays an important role in agriculture. For instance, an experiment has to be made through which the effects of five different varieties of fertilizers on the yield of a certain crop, say wheat, it to be judged. In such a case the varying fertility of the soil in different blocks in which the experiment has to be performed must be taken into consideration; otherwise the results obtained may not be very dependable because the output happens to be the effect not only of fertilizers, but it may also be the effect of fertility of soil. Similarly, there may be impact of varying seeds on the yield. To overcome such difficulties, the L.S. design is used when there are two major extraneous factors i.e., the varying soil fertility and varying seeds.

6. Randomized block design (R.B. design): It is an improvement over the C.R. design. In the R.B. design the principle of local control can be applied along with the other two principles of experimental designs. In the R.B. design, subjects are first divided into groups, known as blocks, such that within each group the subjects are relatively homogeneous with respect to some selected variable. The variable selected for grouping the subjects is believed to be related to the measures of the dependent variable. The number of subjects in a given block would be equal to the number of treatments and one subject in each block would be randomly assigned to each treatment.

		Fertility Level				
		I	II	III	IV	V
	X1	A	B	C	D	E
	X2	B	C	D	E	A
Seeds	X3	C	D	E	A	B
	X4	D	E	A	B	C
	X5	E	A	B	C	D

In general, blocks are the levels at which we hold the extraneous factor fixed, so that its contribution to the total variability of data can be measured. The main feature of the R.B. design is that in this each treatment appears the same number of times in each block. The R.B. design is analysed by the two-way analysis of variance (two-way ANOVA)* technique. The Latin-square design is one wherein each fertilizer, in our example, appears five times but is used only once in each row and in each column of the design. In other words, the treatments in a L.S. design are so allocated among the plots that no treatment occurs more than once in any one row or any one column. The two blocking factors may be represented through rows and columns. The following is a diagrammatic form of such a design with respect to five types of fertilizers, viz., A, B, C, D and E and the two blocking factor viz., the varying soil fertility and the varying seeds.

7. Factorial designs: Factorial designs are used in experiments where the effects of varying more than one factor are to be determined. They are specially important in several economic and social phenomena where usually a large number of factors affect a particular problem. Factorial designs can be of two types: simple factorial designs and complex factorial designs.

In case of simple factorial designs, we consider the effects of varying two factors on the dependent variable, but when an experiment is done with more than two factors, we use complex factorial designs. Simple factorial design is also termed as a 'two-factor-factorial design', whereas complex factorial design is known as 'multifactor-factorial design.' Simple factorial design may either be a 2 × 2 simple factorial design, or it may be, say, 3 × 4 or 5 × 3 or the like type of simple factorial design. We illustrate some simple factorial designs as under:

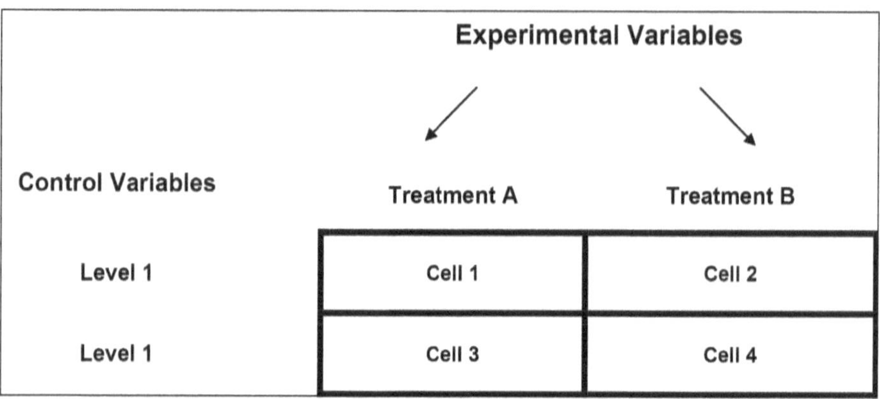

Illustration: (2 × 2 simple factorial design). A 2 × 2 simple factorial design can be depicted as follows: In this design the extraneous variable to be controlled by homogeneity is called the control variable and the independent variable, which is manipulated, is called the experimental variable.

Then there are two treatments of the experimental variable and two levels of the control variable. As such there are four cells into which the sample is divided. Each of the four combinations would provide one treatment or experimental condition. Subjects are assigned each treatment in a random manner, in the same manner as in a randomized group design.

Study I Data

		Training		Row Mean
		Treatment A	Treatment B	
Control (Intelligence)	Level I (Low)	15.5	23.3	19.4
	Level II (High)	35.8	30.2	33.0
	Column Mean	25.6	26.7	

Study II Data

		Training		Row Mean
		Treatment A	Treatment B	
Control (Intelligence)	Level I (Low)	10.4	20.6	15.5
	Level II (High)	30.6	40.4	35.5
	Column Mean	20.5	30.5	

The means for different cells may be obtained along with the means for different rows and columns. Means of different cells represent the mean scores for the dependent variable. The column means in the given design are termed the main effect for treatments without taking into account any differential effect that is due to the level of the control variable. Similarly, the row means in the said design are termed the main effects for levels without regard to treatment.

Thus, through this design we can study the main effects of treatments as well as the main effects of levels. An additional merit of this design is that one can examine the interaction between treatments and levels, through which one may say whether the treatment and levels are independent of each other or not.

Recap & Review Section

SUMMARY Chapter 3

After problem identification, the next step is to formulate the objective of research post literature review. A literature review is a significant step to review the collection of the most relevant and significant publications regarding that topic or problem in order to provide a comprehensive look at what has been said on the topic and by whom and what are the gaps. The formulation of the objective is set after a literature review that gives direction to a study. The researcher should also propose a set of solutions to the problem, that is called a hypothesis. The hypothesis is of various forms such as Simple Hypothesis, Complex Hypothesis, Logical Hypothesis, Empirical Hypothesis, Statistical Hypothesis, Null Hypothesis (Ho), and Alternative Hypothesis (H1).

Having selected the problem, literature review, formulating objective, and hypothesis, the researcher has to prepare a plan of action called research design. The research design includes a series of decisions regarding definitions, scope, methods, techniques, procedures, time expenditure, and administration process. This part covers the total spectrum of research endeavor in a simple step by step manner.

Caselet 2 – Ajooni International

Vishal had joined a month back and was due to meet Tanvir. Vishal opened the door and walked into Tanvir's room. Tanvir asked him to be seated and said, **"so doctor, what is the diagnosis?"**

Vishal Nair had been recently hired as the company Leadership Coach at Ajooni International. The need for the hiring came, Tanvir Narang, the MD, felt that he was fed up with the team of non-performers. He had hired the assistant managers, managers and decision-makers from the most prestigious institutions having 5yrs of minimum work-experience. Each one came with a proven track record. The compensation was competitive, yet nothing was moving.

When Vishal went to meet Himanshu Chabbra, the bright star who had joined three months, back, Himanshu was reported absent and seemed to be suffering from hypertension and sugar. His colleagues were not aware that Himanshu had not come for the past one week. During his conversation with Tanvir's secretary, he could hear Ms.Kajol, the HR head, yelling at the top of her voice at a new recruit. After 4 weeks of joining, she was sharing his job role. Managers were laid-back, extremely critical, and not moving.

Tanvir also made some structural changes as per the nature of a business once it merged with a couple of startups. The company offers good infrastructure, attractive compensation, but it is like a stagnant pool of the best talent.

Questions

1. Formulate the above case into a research problem and state the objectives of the study.
2. Develop the working hypothesis for the study.

Check Your Knowledge

CYK 1 Suggest a suitable null hypothesis to the situation presented below:

Individuals who listen to music whilst revising will achieve significantly higher exam grades than will individuals who revision in silence. **Hypothesis I**: There will be no difference in exam grade between those individuals who revise whilst listening to music and those individuals who revise in silence

Hypothesis II The more music an individual listens to when they are revising, the higher their exam grade will be & vice versa

Hypothesis III Individuals who listen to music whilst revising for their exam will achieve significantly lower exam grades than will individuals who revise in silence

Hypothesis IV There will be no relationship between examination grade and the amount of music or silence experienced during revision.

Answer (d)

CYK 2 In the above-mentioned question, which of these hypothesis qualifies to be a directional hypothesis.
a. Hypothesis I
b. Hypothesis II
c. Hypothesis III
d. Hypothesis IV

Answer (b)

Questions

Q1. What is the difference between exploratory, descriptive, and causal research?
Q2. List the major components of the research design.
Q3. What are the potential sources of error that can affect a research design?
Q4. How does formulating a research design differ from developing a problem?
Q5. Differentiate between exploratory and conclusive research.
Q6. What are the major purposes of descriptive research?
Q7. Define a research design? Illustrate with examples.
Q8. While exploratory research design records lowest accuracy of findings, every research is recommended to include them. Justify the statement with suitable examples.
Q9. Elucidate, 'The majority of the research designs are exploratory cum descriptive in nature in business research'.

Q10. Distinguish between:
1. Exploratory and descriptive research designs
2. Conclusive vs. Causal Research

Application Questions

1. KK jeweler is a small jewelry store from Ludhiana owned by Kundan Kumar. He is into the business of designing traditional Kundan jewelry. He believes that participating in an Exhibition in INDIA Expo 2021 will boost his sales as this will give him exposure to Indian & foreign clients. It is the month of March & he has to decide by September whether or not to Exhibit.

Suggest a suitable research design for this study and justify your selection. What would be the variables, hypothesis, and population under study?

2. Assume you are a consultant hired to evaluate the effectiveness of an industrial safety program undertaken by a large manufacturing organization. The safety program is a behavioral one that provides rewards such as monetary bonuses or extra paid vacation days, for safety behaviors in terms of accident free days, weeks, etc. The task is to devise an approach (a research strategy, a design, a set of measures, and a general analysis strategy) that will allow you to evaluate the safety program.

When developing a plan, be sure to address at least the following issues:
1. The type of research design. Compare and contrast with other possible designs.
2. Form Null and Alternative Hypothesis for the plan suggested.

Data Collection & Presentation

> **Keywords:** *Data Forms, Primary data, Secondary data, Experimental data, Data Adequacy, Data Accuracy, Tabulation-Simple & Complex, Observation, Testing effect, Interview, Types of interview, Questionnaire, Brainstorming, Delphi Technique, Projective Techniques, Case Study, Data errors, Data Editing, Data presentation, Quantitative research, Qualitative research, Types & Forms of Questionnaire, Open Ended & Close ended questions, Double barrelled questions, Loaded & leading questions.*

Data collection is defined as the procedure of collecting, measuring, and analyzing accurate insights for research using standard validated techniques. It involves gathering information on variables under study in a systematic fashion, enabling the researcher to find answers to the pre-defined research questions, test hypotheses, and arrive at outcomes. Data collection remains a component of research in all fields of study, including humanities, social sciences, business management, etc. The methods of data collection might vary in each discipline, but the accuracy & honesty in collecting data in all remains sacrosanct.

The ultimate objective of data collection is to accumulate rich and reliable information, statistical analysis tools may be incorporated for data-driven decisions. In dealing with any real-life problem, the data at hand are often inadequate, and hence, it becomes necessary to collect appropriate data. There are many ways of collecting the appropriate data, which differ considerably in the context of money, costs, time, and other resources at the disposal of the researcher.

Forms of Data

The task of data collection begins after the research problem has been defined and the plan formulated. While deciding about the method of data collection to be used for the study, the researcher should keep in mind two types of data viz., primary and secondary. It is important to know, however, that exclusivity in both the forms may not be possible to maintain and the third form of combination data might emerge. The accumulation of data in a systematic and controlled manner to facilitate research in terms of hypothesis formulation and to achieve suitable outcomes is called data collection.

Different Forms of data:
– Primary data
– Secondary data
– Combination data

The primary data are those which are collected afresh. It is collected for the first time and thus happens to be original. Whereas secondary data are those have been already been collected by someone else and has passed the statistical process. The researcher would have to decide which sort of data to be used for the study (primary or secondary). We describe the different methods of data collection, with the pros and cons of each method.

	Primary Data	**Secondary Data**
Definition	This is first-hand data collected by the researcher	This is data pre-existing on multiple sources
Nature	This is raw data open to the compilation and finding application as suited to researchers study	This is compiled data suited to fit an already established research
Editing	Usually, this does not require editing as it is collected as per a specific research question	Usually, this requires editing as it has been collected for previous research and finding a fit into another
Reliability	Relatively High	Relatively low
Validity	Relatively more as this is time & place specific	Relatively less due to time & place disconnect
Time & Cost involved	Usually, more time consuming & expensive	Usually, less time consuming & in-expensive
Suitabilty	More	Less
Flexibilty	High	Low
Adaptabilty	High	Low

The importance of ensuring accurate and appropriate data collection:

Data forms the basis of all decision making and assessments in any research. The process, as well as outcomes, are hugely impacted by the accumulation & assimilation of data. As such, regardless of the field of study or preference for defining data (quantitative, qualitative), accurate data collection is essential to maintaining the integrity of research. Both the selection of appropriate data collection instruments (existing, modified, or newly developed) and specifying instructions are of prime relevance and would reduce the likelihood of errors. Good data collection requires a clear process to ensure the data you collect is clean, reliable, and consistent.

Based on their source and approach to procurement, data classification falls into two primary forms.

Primary Data

Primary data consist of information collected first hand by the researcher. This data involves the use of instruments such as surveys involving questionnaires, interviews (individual or panel), focus groups, or observation etc. Primary data, as such, yields a record containing first-hand information, which is original data. Primary data provides the most accurate and up-to-date inputs and also has the advantage of tailor-made specifications. The degree of flexibility is much higher than that in secondary data since the collection instruments can be modified to suit the researcher's specific objectives.

This data has never been collected or sought before, whether in any specific way or at any specific period. Researchers use this type of data when what they are seeking in the research problem is not already available or, if available, is not valid or substantial enough.

> **PRIMARY DATA**
> - *Activity Sampling Technique*
> - *Brainstorming*
> - *Case Study*
> - *Diaries Method*
> - *Delphi Technique*
> - *Experimental Method*
> - *Focus Group*
> - *Interviews*
> - *Link Analysis*
> - *Observation*
> - *Questionnaire*
> - *Principal Component Analysis*
> - *Projective technique*
> - *Process Analysis*
> - *Survey*
> - *Statistical Method*
> - *Time and Motion Study*

The major drawback of this data, however, is that it may involve a lot of cost and effort. Also, in case of organizational or institutional involvement, there could be issues like confidentiality, which might pose a challenge. This data, as such, requires permission and authorization to collect.

Secondary Data

Secondary data, on the contrary, is primarily data collected by someone else. Any published or unpublished inputs which the source is mentioning are secondary. This form of data usually describes, summarizes, analyzes & evaluates inputs derived from primary sources. This type of data is made available from relevant studies done by other institutional researchers or organizations. Secondary data holds validity and is reliable but must be identifiable with a careful understanding of the collection,

> **SECONDARY DATA**
> - *Books*
> - *Biographies*
> - *Databases*
> - *Data archives*
> - *Desk Research*
> - *Internet articles*
> - *Newspapers*
> - *Published censuses or other statistical data*
> - *Records*
> - *Research articles by other researchers (journals) etc.*

objectives, and instruments used. Researchers employ this data as it is easier to collect and relatively cheaper to procure.

It may be noteworthy to mention here that while most researchers use secondary data (literature review) as a take-off point, this is no way sufficient and must be supplemented with primary sources.

An extension of the Primary data & Secondary data would be a third form called the Combination data. All researches begin with secondary data, which if found in-sufficient or less reliable or less suitable, are backed by primary data. This form of using both Primary & Secondary data alongside research is called using Combination data.

Combination Data

Using a combination of both primary and secondary data, applying secondary research initially and then backing it up with primary research to block any lacunas in the study is the core basis of this approach. It gives researchers a more comprehensive picture.

While secondary data continues to be much readily accessible and inexpensive, it is essential to test the secondary data against several considerations:

1. **Data measurement units**: The researcher has to ensure constancy in the use of unit definitions as those in the earlier investigation.
2. **Adequacy**: Adequacy of the data and deciding if it is substantial enough depends on the requirements of the survey problem as well as the geographical area covered or proposed to be covered by the available data. It is always a good idea to study the purpose and objectives for which we are collecting data.
3. **Accuracy:** The researcher has to understand and act as per the degree of accuracy necessary and critical to the research.
4. **Time & Condition of Collected data:** It is imperative to ascertain before using available data, the time & conditions under which we are collecting. Allocating data collected to a specific time frame would help establish its current usefulness.
5. **Comparison:** Investigators should ensure that the secondary data is logical, consistent, and comparable. Also, if there are several data sources available, they could be unrealistic when offering conflicting statistics.
6. **Test Checking:** The relevance of the secondary data must be assured only when checked against totality in the results achieved. This checking would also involve a check on the data collection technique and instruments involved.

Techniques of Data Collection

A variety of techniques to accumulate both quantitative as well as qualitative data may be in use. Some frequently used techniques include:

Observation

Gathering data by watching behavior is called Observation. This technique is based on the passive non-involvement of the researcher and allows the respondents to react as they would typically do. Observations can be **overt** (when the respondents know the researcher is observing; **participative observation**) or **covert** (participants ignorant of being observed; **non-participant observation.**). The benefits of covert observation is that people are more likely to behave as they naturally do if they do not know they are

> **Testing Effect:** An effect where respondents suppress or disguise their true behaviour or thoughts and fake behaviour because they know that they are being tested upon

under observation. This effect or error where respondents tend to suppress their actual responses in the garb of fake or made-up reactions because they know they are being tested is known as **testing effect**.

Unobtrusive (without interference), non-participant data collection helps to reduce the testing effect in a big way. However, overt observations might sometimes be resorted to, because of ethical issues. Observations can also be either **direct** or **indirect**. Direct observation is when the observer is watching interactions, processes, or behaviors as they occur, for example, observing a doctor at his clinic with his patients. Indirect observations are when we watch the results of interactions, processes, or behaviors; for example, measuring the number of patients in the waiting queue or observing hospital staff and reactions towards the doctor to make inferences about his popularity & goodwill. Further observations where the observer's physical presence is

> **Bottlenecks due to errors in data collection may lead to:**
> - *Inaccuracy or failure in answering research ques-tions.*
> - *Inability to repeat the study.*
> - *Vague or absurd findings leading to wastage of re-sources applied.*
> - *Misleading for future direction of research.*

unavoidable on account of inaccuracies in data collection that might crop in, a solution could be in the form of **Disguised observation.** i.e., the researcher poses as a part of the group, and his presence and status in the group remain unannounced, so he blends as a part of the group and can collect accurate and substantial inputs.

Interview

The interview consists of verbal questioning. Generally, an interview comprises of a two-person conversation, started by the interviewer. The purpose of the interview is to obtain research-relevant information desired on the inputs specified by the research objectives.

Some noticeable characteristics of an interview are:

- Personal communication
- Equal status (the status of the interviewer as that of the interviewee are equal)
- Time-based relationship between interviewer and the interviewee
- Scope of flexibility in the format & conduct of the interview
- Instant response

Types of interviews:

Unstructured: There are no prescribed specifications on the language or sequencing of questions to be posed. This form of interview generally starts on a very informal note, while subsequent probing might follow. The interviewer frames questions as and when desired. The format of this interview is, therefore, very flexible and open to many variations as per the interviewer's discretion.

Structured: This format finds its basis upon the structured interview-guide, which in nature and approach is very similar to the questionnaire. It consists of a set of specific and particular questions that are pre-decided by the interviewer and leaving no scope for alterations. The structured approach offers more objectivity in assessment and facilitates comparisons amongst respondents.

Standardized: In these interviews, answers to questions are standardized and are determined or fall into a set of response categories pre-defined for this purpose. The research respondents are to choose one of the given options suggested as the most probable or exact answer. Standardization forms a part of the close-ended technique. Although it is inflexible in approach, it provides clear assessment parameters.

Unstandardized: No options in anticipation are provided. Open-ended in approach and allow much flexibility, yet open to bias by the researcher. This approach is used mainly in qualitative research.

Individual: A format in which the researcher involves only one respondent at a specified time slot.

Group interview: Simultaneous interviewing of more than one respondent. The group may be small or large depending upon the objectives & problems at hand.

Self-administered: The respondent is provided a question list along with an instruction manual on how to write answers appropriately in the interview form. Self-administering becomes more like a questionnaire technique of survey.

Unique: in this approach, the interviewer collects complete information together in only one interview. This interview is detailed and comprehensive.

Panel interviews: The interviewer attempts to collect inputs from the same group of respondents on an ongoing basis, i.e., two or more times at regularly spaced out intervals. If the choice of the respondents differs in various stages for probing the same question, this becomes a Trend Study.

Soft interview: This form of interview is more of a guidance delivery form. The interviewer guides the respondents through the interview without pressurizing them. The candidates are totally at ease & this is informal and non-probing.

Hard or stress interview: The interviewer tries to cross-check the validity and completeness of the answers obtained. Stress interviews may involve frequent warnings to the respondents about not attempting to lie and forcing them to offer answers when hesitant.

Personal interviews: These involve one-to-one or direct contact between both the interviewer and the interviewee. Personal interviews can be conducted through online mode.

Non-personal interviews: This interview involves no one-to-one contact and the information collection is made possible over the telephone, video conferencing, or another medium.

– Focus group

A focus group, according to Lederman (see Thomas et al. 1995) is, "a technique involving the use of in-depth group interviews in which participants are selected because they are purposive, although not necessarily representative, sampling of a specific population, this group being focused on a given topic".

The selection of participants in this research is basis the criteria that they have something to say on the topic. They come with similar backgrounds and are within the age-range, have similar socio-characteristics, and would be comfortable talking to the interviewer and amongst each other (Richardson & Rabiee, 2001). This approach to selection relates to the concept of 'applicability', in which focus groups could provide information about a range of ideas and feelings that individuals have about specific issues, as well as illuminating the differences in perspective between groups of individuals. Participants should share similar characteristics: gender group, age-range, ethnic, and social class background.

Most researchers recommend that participants should not know each other, thus encouraging more honest and spontaneous expression of views and a more extensive range of responses. It also prevents set behaviors relating to pre-existing relationships and patterns of leadership in the group (see Thomas et al. 1995).

Kitzinger (1994), on the other hand, advocates the use of pre-existing groups, as acquaintances could relate to each other's comments and maybe in a better position to challenge one another.

– Questionnaire

A questionnaire is a set of questions in the written form for gathering information from a vast range of individuals. Handing out of questionnaires by mail, telephone, using face-to-face interviews, as handouts, or electronically (i.e., by e-mail or through web-based questionnaires) is possible.

A questionnaire which sometimes may not be handed out as such and involves researchers self-presence in filling up the answers while the respondent voices them is called a schedule.

Comparison Parameter	Questionnaire	Schedule
Definition	It consists of a series of questions in a written format.	It is a set of statements in a written form but to be administered verbally by the researcher.
To be filled up by	Respondent	Researcher
Response Rate	Low	High
Cost involved	Low	High
Expected Coverage	Large	Small
Resondents identity	Not Known	Known
Respondents qualifier	Basic literate minimum	No literacy level required
Physical appearance	Relevant	Insignificant
Scope of biases	Less	More

When & where should questionnaires be used? (Understanding data requirements to problem objectives)

When resources are limited, and you need data from many people. *Covering huge sample sizes is the most cost & time effective way in this approach. The researcher can disseminate questionnaires relatively inexpensively. The costs will increase if there is a need to do many follow-ups to get a sufficient response rate.*

To gather data about knowledge, beliefs, attitudes, and behaviors. *Questionnaires help gather information that is unique to individuals, such as attitudes or knowledge. Being formal & structured in approach, they are prone to lesser objections and higher efficacy in gathering responses.*

When the privacy of participants needed to be maintained. *Questionnaires help maintain participants privacy because participants responses can be anonymous or confidential. Pri-vacy is especially important if the researcher is gathering sensitive information. Maintaining privacy concerns increases the willingness of respondents to participate.*

The most significant advantage associated with a questionnaire is that since it involves lesser physical involvement of the researcher, it is possible to administer over diversely spread out geographical locations. The questionnaire technique is, as such, the most widely used technique for survey methods involving large sample sizes.

– Brainstorming

Brainstorming involves a series of discussions over multiple topics to arrive at a list of multiple options. The objective is to start the exploratory process of 'storming the brain with many ideas'. These may be later individually taken up and discussed at length for feasibility analysis.

Typically brainstorming follows a 4 step approach:

Start with increasing quantities: This step focuses on enhancing the divergent population, aiming to facilitate problem-solving through the maximum since quantity breeds quality. The assumption is that the higher the number of ideas generated, the greater the chance of producing a radical and effective solution. Encouraging people to explore and add new dimensions forms the basis of this step.

Avoiding judgment: As far as possible, brainstorming tries to stay off the judgmental approach. Since the objective is to increase the number of inputs, being critical or judgmental might be damaging. Avoiding may introduce hesitation amongst respondents to offer inputs, so the researcher should generally avoid it.

Openness to unusual ideas: Instead of collecting a vast and long list of ideas, unusual ideas may be welcomed. They can be generated by looking from new perspectives and suspending assumptions. Unusual and sometimes even absurd ideas may eventually lead to reasonable solutions.

Combine and improve ideas: Good ideas may be combined to form a single better idea. Synergistic pairing & coupling of ideas helps to improve efficacy.

– Delphi technique

The Delphi technique (popularly advocated as the expert opinion technique) is a widely used method for gathering data from respondents within their specified domain of expertise. The technique employs designing a group communication process that aims to achieve a convergence of opinion on a specific real-world issue. The Delphi technique is well suited as a method for consensus-building or arriving at common conclusions by using a series of questionnaires delivered using multiple iterations to collect data from a panel of selected respondents. The Delphi technique is usually applied:

1. To determine or develop a range of possible outcomes or alternatives.
2. To seek out information that may later generate a consensus on the part of the respondent group, thus enabling decision making.
3. To correlate informed judgments on a topic spanning a wide range of disciplines.
4. To educate and create awareness among the respondent group on the diverse and interrelated aspects of the topic.

– Projective techniques

The technique involves a projection of the respondent's perceptions and attitudes. Projective techniques vary in the degrees of their structure. For example, attitude scales whereby using an individual's score to make inferences about that person's attitude towards a particular topic are employed. These tend to be highly structured in their format and response options. These techniques are projective since they offer no clear directions; they project a situation that a respondent may dwell into and draw conclusions based on his motivation, personality & perception.

Examples of projective techniques include:

Word association tests: In this test, the respondent is given a stimulus in the form of one word and is asked to speak the first word that comes int his mind after hearing the word. The responses of the respondent are recorded and used to asses the inner feelings towards the research object.

Sentence Completion/Story completion tests: In this techniques respondent's are given an incomplete story or sentence and are asked to complete it. The respondents elaboration of the story/sentence reveals his/her perceptions.

Pictorial Techniques: These involve the use of vague or unintentionally drawn & collected images/pictures. The respondents perceptions may be put to the test by trying to ask him to draw meaningful conclusions out of the abstract based on his/her thought processes, which the researcher is interested in assessing.

Some of the commonly used pictorial tests are:

- Rorschach's Inkblot test
- Thematic apperception test
- Rosenweig's test (Balloon technique)
- Holtzman's test (HIT)
- Tomkins Horn Picture arrangement test

Role Play: This technique, as the name indicates, involves the participation of a respondent by way of enacting the situation and living characters the researcher wants the respondent to identify. The situational elements in a role play Exhibit the respondents attitudes & perceptions.

– Experiments

Experiments are most appropriate in establishing the cause and effect relations. In an experiment, data collection is in such a manner that it permits relatively unambiguous interpretation. In the practical & most realistic approach of the sciences, experiments are used to determined and prove cause-and-effect relations. Experimentation forms the basis of research methodologies. Designing of experiments provides a fundamentally rational analysis of research findings. It also offers a role model or benchmark against which other research designs can be judged and compared.

Boyd, Westfall, and Stanch define an experiment as follows: "An experiment is a research process in which one or more variables are manipulated under conditions that permit the collection of data that shows the effects, if any, of such variables in an unconfused fashion."

As such, experiments measure the impact of one set of variables or factors on another under controlled conditions. The conditions are controlled & manipulated by the researcher. The objective of control is to focus on specific inputs desired as a part of the problem solution. These conditions may also be essential to measure the specific data in the most accurate manner or precise format.

The experimental method scores an advantage over the others in the fact that researchers can analyze the actual cause-and-effect relations between any two variables that are pertinent or critical to the specific research. Other variables can either be eliminated or else controlled and present to the minimum or lowest bit.

Primarily experiments are of 2 types:

Laboratory (simulation conditions):

Designing laboratory experiments to replicate real-world situations in the laboratories. Testing of subjects in laboratories were extraneous variables are controlled. The tests could involve showing a TV commercial or a newspaper advertisement. It could also be witnessing a program prepared by trained artists.

Field (actual conditions):

Field experiments involve conducting tests in the field or location where subjects usually are identified. Test subjects may be questioned or shown stimuli. They could even be requested to try some products. Their responses are sought & measured there and then and after that recorded for further action.

This method though consistent, is time-consuming, expensive, and involves more significant efforts. In situations where cost and operational issues are not the fundamental limitations, field experiments seem to be the most suitable & preferred choice. The accuracy in field experiments is much more than that in the laboratory.

– Case study

The case study method involves detailed, holistic investigation and can utilize a range of different measurement techniques. A detailed analysis of a person or group, especially as a model of medical, psychiatric, psychological, social phenomena, or data can be collected over a while, and it is contextual (relative to a particular industry). Narrating histories and stories about the company are also something that is under assessment & documentation. This technique applies not just empirical data but moves beyond; for example, stories and anecdotes about how the company interacts with the marketplace are also in use. Case studies guide as an example of a real-world scenario for future reference.

Overview of Basic techniques to Collect Information:

Technique	Objective	Advantages	Disadvantages
Observation	To gather accurate information about people & processes.	– view operations of a program as they are actually occurring – can adapt to events as they occur – natural circumstances cut fake responses	– can be complex to categorize observations – can influence behaviors of program participants – can be expensive – can be open to biasing
Interviews	When wanting to understand in totality someone's impressions or experiences.	– get full range and in-depth information – develops bonding with client – allow flexibility	– time consuming – difficult to analyze and compare – expensive – open to biasness
Questionnaires, surveys, checklists	When need to quickly and easily get lots of information from people.	– can maintain anonymity – inexpensive to administer – easy to compare and analyze – administer to many people – can get lots of data – many sample questionnaires already exist	– might not get careful feedback – are impersonal -in surveys, may need sampling expert – lack of interest of respondent
Focus groups	When exploring a topic in depth through group discussion.	– can be efficient way to get much range and depth of information in short time – can convey key information about programs	– can be hard to analyze responses – difficult to schedule 6-8 people together
Case studies	To fully understand subject's experiences in a program, and conduct comprehensive examination through cross comparison of cases.	– depicts experience in program input, process and results – powerful means to portray program to outsiders	– usually quite time consuming to collect, organize and describe

Designing Questionnaires

A good questionnaire plays a pivotal role in all researches. Therefore it is essential to take utmost care to see that the questionnaire designing is proper. It makes sure that there is uniformity in data collection and ensures all respondents are responding to the same question. Without this, the information gathered is practically impossible to analyze. Besides, a well-designed questionnaire will typically cost less than a poorly designed one. A good questionnaire acts as a control device in research.

[A] Designing a good questionnaire consists of a series of steps which may be:

1. Deciding the information requirements-

The initial step would be to decide a list of all the things that the researcher needs to collate from the respondent. A systematic questionnaire designing can bring out results that will reveal all that is under exploration.

It would be a great idea to start by writing down what needs to be asked in a few clear sentences and then accordingly move on to designing the questionnaire. The researcher must always focus on information required as it also helps sought from secondary data. As it comes to secondary data, the researcher must be aware of the work already done on similar problems in the past. These factors are under exploration, and finally, how the present questionnaire can draw its guidelines from what is pre-existing.

2. Specifying the target respondents

The researcher must, in the next step, clearly define the population from which he aims to select the sample data. For example, researchers quite frequently have to decide whether or not to restrain in covering only existing users of the product or whether to extend coverage to include non-users. Following this, researchers would have to draw up the sampling frame. Subsequent to designing the questionnaire, the researcher must consider factors such as age, education of the target respondents.

3. How is the information going to be used?

It is imperative to understand the usage of all the information that will be collected. A guideline here would be to ensure coverage of everything required when it comes to analyzing & interpreting the answers. e.g., maybe the research involves comparative assessments of answers given by men and women. Information collection is doable only if maintaining the gender record of each respondent is possible through the questionnaire.

4. Selecting the correct method of reaching out to the target respondents

The significant methods used to the administered questionnaire in survey research are:

(a) Personal interviews
(b) Group or focus interview
(c) Mailed questionnaires
(d) Telephone interviews.

(e)   Face-to-face survey

(f)   Web surveys

All of the methods, besides many others, have their pros & cons. For example, while online surveys are inexpensive, the response rate can be low. Face-to-face though expensive will generate the most explicit responses; web surveys are again cost-effective, but witness hit and miss on response rates.

5. Qualitative or Quantitative

Whether the research has more inclination on numbers (e.g., 87% of respondents stated this) or else is the researcher more interested in trying to interpret feedback from respondents in an attempt to bring out common conclusions.

The method finally adopted and used would be determined by the subject matter under research and the types of respondents under study.

6. Decide on question content

Careful thinking of every question is imperative. There could yet be a strong temptation to include questions before critically evaluating their contribution to the research objectives & achievement. As specified in the formal research proposal, the researcher should not include any question until unless the data it gathers leads to use in testing the hypotheses already established during the research design.

Only on two occasions, we can include the seemingly '**redundant**' questions:

- Opening questions or warm-up questions that are easy to answer and 'break the ice'. These help in breaking the predisposition of the research being "threatening" and make it enjoyable. Besides, they can significantly assist in gathering the respondent's involvement and also help to establish a rapport.
- Using 'Dummy' questions to disguise the real purpose of the survey and also the sponsoring source of the study.

[B] Forms of questions

Survey questions follow two primary forms i.e., Closed & Open-ended.

Close-ended questions are the most suggested questions because they offer the following advantages;

- Provide the respondent ease of indicating his answer i.e., no need to plan out the articulation of the answer.
- Prompt the respondent so that he/she has to rely less on his memory to recover an answer.
- Responses are easy to classify, thus making analysis straightforward.
- Permit the respondent to specify the choice of answer categories which seem most suitable for his purpose.

Open-ended questions offer no suggestions and do not limit the respondent's thought process. They are open to the respondent to explore. Example: "What do you know about COVID-19?"

Open-ended questions offer the following advantages:

1. They allow the respondent flexibility to answer in his own words, thereby eliminating influences that may come by any specific alternatives offered in the questionnaire.
2. They may reveal the issues and offer insights into what the respondents consider most important, and this may lead to findings which though not anticipated initially, could be useful to the survey.
3. Respondents can 'qualify' their answers and emphasize the strength of their opinions.

However, while seemingly useful open-ended questions are also associated with specific problems which may be:

1. Respondents might find it difficult to 'articulate' their responses. They may be at a loss of words to thoroughly explain their attitudes or voice their motivations.
2. Respondents may hesitate to give a full answer simply because of forgetting to mention important points.
3. Data collected here is in the form of comments – it would involve further coding and interpretation to a manageable category. This approach is time-consuming and would also have numerous errors in recording and interpreting.

[C] Pre-testing Questionnaire

Self-check series of questions should be posed by the researcher while developing the questionnaire:

"Would the respondent be able to answer the question correctly?"

An inability to answer a question arises from three sources:

- No prior exposure to the answer, e.g., "How much is your husband earning?"
- Forgetting, e.g., "At what price did you buy when you last this bought maize meal?"
- Inability to articulate the answer: e.g., "What enhancements would you wish to witness in food preparation equipment?"

"Are there any external events that might lead to biasing in responding to the question?"

For instance, judging the popularity of non-vegetarian products soon after a related epidemic is quite likely to have an impact on the responses.

"Do the words mean the same to all respondents?"

For example, "How many members are there in your family?"

Ambiguity in such a question could arise since it is open to individual interpretation on whether to speak about the immediate or extended family.

"Are there any loaded words or phrases leading in any way?"

For example, "What did you most dislike about the product you just tried?"

The respondent misses the opportunity to indicate the positives of the product. A relatively less biased approach would have been to start with a preliminary question like, "what is your opinion about the product you have tried?" and allow the answer to be 'like or dislike'.

"Is there any ambiguity in the questions?"

Careless designing of questions can lead to the inclusion of two options in one question. For example: "Do you appreciate the speed and reliability of your tractor?" This type would be a double-barrelled question. The respondent is allowed to answer only 'yes' or 'no,' whereas he might like the speed, but not the reliability, or vice versa. Thus it is difficult for the respondent to answer and equally painful for the researcher to interpret the response.

> **Double barrelled question:** *A question that asks two questions at the same time. They confuse respondents and cannot be interpreted because the researcher has no clear indication to the part of answer, the respondent is trying to attempt*

Avoiding the use of ambiguous words is suggested, For example: "Do you regularly service your tractor?"The respondents comprehension and interpretation of the term 'regularly' might differ from person to person. While some may consider regularly means once a week, others may take it to be once a year. As such inclusion of such words causes interpretational difficulties for the researcher.

"Are any words or phrases vague?"

Questions such as 'What is your income?' could be vague, and one is likely to get many alternatives or different responses with different dimensions. Interpretations of the question in different terms could come from different respondents, for example:

- Hourly pay?
- Weekly pay?
- Yearly pay?

The researcher should specify the 'term' within which the responses can deliver enhanced clarity.

"Are there any questions that may sound too personal in nature?"

The researcher must take into consideration the various customs, cultural values, morals, and rituals in the community under study. For instance, in many communities, there could be a considerable reluctance to discuss specific issues with strangers. Though the degree to which discussion on topics is taboo varies across various areas, issues like level of education, income, and religious notions may be finding a generic resistance and embarrassing respondents who may then refuse to answer.

Exhibit 3: Key Questionnaire design considerations

1. Keep the questionnaire as short as possible

Respondents lose interest in questionnaires that are long and seemingly tedious.

If the questionnaire is too long, removing some questions which might be not so critical is essential. Evaluate the information each question would reveal and then decide whether or not it is required for the research.

2. Use direct and straightforward language. The respondent must comprehend the questionnaire and its questions. The language of the questions, as such, should be simple, brief, and to the point. Use of uncommon words, jargon, or long sentences may lead to ambiguity and defeat the purpose of the survey.

3. Introduce the questionnaire with general 'warm-up' questions. Involve the respondents interest by asking these simple questions.

Eg. When was the last time you came to this restaurant?

Asking tougher questions like those on income later, or else the respondent loses interest and may not cooperate.

4. Sequencing of the questionnaire.

Respondents sometimes may only complete the questionnaire partially. It is advisable to sequence the essential items at the very beginning since the partially completed questionnaire would still be relevant as they would contain important information.

5. Leave enough space to record the answers.

If including questions with long answers open-ended, make sure enough space to write in the possible answers is available. Though it sounds obvious, there is a possibility of overlooking!

6. Pre-test the questionnaire before releasing its audience

Despite the time and effort put into designing the questionnaire, there is no substitute for pre-testing it before releasing it to the audience. Pre-test it on colleagues or friends before involving the respondents. This would help in tracking the timing of the questionnaire and to make any final changes as per the feedback from colleagues.

The pretesting of the questionnaire would be able to offer the following solutions:

- Whether the questions are correctly worded to achieve the de-sired results.
- Whether the questions have been correctly sequenced.
- Whether the questions offer clarity and understanding by all classes of respondents.
- Whether there is a need for additional questions or should some questions be left out.
- Whether the instructions offered to interviewes are adequate.

[D] Formatting the questionnaire

The questionnaire formatting forms an essential part of designing since it enhances the receptivity, in turn responsiveness. The sequential pattern & important considerations suggested here would be:

- **Opening or warming up questions**

The first question is critical because it constitutes the respondent's first exposure to the interview and, as such, sets the tone for the questions to follow. If respondents find this first question itself difficult to understand or uncomfortable to answer or beyond their knowledge set, they are likely to resist immediately. If, on the contrary, the opening question is found easy and pleasant, the level of motivation to continue goes up.

- **Question flow**

Questions flow should be in some kind of chronological order, such that one quickly leads to the next. Questions on one subject, or one aspect of a subject, should be clubbed together. Respondents might feel it difficult to keep juggling from one issue to another, or else to keep coming back to the same subject were they expressed opinions.

- **Variety of questions**

It is vital to introduce variety, or else the respondents may lose interest due to repetitive or monotonous issues. Introducing variety generally not only improves response but keeps the interest alive. An open-ended question intervening between the close-ended may provide a much-needed breather from a long series of questions during which respondents have been forced to confine their responses to pre-coded categories. The graphic rating scale also continues to be a suggested technique to make the questionnaire much more enjoyable.

- **Closing the questions**

Leaving out the questions that appear potentially sensitive to the end in order to avoid respondents breaking off the interview before several necessary inputs are collected.

- **Layout of the Questionnaire**

While developing the questionnaire, emphasis should be paid to the presentation and layout of the interview besides others. The interviewer's role is to make the survey process as simple and as straight-forward as possible.

- **The physical appearance of the questionnaire**

The physical appearance or look of the questionnaire can significantly impact the quantity and quality of data compiled. Poor design of questionnaires would generally create an impression of being too complicated and involving too big a time commitment. Unnecessarily confusing layouts make it hugely difficult for both the interviewers and the respondents in the case of self-administered questionnaires. Due attention to these few necessary details can create a favorable impact on the data obtained.

- **Using booklets**

The use of booklets, in the place of loose or stapled sheets of paper, makes it easier for the interviewer or respondent to progress through the document. Moreover, fewer pages tend to get lost.

- **Simple, clear formats**

The clarity of the questionnaire presentation can also help to improve the ease with which interviewers or respondents can complete a questionnaire.

- **Creative use of space**

Questionnaires that make use of blank space appear more comfortable to use, enjoy higher response rates, and contain fewer errors when completed.

- **Use of color coding**

Colour coding can help in the administration of questionnaires. It is often the case of including several types of respondents within a single survey (e.g., wholesalers and retailers). Printing the questionnaires on two different colors of paper can make the handling easier.

- **Interviewer instructions**

Placing interviewer instructions alongside the questions to which they pertain. Instructions on where the interviewers should probe for more information should be placed right next to the relevant question.

- **Ending the questionnaire**

A note of acknowledgment to the respondent or a simple 'thank you for your cooperation', at the end of the questionnaire, leaves a pleasant association with the respondent and should be included.

Processing of Data

Data processing primarily involves **editing, coding, classification,** and **tabulation** of data, so that it becomes amenable for data analysis. The processing of data starts after the data collection. Once data collection is over, the next step is to organize and process data by editing and tabulating it to arrive at a meaningful conclusion.

Editing of Data

Editing is the first stage of data processing. It is a procedure that uses available information and assumptions to substitute inconsistent value in a data set. Editing, therefore, is the process of examining data collected to detect error, omission, and correct them for further analysis. This is important because the information gathered during data collection may lack uniformity. In a summarised form, the data collection instruments discussed in the previous topic would lead to the accumulation of raw data in huge volumes. However, it becomes incredibly crucial to screen this data against possible errors and assign suitable codes to facilitate meaningful interpretations.

Typically data collected might be subject to the errors in the following categories:

1. **The respondent error**-when error occurs on account of a mistake made by the respondent.

2. **Non-respondent error** – a non-respondent error includes mistakes that could be made by either an interviewer or by other persons involved in creating electronic data to represent the responses. As long as errors prevail in the data, the process of transforming it from raw data into meaningful inputs would be a risky and tedious job. Editing, therefore, becomes an extremely critical stage for interpretation & understanding. Apart from ensuring quality data, this will also facilitate coding and tabulation of data. Editing involves careful scrutiny of the completed questionnaires.

> ***EXAMPLE OF EDITING***
>
> ***Q. How long have you been working in this organization?***
>
> ***A. 15years***
>
> *However, the next question brings forth a different situation.*
>
> ***Q. How many years has it been since you completed your formal education?***
>
> ***A. 11 years***
>
> *As this answer contradicts the earlier one (because this qualification is a prerequisite for entry in this organization) we need to adjust to synchronize this information.*
>
> *This example is an illustration of data editing. Editing depicts the process of checking, adjusting, and manipulating data for safeguarding against omissions, ensuring consistency, and making it legible. Data, once edited, is prepared and ready for analysis.*

[A] Types of Editing

The editing can be done at two stages described below:

1. Field Editing
2. Central Editing

(1) Field Editing

The field supervisor conducts preliminary field editing right at the time of data collection. It consists of a review of the reporting forms by the investigator for completing or translating what the latter has written in abbreviated form at the time of interviewing by the respondent. This form of editing is necessary in view of the writing of individuals, which vary from individual to individual and sometimes difficult for the tabulator to understand. This sort of editing should be done as soon as possible after the interview, as it may be necessary sometimes to recall the interview inputs. While doing so, care should be taken to ensure that the investigator does not correct the errors of omission by simply guessing what the respondent would have answered if the question was put to him.

Field editing serves the purpose of:

1. Identifying omissions such as a blank page on a questionnaire or an interview form.
2. Checking for legible handwriting in open-ended responses.
3. Clarifying responses which may be logically or conceptually inconsistent.

(2) Central Editing/In-House

Even though field editing is highly desirable, it may not be practically possible to apply it to many situations, especially those involving small questionnaires. Early reviewing of the data may not always be possible. Central editing investigates & probes the results of compiled data collected. The research organization usually has a centralized office staff dedicated to performing the editing and the coding function.

[B] Situational Requirements for Editing

- **Editing for Completeness**

In cases where the respondent would have answered only the second part of a two-part question or otherwise left an answer incomplete, we need to clarify and make changes accordingly.

For Example: The given set of question presents a situation in which an in-house editor would have to adjust answers for completeness:

Q1. Does, your organization, has more than one stand-alone workstations?

A. _ Yes _ No

Q2. (contd) If yes, how many? _____

- **Item 'Non-response' or 'No-response' answer is** a term that defines unanswered questions in an otherwise answered questionnaire. It is important to include clear instructions on how to tackle this. In many cases, the golden rule to adopt is to do nothing with the missing data and to leave it blank. However, when the association between two questions is significant, e.g., a question on job satisfaction and compensation, an approximation on a plug value might be chosen. The approach than could be to plug in an average or neutral value, wherever there is an instance of missing data.

- **Editing Questions Answered Out of Order**

In certain situations, the respondent may have answered already in an open-ended statement. In such cases, the respondent might show a lack of interest since he has already answered. It is as such recommended to maintain sequence and add these inputs as and when required.

If the research involves listing answers to all questions in a specific order, the researcher may shift precise answers to the sections relating to the skipped question.

- **Editing 'do not know' responses**

Under certain situations, respondents may answer with a, 'do not know'. This response seems to hint at unfamiliarity in question content. Also, logically, a 'do not know' response implies the same as 'no opinion'. However, specific reasons attribute to this response over the logical does not know. The respondent gives a reluctant do not know when he knows but does not want to answer the question. For example, questions on income might seldom get such responses.

On other occasions, the respondent may take the question to be too personal and refrain from answering the question. Next could be a situation where the individual does not comprehend the question; the response may then be confused, 'I do not know' the answer.

[C] Flaws in Editing

Primarily flaws could be on account of subjectivity that can enter into the editing process. The data editors involved should have the training, intelligence, experience, and objectivity in approach. A systematic procedure for questionnaire assessment needs to be developed by the researcher so that the editor has a clear set of defined decision rules to follow. Any conclusions such as, interpreting missing values, involve reviews such that they limit the chance for the editor's subjectivity to create an influence on the response.

Coding of data

Coding is translating answers into numerical values or assigning numbers to the various categories of a variable to be used in data analysis. It is done by using a codebook, code sheet, and a computer card. Coding is done on the basis of the instructions given in the codebook. The codebook gives a numerical code for each variable.

The coding of data implies a process involving the categorization of data into groups and symbols/numerical or both assigned to each item. It involves categories for which assigning of individual codes are in use. It helps in reducing information for analytical interpretation. Manual (for coding) preparation needs to be prepared before the collection of data, and the following rules should be taken care of:

- Each respondent to be given a code number;
- Qualitative questions should have codes, but the qualitative variable may or may not have codes. For example, if we want to calculate or compute average quarterly income than a quarter or monthly income should not be coded;
- All responses, including 'No Opinion', 'No response', 'Not Sure', 'Do not Know', and all, are to be coded.
- Response of all questions to be studied, and codes decided by examining the essence of the answer.

Data classification/distribution

Sarantakos (1998: 343) defines the distribution of data as a form of classification of scores obtained for the various categories for a particular variable. There are four types of distributions:

- Frequency distribution
- Percentage distribution
- Cumulative distribution
- Statistical distributions

Frequency distribution: In social science research, the frequency distribution is very commonly used. It presents the frequency of occurrences of certain categories. This distribution appears in two forms:

- Ungrouped: Here, the scores are not collapsed into categories.
- Grouped: Here, the scores are collapsed into categories, so that 2 or 3 scores are presented together as a group.

Percentage distribution: It is also possible to give frequencies not in absolute numbers but in percentages.

Cumulative distribution: It tells how often the value of the random variable is less than or equal to a particular reference value.

Statistical data distribution: In this type of data distribution, some measure of average is found out of a sample of respondents. Several kinds of averages are available (mean, median, mode), and the researcher must decide which is most suitable purpose. Once the average has been calculated, the question arises: how representative a figure it is, i.e., how closely the answers are affiliated around it. Are most of them very close to it, or is there a wide range of variation?

Tabulation of data

Tabulation involves the careful sorting and presentation of data in rows and columns in order to make it more presentable. Also, this presentation enables clarity of comparison & assessment and ease of using supportive spreadsheets for quicker calculations. To sum it up, tabulation helps in drawing the inferences or conclusions from the provided statistical figures converting raw data into meaningful inputs.

Tabulation provides the necessary spadework for analysis and interpretation. As such, an appropriate method must be thought upon carefully, taking into consideration the scope and objectives of the research.

Types of Tabulation

Tabulation is classified into two parts:

a) Simple tabulation
b) Complex tabulation

Simple tabulation reveals information regarding one or more than one independent question. On the contrary, **complex tabulation** reveals information regarding two mutually dependent issues.

One-Way Table

All questions which find an answer in ONE WAY TABLE are independent of each other. It is as such an example of a simple tabulation.

The table gives clear indications of the population in various zonal areas of a specified geographical location.

One-Way Table

ZONE	POPULATION (in millions)
North	13.564
East	12.987
South	9.779
West	15.879

Two-Way Table

ZONES	POPULATION (in millions)		
	Male	Female	Total
North East South West			

The two-way table Exhibits information about two mutually dependent questions, i.e., it studies the impact of two variables simultaneously. For example, we need to present not only the information on the population as per zones but also population count and also gender break up amongst the population. Hence, the better alternative is to use two-way table.

Three-Way Table

Three-Way Table reflects information about three mutually dependent and inter-related issues. For example, the one-way table will reveal information about the population, and the two-way table will speak about information about the population and also gender distribution. Now we can extend the same table to a three-way table by also adding literacy status. Thus the collected statistics will reveal the following, three mutually dependent and inter-related issues:

- Population in various zones
- Their gender-based distribution.
- Their literacy status

Zones	Population (Millions)								
	Male			Female			Total		
	Literate	Illiterate	Total	Literate	Illiterate	Total	Literate	Illiterate	Total
North East South West									

Higher-Order Tables

Value	Profession	N	Mean	Standard Deviation
Openness to change	Architect	152	3.82	0.69
	Engineer	168	3.56	0.60
	Quantity Surveyor	80	3.28	0.65
	Total	400	3.59	0.77
Conservation	Architect	152	3.13	0.72
	Engineer	168	3.15	0.74
	Quantity Surveyor	80	3.45	0.66
	Total	400	3.27	0.83
Self-transcendence	Architect	152	3.73	0.64
	Engineer	168	3.34	0.68
	Quantity Surveyor	80	3.29	0.73
	Total	400	3.49	0.78
Self-enhancement	Architect	152	3.09	0.71
	Engineer	168	3.78	0.68
	Quantity Surveyor	80	3.75	0.69
	Total	400	3.62	0.79

Similarly, the variables under study can find further extensions to construct a higher order table. These tables try to provide information about a large number or series of interrelated questions. They may include maybe four-way, five-way, six-way.

Data Presentation

Presentation of **data** refers to an Exhibition or putting up **data** in an attractive and useful manner. Presentation help in interpreting the data, collected, and edited from various sources and techniques. The three main forms of presentation of data are: **Textual** presentation, **Data** tables, and **Diagrammatic** presentation. Before analysis, it is vital to highlight the various techniques of data presentation to reveal inputs with clarity & objectivity.

There are many ways of presenting data, and choosing the most appropriate, relevant, and statistically correct tool would be a significant part of the research design.

Data presentation techniques

Exhibit 4: Tabular and Diagrammatic Presentation Techniques

FREQUENCY	
FREQUENCY DISTRIBUTION	Data can be presented in various forms depending on the type of data collected. A frequency distribution is a table showing how often each value (or set of values) of the variable in question occurs in a data set. A frequency table is used to summarize categorical or numerical data. Frequencies are also presented as relative frequencies, that is, the percentage of the total number in the sample. **Frequency distribution of peptic ulcer according to site of ulcer / Percentage** Gastric ulcer — 24 — 30.0 Duodenal ulcer — 50 — 62.5 Gastric and duodenal ulcer — 6 — 7.5 TOTAL — 80 — 100
GRAPHICAL	
BAR	Bar graphs present non-continuous (discrete data). These may figure horizontally or vertically. Each bar must be plotted with the same width and the same distance apart.
HISTOGRAM	Histograms are similar to bar graphs in use when the data needs presentation on a continuous series, e.g., precipitation data on a climate graph. They may again be either horizontal or vertical.

LINE GRAPH	Line graphs represent continuous data, e.g., data collected on an ongoing time frame. These can be in use it to show multiple datasets and have both independent and dependent variables.	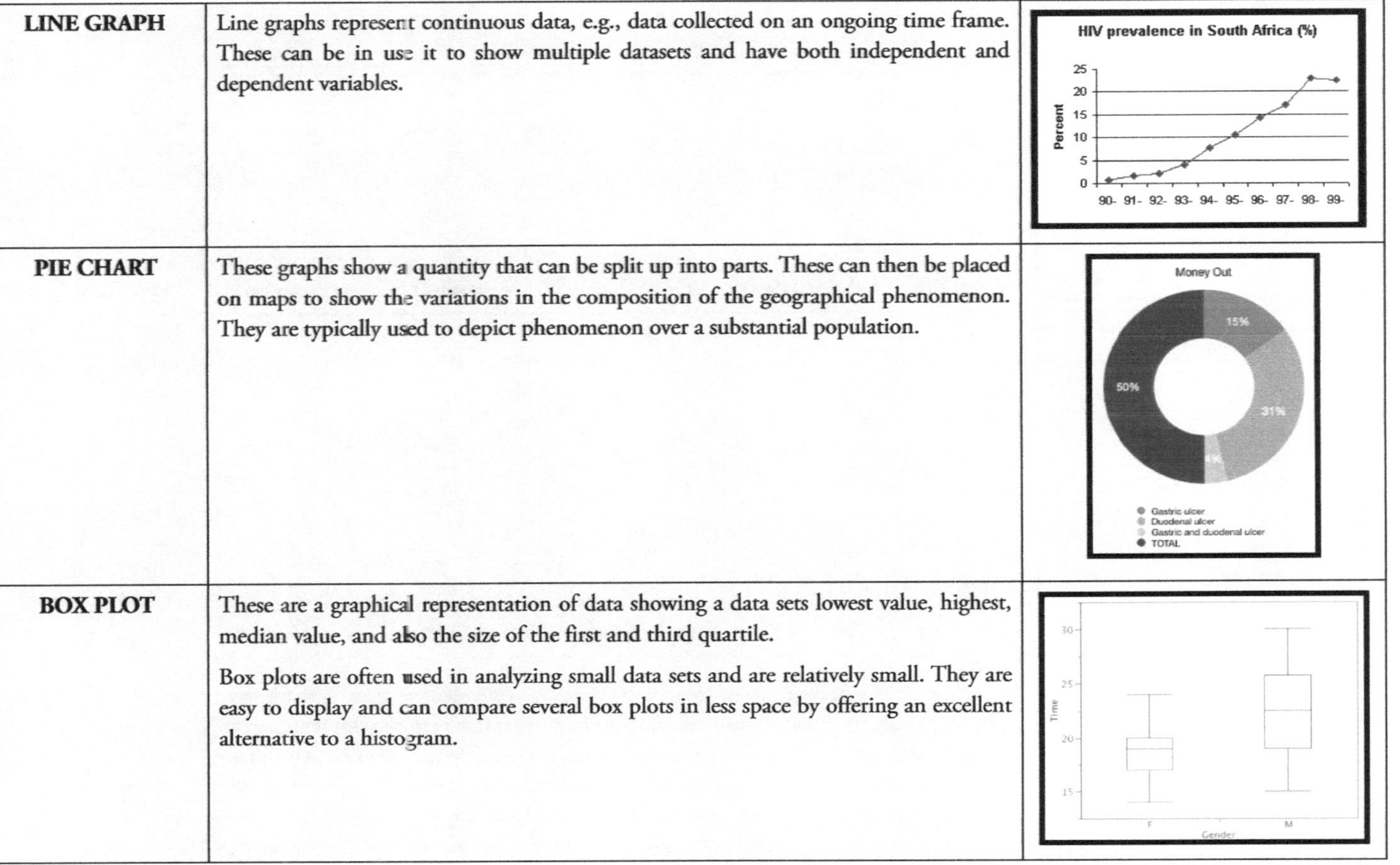
PIE CHART	These graphs show a quantity that can be split up into parts. These can then be placed on maps to show the variations in the composition of the geographical phenomenon. They are typically used to depict phenomenon over a substantial population.	
BOX PLOT	These are a graphical representation of data showing a data sets lowest value, highest, median value, and also the size of the first and third quartile. Box plots are often used in analyzing small data sets and are relatively small. They are easy to display and can compare several box plots in less space by offering an excellent alternative to a histogram.	

Continued…

OGIVE	Ogives, also called cumulative histograms, pertain to graphs that are used to determine how many data values fall above or below a particular value in a series of data. They require cumulative frequencies calculations from the frequency table by adding each consecutive frequency to the total achieved frequencies by adding all data values before it. The final total of the cumulative frequency must always equal the total number of data values because all frequencies are already included in the prior total.	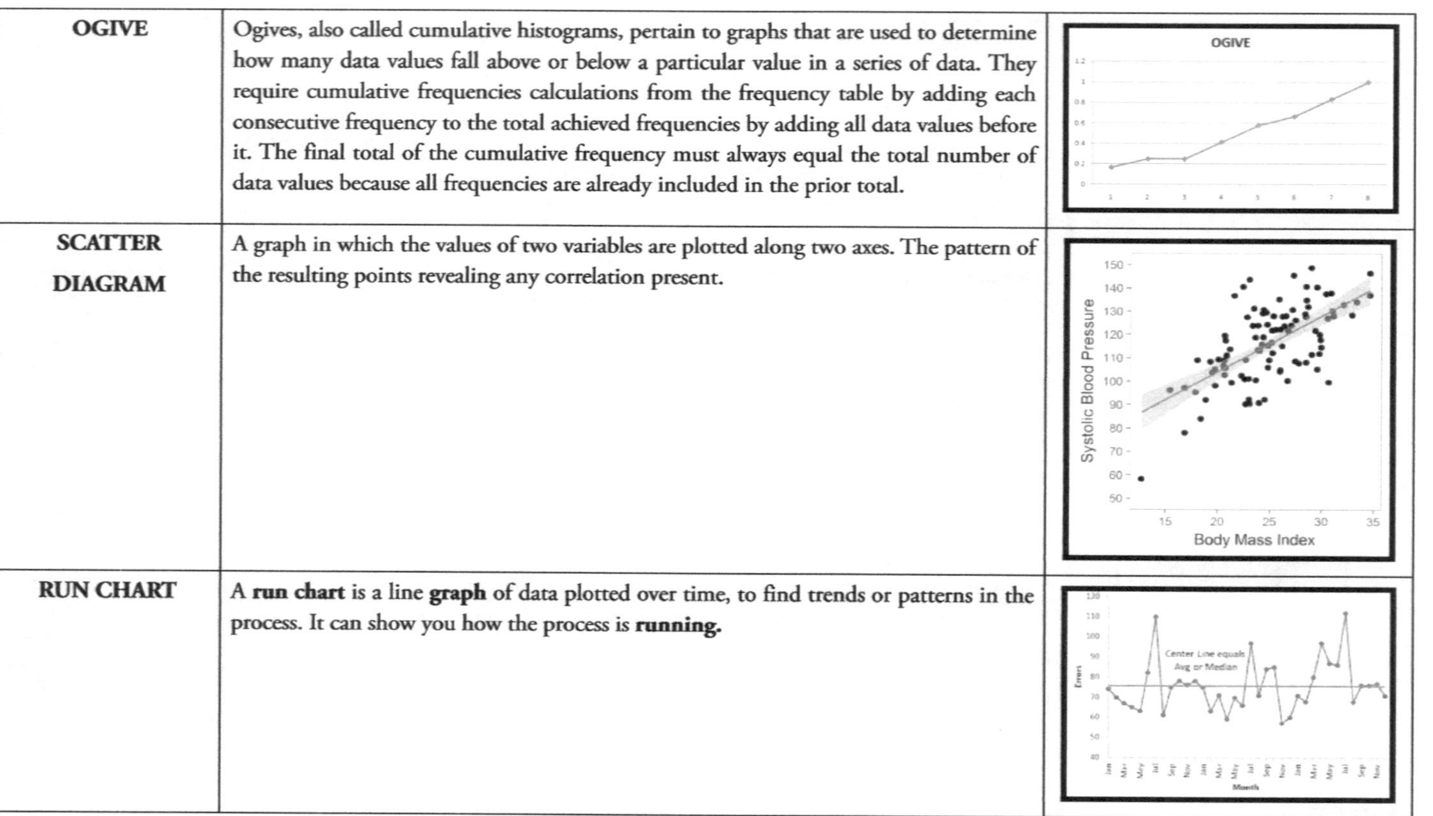
SCATTER DIAGRAM	A graph in which the values of two variables are plotted along two axes. The pattern of the resulting points revealing any correlation present.	
RUN CHART	A **run chart** is a line **graph** of data plotted over time, to find trends or patterns in the process. It can show you how the process is **running.**	

Recap & Review Section

SUMMARY Chapter 4

In this chapter, we have elaborated the meaning of data, methods of collection, advantages, and disadvantages with the limitation of data collection. Data is information collected from various processes for a specific purpose. The statistical data described are of three types Primary, secondary, and combined. A significant consideration of data should be reliable, suitable, adequate; otherwise, it may result in a misleading conclusion.

There are various methods in collecting data, i.e., observation, interview, focus group, questionnaire, delphi technique, projective, and case study. Every method has its own usage. Hence, no one method is suitable in all situations. A suitable method can be selected as per the need of the researcher.

Once the data collection is over, the next essential steps are editing and coding, followed by tabulation and presentation. Editing, being the first stage, helps in maintaining consistency in the quality of data by the process of examining. Coding makes further computation by assigning some symbols to the answer for efficient analysis of data. The data is then tabulated, and its extensions is provided in summarising data and comparing different sets of data. Finally, we present the data visually and graphically/diagrammatically.

Caselet 3 – The Netflix Dilemma

Netflix functions under the sole purpose of subsidizing the extended costs that movie renters incurred after passing their due dates for movie and DVD returns. Netflix was established in 1997, and its core business was to rent DVDs to individuals using the internet through home deliveries. As time passed by, the company has shifted its core business to online streaming due to increased usage of the internet. However, DVD rental, which is referred to as DVD by mail, is still among its business market together with other markets such as video-on-demand services.

(a) Streaming media: With the popularity of the internet, streaming media has been the core business for Netflix. It offers streaming services to over 167 million subscribers (2019) within and outside the United States. It allows users to stream movies and TV show episodes at their convenience.

(b) DVD rental: Netflix rents out DVDs through the internet and distributes them to consumers using the strategically placed distribution centers across the country. This rental was the core business of the company when it began, and it has grown to be a very significant aspect of Netflix.

(c) Video on Demand Video on Demand: which involves the streaming of videos and audios whenever one feels like, unlike having to watch according to the program lineup. This aspect is a recent venture by Netflix, and seemingly, it is also gaining popularity and its market expansion.

Netflix's Competitive Advantage

Netflix was among the very first DVD and movie rental companies to take advantage of the internet era. It gave the company enough time to blend in and create a sustainable market for its self. Diversifying into other innovative markets such as the 'Video on Demand' and the streaming media markets. This enabled it to expand its markets and create its potential for making more money. The company was established in 1997 by Reed Hastings. The home delivery system for DVD rentals gives the company an advantage over most of the other companies in the same business. It has strategic distribution centers all over the country that allow the company to deliver rented DVDs to customers within the shortest time possible. Around 92% of rentals done in a day are delivered to the customers. Its delivery system is a striking aspect that has made its market increase tenfold ever since its inception.

Other outstanding features that may be attractive to customers and have been increasing its market as the day pass by are the two distinctive features that continue to be in Netflix accounts. They added the ability for one account to have multiple favorite lists. This feature allows various family members who use one Netflix account to have a variety of favorite lists. An addition of the community option known as 'Friends' that allows users to share their favorite lists, among other features such as ratings and preferences with friends.

The majority of its subscribers being from the United States of America. Its expansion move to other countries was also a strategic move, starting with Canada in 2010 and to over 160 other countries in January of 2016. Its market increased proportionally with every expansion to the various countries it expanded to (The Brain behind Netflix). Diversification and readiness to embrace technology have always been a strong suit of the company. The addition of High-definition DVD rentals to its current market will increase its sales and customer base much more. It has also ventured into the TV and film industry by releasing TV-Shows under the market-brand "NETFLIX ORIGINAL."

Questions

1. To help NETFLIX achieve its target of understanding what Indian Viewers want, what secondary data sources would you suggest?
2. You have to conduct a primary study on Netflix in the Indian market, what data collection methods will be used, and why.

Caselet 4 – Travel Agency

Gurgaon is an upcoming cosmopolitan city in the North of India. It houses people from all over the country with varied cultures and interests. With higher income at their disposal, the people of Gurgaon are now keener than ever to undertake various tours across the country. There are several Travel agencies and Tour/Travel operators in the city. Sharma Travels had started its business just a few months ago and was excepting to double or triple its business in the coming festive season or the later holiday season. In this highly competitive business arena, Mr. Sharma has decided to conduct a survey to determine how much business Gurgaon has to offer and also wanted to know whether the residents are aware of Sharma Travels. He thought that this survey would also determine the effectiveness of his advertising strategies. Besides the above aspects, Mr. Sharma wants to gain additional knowledge on several facets, such as peoples traveling options, frequency of travel, their budgets, their satisfaction/dissatisfaction levels with their present travel agencies, and other related characteristics.

Questions

1. As a student of management research, you need to design a detailed questionnaire to satisfy Mr. Sharma's queries on the aspects mentioned above besides other facets, such as demographics, and all which you think might be of additional help to Mr. Sharma in his venture.

2. Extend the questionnaire to include the impact of lockdown due to COVID-19 in the travel business.

Check Your Knowledge

CYK 1 Which of the following statements is true?

a. Open-ended questions provide quantitative data based on the researchers predetermined response categories;

b. Closed-ended questions provide quantitative data in the participant's own words;

c. Open-ended questions provide qualitative data in the participant's own words;

d. Closed-ended questions directly provide qualitative data in the participants own words;

Answer (c)

CYK 2 Which of the following does not come under the case of secondary research?

a. The telephonic survey of a company asking consumers about product usage.

b. Published market report

c. Trade association report

d. News clippings

Answer (a)

CYK 3 Information about a market that is already collected or published is known as

a. Secondary data

b. Outdated data

c. Tertiary data

d. Primary data

Answer (a)

CYK 4 Which of the following best describes quantitative research?

a. The compilation of statistical data;

b. An attempt to confirm the researchers hypotheses;

c. Exploratory research;

d. Research that attempts to generate a new theory

Answer (a)

CYK 5 What data presentation technique would best represent the percentage of shoppers aware of unit pricing?
a. Bar graph
b. Histogram
c. Pie-Chart
d. Ogive

Answer (c)

CYK 6 What data presentation technique would best represent the percentage increase in the number of unit shoppers over the last five years?
a. Box plot
b. Stem & leaf display
c. Pie-Chart
d. Ogive

Answer (d)

CYK 7 What data presentation technique would best represent the degree of purchases in the product categories of:
- **Cosmetics**
- **Garments**
- **Frozen food**

a. Bar graph
b. Stem & leaf display
c. Pie-Chart
d. Histogram

Answer (a)

CYK 8 Match the given questions to the type of errors in the question framing:

a. Are the passengers satisfied with the food and services onboard?	(i) Loaded question
b. How much would you prefer a chocolate flavour over vanilla?	(ii) Double-barreled question
c. Are you satisfied with the laptop currently being used	(iii) Vague question

a-ii, b-i, c-iii

Questions

Q1. Distinguish between the following:
Primary and Secondary data
Questionnaire and Case Study
Observation and Focus group Interview

Q2. Why is it essential to obtain secondary data before primary data?

Q3. What are the criteria to be used when evaluating secondary data?

Q4. Why is it desirable to use multiple sources of secondary data?

Q5. What is the nature of the information collected by surveys? How can surveys be classified?

Q6. Anoop Jain has decided to become a freelance organization Development Consultant and advise his clients on:

a) HR Servies

b) Mergers and Acquisition

What would be the nature of the information that would assist Anoop? How would secondary data sources help him here? From which sources Secondary data can be collected.

Q7. What is the observation method? What are the different types of observation methods available to the researcher? Elaborate with suitable examples.

Q8. What is primary data collection and its different types?

Q9. What are the projective techniques? What are the different types of techniques available to a researcher? Explain with suitable examples.

Q10. Explain how the mode of administration affects questionnaire design.

Q11. What are the reasons that respondents are unwilling to answer specific questions? What initiative can the researcher take to request information that seems legitimate?

Q12. What are the guidelines available for deciding on question-wording? What is a leading question? Give an example.

Q13. What guidelines are available for deciding on the form and layout of a questionnaire? Describe the issues involved in pre-testing a questionnaire.

Q14. Develop at least five double-barreled questions related to online stream viewers. Also, develop corrected versions of each question

Application Question

1. You have been approached by Indian Famous Designer Ravi Bajaj, who wants to start an economy line and would like to know:

a) How is the fashion market composed?

b) What is the profile of the avid fashion followers?

Conduct an interview (structured interview) to obtain information about:

a) Demographics

b) Lifestyle

c) Role models

2. You have been assigned the task on behalf of Radio Mirchi to get information from the sample group taken from Gen-Z (those born after 2000). You need to collect information on:

a) What kind of new programs should we air?

b) What would be the requirement for hiring RJ 's (Radio Jockey)?

Suggest a suitable choice of technique and discuss the plan in detail.

3. Essex markets were a chain of supermarkets in medium-sized California City. The supermarket caters to a variety of products, both branded and manufactured labels.

For six years, it had provided its customers with unit pricing of grocery products. The unit prices being given in the form of shelf tags that showed the final price of the items and its unit price (the price per ounce, for example). The program was costly. The tags had to be prepared and updated. Further, because they tended to become dislodged or moved, considerable effort was required to make sure that they were current and in place.

A study was undertaken to evaluate unit pricing. Among the research questions in the study were the following:

1.   What percentage of shoppers were aware of unit pricing?
2.   What is the percentage increase in the number of unit shoppers over the last five years?
3.   What is the degree of purchases in the product categories of:

- Cosmetics
- Garments
- Frozen food

It yielded that a 5-page questionnaire completed by about 1000 shoppers would be needed. The respondent would need to answer it, in the store in about 15 minutes, or the respondent could be asked to complete it at home and mail it in.

Suggest suitable data representation techniques to support each of the observed questions.

Sampling Fundamentals

> **Keywords:** *Sample, Population, Sampling plan, Sample size, Sample element, Sampling frame, Probability & Non Probability sampling, Standard error, Random Sampling, Stratified sampling, Cluster sampling, Area sampling, Convenience sampling, Quota sampling, Snowball sampling, Judgemental sampling.*

Meaning

Sampling, by definition, is the selection of some part of aggregate, based on which an inference about the aggregate is drawn. It is as such the process of extracting information about a population by examining only a section of it. The sample, therefore, represents the population from which it is drawn. It is widely used in research work and surveys where the approach is to make generalizations based on samples.

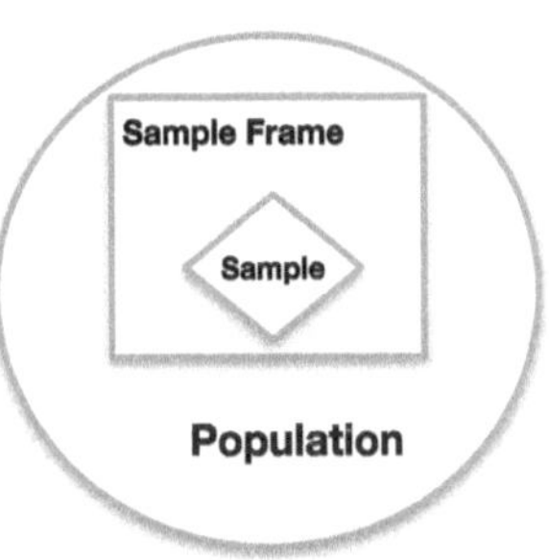

Sample Frame

The researcher might pick up or identify only a few items from the universe/ population for study purposes. This selection is undertaken on the assumption that the sample data will be representative of the entire population.

The items picked up together comprise a sample, the selection process is called sample design, and finally, the survey conducted on the sample is categorized as a sample survey. The sample should represent the population characteristics free from bias such that it is useful in arriving at valid and reliable conclusions. If you want to get information about a large group of individual people or things, for example, students or cars, it usually is impossible to get all of them to answer your questions or to examine all the things 'it would take too long and be far too expensive'. The solution is just to ask or examine some of them and hopes that the data you get are representative (or typical) of all the rest. If the data you collect is the same as you would get from the rest, then you can draw conclusions from those answers which you can relate to the whole group. This process of selecting just a small group of cases from out of a large group is called sampling.

When we talk about the population in research, it does not necessarily mean a number of people; it is a collective term used to describe the total quantity of things (or cases) of the type which are the subject of your study. So a population can consist of certain types of objects, organizations, people, or even events. Within this population, there will probably be only certain groups that will be of interest to your study, for instance, of all school buildings, only those in cities, or of all limited companies, only small to medium-sized companies. This selected category is your sampling frame. It is from this sampling frame that the sample is selected.

> *Key Sampling Considerations*
>
> *Population/Universe* – *the entire group of units which may be considered under the scope of the study.*
>
> *Sample frame* – *the comprehensive set of items of the population from which a sample is to be obtained.*
>
> *Sample element* – *the selected unit of the target population which qualifies for the study.*
>
> *Sample size* – *the part of the population, given in numbers, chosen for a survey or experiment.*
>
> *Sampling method* – *the techniques used to select members from the population which form a part of the study.*
>
> *Sample Unit* – *the singular value within a sample database, i.e., each unit within a chosen sample.*
>
> *Sampling Error* – *the difference between a sample statistic said to represent a population and the actual value of the parameter based on the entire population.*

Need for Sampling

Sampling is used in practice for a variety of reasons such as:

1. Sampling can save time and money. A sample study is usually less expensive than a census study and produces results at a relatively faster speed.
2. Sampling may enable more accurate measurements because a sample study is conducted by trained and experienced investigators.
3. Sampling remains the only way when the population contains infinite members.
4. Sampling is the only choice when a test involves the destruction of the item under study.

Census vis-a-vis sampling are two approaches to collecting survey data about the population. **Census** is a quantitative method involving all the members of the population understudy. On the contrary, **sampling** is choosing a data set from the large population, which is a representative of the entire population. The choice of taking the sample under consideration or extending the research to cover the entire population depends upon the multiple parameters as illustrated below:

Type of study	Sample	Census
Definition	Collecting data about a chosen set which represents the total population	Collecting data about the entire population
Budget	Small	Large
Time available	Short	Long
Population size	Large	Small
Nature of population	Homogenous	Heterogenous
Variance in the characteristics	Small	Large
Attention to individual cases	No	Yes
Sampling Error	Present	Missing
Cost of sampling errors	Low	High

Sampling Theory

Sampling theory studies the relationship that exists between the universe and samples drawn from the population. Sampling theory is applicable only to random samples. For this purpose, the population or a universe may be defined as an aggregate of items possessing common traits. In other words, a universe is the entire group of items about which knowledge is sought. The universe may be finite or infinite. The finite universe is one that has a definite and specific number of items, but when the number of items is uncertain and infinite, the universe is said to be an infinite universe.

The theory of sampling studies the relationships that exist between the universe and the sample or samples drawn from it. The main problem of sampling theory is the problem of the relationship between a parameter and a statistic. The theory of sampling is concerned with estimating the properties of the population from those of the sample and also with gauging the precision of the estimate. This sort of movement from particular (sample) towards general (universe) is what is known as statistical induction or statistical inference. In more clear terms "from the sample, we attempt to draw an inference concerning the universe. In order to be able to follow this inductive method, we first follow a deductive argument, which is that we imagine a population or universe (finite or infinite) and investigate the behavior of the samples drawn from this universe applying the laws of probability." The methodology dealing with all this is known as sampling theory.

Sampling theory is designed to attain one or more of the following objectives:

(i) Statistical estimation: Sampling theory helps in estimating unknown population parameters from the knowledge of statistical measures based on sample studies.

In other words, obtaining an estimate of the parameter from statistic is the main objective of the sampling theory. The estimate can either be a point estimate, or it may be an interval estimate. A point estimate is a single estimate expressed in the form of a single figure, but the interval estimate has two limits viz., the upper limit and the lower limit within which the parameter value may lie. Interval estimates are often used in statistical induction.

(ii) Testing of hypothesis: The second objective of sampling theory is to enable us to decide whether to accept or reject a hypothesis. The sampling theory helps in determining whether observed differences are actually due to chance or whether they are really significant.

(iii) Statistical inference: Sampling theory helps in making generalizations about the population/universe from the studies based on samples drawn. It also helps in determining the accuracy of such generalizations. No sample will be exactly representative of a population. If different samples, using identical methods, are taken from the same population, there are bound to be differences in the mean (average) values of each sample owing to the chance selection of different individuals. The measured difference between the mean value of a sample and that of the population is called the sampling error, which will lead to bias in the results. Bias is the unwanted distortion of the results of a survey due to some parts of the population being more strongly represented than others.

Methods of Sampling

Since the primary aim of research continues to be able to put forth valid conclusions, the choice of participants becomes very critical when approaching the research. Since it may not be possible to collect data from every single individual who is a part of the population under study, as this would involve huge expenses and time, a practicable alternative comes in the form of using a small group of individuals. This smaller group, which is drawn from and is representative of the population, is termed 'a sample'. Researchers involve sampling techniques to pick & choose the participants for the sample. These techniques aid in minimizing cost while simultaneously maximizing generalization.

Multiple sampling techniques may be used to identify sample individuals under study. Broadly techniques may be divided into probability and non-probability.

Basis for Comparison	Probability Sampling	Non-probability Sampling
Meaning	It is a sampling technique in which the subjects of the population get an equal opportunity to be selected as a representative sample	It is a sampling technique in which the subjects of the population do not get an equal opportunity to be selected as a representative sample
Alternatively Known as	Random Sampling	Non-random Sampling
Basis of Selection	Random	Arbitrarily
Opportunity of selection	Fixed and known	Not specified and unknown
Research	Conclusive	Exploratory
Result	Unbiased	Biased
Inferences	Statistical	Analytical
Hypothesis	Tested	Generated

Probability Sampling

Probability Sampling is a sampling technique in which sample from a larger population are chosen using a method based on the theory of probability. Specific techniques are used for selecting representative samples from populations of different characteristics, such as simple random sampling, stratified sampling, cluster sampling, etc.

Every individual constituting a part of the population is identified, and each has a certain specific probability of being selected, i.e., every individual in the population has a fair & equal chance of being selected.

A randomly adopted process decides the final sample-based on each individual's probability.

Under the category of probability sampling the various techniques that may be used are:

1. Simple Random Sampling
2. Systematic Sampling
3. Stratified Random Sampling
4. Cluster Sampling
5. Area Sampling
6. Multistage Sampling

1-Simple Random Sampling

The most commonly used random sampling method is a simple random method. It is a sampling technique where a sample is chosen from a population by chance or draw of lots & each element of the population has an equal chance of being picked up in the sample. All participants are listed down & sample drawn by draw of lots. This ensures that each individual has an unbiased, fair, and equal chance of being selected. This approach is practicable, fair, unbiased, and easy to adopt. However, with simple random sampling, there is no assurance of complete representativeness of the sample. Simple random sampling refers to any sampling method that has the following properties.

- The population consists of 'N' objects.
- The sample consists of 'n' objects.
- Numbering of each member of the population under investigation in a serial order.
- Determine the starting point of selecting sample by randomly picking up.

The samples can be drawn in two possible ways.

The sampling units are chosen without replacement in the sense that the units once are chosen are not placed back in the population.

The sampling units are chosen with replacement in the sense that the chosen units are placed back in the population.

1. Simple random sampling without replacement (SRSWOR):

SRSWOR is a method of selection of n units out of the N units one by one such that at any stage of selection, **any one of the remaining units has the same chance of being selected**, i.e., 1/ N.

2. Simple random sampling with replacement (SRSWR):

SRSWR is a method of selection of n units out of the N units one by one such that at each stage of selection, **each unit has an equal chance of being selected**, i.e., 1/ N.

There are many ways to obtain a simple random sample. One way would be the lottery method. Each of the N population members is assigned a unique number. The numbers are placed in a bowl and thoroughly mixed. Then, a blind-folded researcher selects n numbers. Population members having the selected numbers are included in the sample.

2-Systematic Sampling

With systematic random sampling, we create a list of every member of the population, and the sample units are selected from the population at equal intervals in terms of time, space or order. In other words, from the list, we randomly select the first sample element from the first k elements on the population list. Thereafter, we select every kth element on the list. This method is different from simple random sampling since every possible sample of n elements is not equally likely.

Suppose the N units in the population are numbered 1 to N in some order. Suppose further that N is expressible as a product of two integers n and k so that N = nk.

To draw a sample of size n,

- Select a random number between 1 and k.
- Suppose it is 'i'.

- Select the first unit, whose serial number is i.
- Select every kth unit after ith unit.
- Sample will contain i,i + k,1+ 2k,...,i + (n-1)k serial number units.

So the first unit is selected at random, and other units are selected systematically. This systematic sample is called a kth systematic sample, and k is termed as the sampling interval. This is also known as systematic linear sampling. Example: Let N = 50 and n = 5. So k = 10. Suppose the first selected number between 1 and 10 is 2. Then systematic sample consists of units with the following serial numbers 2, 12, 22, 32, 42.

3-Stratified random sampling

With stratified sampling, the population is divided into groups, based on some characteristic. Then, within each group, a probability sample (often a simple random sample) is selected. In stratified sampling, the groups are called **strata**. When we sample a population with several strata, we generally require that the proportion of each stratum in the sample should be the same as in the population. Stratified sampling techniques are generally used when the population is heterogeneous, or dissimilar, where certain homogeneous, or similar, sub-populations can be isolated (strata). Simple random sampling is most appropriate when the entire population from which the sample is taken is homogeneous.

The basic idea behind the stratified sampling is to:

- Divide the whole heterogeneous population into smaller groups or subpopulations, such that the sampling units are homogeneous with respect to the characteristic under study and heterogeneous with respect to the characteristic under study between/ among the sub-populations. Such subpopulations are termed as strata.
- Treat each subpopulation as a separate population and draw a sample by SRS from each stratum.

[Note: 'Stratum' is singular and 'Strata' is plural].

Some reasons for using stratified sampling over simple random sampling are:

(a) the cost per observation in the survey may be reduced;

(b) estimates of the population parameters may be wanted for each sub-population;

(c) increased accuracy at a given cost. Splitting the entire population into equal groups or strata's and thereafter repeating the above technique to ensure more uniformity.

We use the following symbols and notations:

N: Population size

k: Number of strata

Ni: Number of sampling units in ith strata

$$N = \sum_{i=1}^{k} N_i$$

n_i : Number of sampling units to be drawn from i^{th} stratum.

$$n = \sum_{i=1}^{k} n_i \text{ : Total sample size}$$

Example

Suppose we conduct a national survey. We might divide the population into groups or strata, based on geography – north, east, south, and west or based statewide. Then, within each stratum, we might randomly select survey respondents.

The two approaches further used in stratified sampling are proportional and disproportional stratified sampling.

4-Cluster sampling

With cluster sampling, every member of the population is assigned to one and only one group. Each group is called a cluster. Cluster sampling is a sampling technique where the entire population is divided into groups or clusters, and a random sample of these clusters is selected. All inferences in the selected clusters form a part of the sample. This method is generally used for obtaining a larger and relatively more random selection of subjects. A sample of clusters is chosen, using a probability method (often simple random sampling). Only individuals within sampled clusters are surveyed. The difference between cluster sampling and stratified sampling is with stratified sampling, the sample includes elements from each stratum and the strata are constructed such that they are within homogenous and among heterogenous. With cluster sampling, in contrast, the sample includes elements only from sampled clusters and clusters are constructed such that they are within heterogeneous and among homogenous. However, the method suffers from a major shortcoming of lacking independence.

In cluster sampling

- Divide the whole population into clusters according to some well-defined rule.
- Treat the clusters as sampling units.
- Choose a sample of clusters according to some procedures.
- Carry out a complete enumeration of the selected clusters, i.e., collect information on all the sampling units available in selected clusters.

Examples:

In a city, the list of all the individual persons staying in the houses may be difficult to obtain or maybe not available, but a list of all the houses in the city may be available. So every individual person will be treated as a sampling unit, and every house will be a cluster.

5-Area Sampling

Area sampling is defined as, the entire area containing the populations is subdivided into smaller area segments and each element in the population is associated with one and only one such area segment.

With area sampling we select an area to be sampled. This is then sub-divided into smaller blocks that are then randomly selected and subject to further sub-sampling. It involves sampling from a map, an aerial photograph, or a similar area frame.

For example, a city map can be divided into equal size blocks, from which random samples can be drawn.

6-Multistage Sampling

With multistage sampling, we select a sample by using combinations of different sampling methods. It divides large populations into stages to make the sampling process more practical. A combination of stratified sampling or cluster sampling and simple random sampling is usually used. For example, in Stage 1, we might use cluster sampling to choose clusters from a population. Then, in Stage 2, we might use simple random sampling to select a subset of elements from each chosen cluster for the final sample.

Exhibit 5: Categories of Probability Sampling

Type of Sampling Technique	Description	Cost & Degree of Use	Advantages	Disadvantages	
Simple Random Sampling	Assigning each member of the sample, a number, and then selecting random numbers for identifying the sample.	High in cost & used moderately	Requires bare minimum prior knowledge of population under study	Requires clear sampling frame. Since there is no prior classification of population, open to sampling errors leading to high cost.	
Systematic Sampling	Using natural ordering. The researcher starts at an arbitrary number and thereafter keeps replicating the number to be spaced out across the sample at preselected intervals	Moderate cost & moderately used	Relatively simple to draw, more evenly spread out and easy to check	Periodicity in choosing sample elements may increase variability in the data set.	
Stratified Sampling	Dividing the population into groups & randomly selecting sub-samples from each group.	High cost, moderately used.	Reduces variability by way of ensuring representation of all groups in the sample.	Requires accurate information on each stratum before drawing the sample	

Cluster Sampling	Selecting sampling blocks at the random and thereafter complete observation of blocks to draw a probability sample	Low cost & frequently used	Yields lowest cost when clusters are chosen geographically. Requires pre-listing of clusters, however, individuals within clusters can estimate characteristics of the clusters as well as the population.	May present larger errors for a comparable size of population than other techniques. Pre-listing of clusters might lead to omission or duplication of member elements.	
Area Sampling	Extending the approach of cluster sampling to choose areas with the help locational maps	Low cost & frequently used	Involves lowest cost & easy administration	Prone to biasing & high sampling eror	
Multi stage sampling	Choosing sample elements progressively by using a combination of the previously stated techniques	High cost yet frequently used.	The advantages here would depend on techniques involved	The disadvantages here would depend on techniques involved	

Non-probability sampling

Non-probability sampling is based on selection by non-random means. This can be useful for certain studies, for example, quick surveys or where it is difficult to get access to the whole population. There is a variety of techniques that can be used, such as accidental sampling, quota sampling, and snowball technique.

The population is not entirely known. Thus individual probabilities cannot be known. Common sense or ease is used to choose the sample, but efforts are made to avoid bias and keep the sample representative.

Categories of techniques under non-probability sampling include:

1-Convenience sampling

The sample is composed of individual participants who are relatively easy to approach. Convenience sampling is practically very easy to practice & apply, but the major disadvantage could be that the sample potentially has chances of being biased. We involve in the sample collection, population members who are conveniently available & approachable. Facebook, Insta polls, Social networks, Google forms, etc., may be taken as some examples of convenience sampling.

Convenience sampling technique may prove to be effective during the exploration stage of the research area, and when conducting pilot data collection in order to identify and address shortcomings associated with questionnaire design.

Example

A marketing student needs to get feedback on the 'scope of content marketing in 2025.' The researcher may quickly create an online survey, and send a link to all the contacts over mobile phones, share a link on social media like LinkedIn, Facebook, Tumbler, Twitter, and Instagram.

2-Quota sampling

Identifying different subgroups and selecting participants through convenience from each subgroup is called quota sampling. No formal rules exist. The general steps to follow are:

1. Divide the population into subgroups. These should be exclusive. For example, you might divide employees by type of educational degree.
2. Figure out the proportion of subgroups to the population. For example, employees who have a physical science degree might be 1 out of 4.
3. Choose your sample size. For example, if you are sampling 10,000 people, you might have a quota size of 100.
4. Choose participants, being careful to adhere to the subgroup, population proportion. For this example, 25% of your sample should have a physical science degree. The selection process continues until your quotas are filled.

Quota sampling can be divided into two groups: controlled and uncontrolled.

Controlled quota sampling involves the introduction of certain restrictions in order to limit the researcher's choice of samples.

Uncontrolled quota sampling, on the other hand, resembles a convenience sampling method in a way that the researcher is free to choose sample group members according to his/her will. Example

Let's assume your research objective is to evaluate the impact of cross-cultural differences on employee motivation in Prism Philosophy (Prism World Pvt Ltd.) in India and the United Kingdom. You need to assess the effectiveness of employee motivational tools taking into account gender differences among the workforce.

Quota sampling can be applied in the following manner:

a) Dividing the population into specific groups: Prism employees in India and the U.K. as the sampling frame need to be divided into the following two groups according to their cultural background:

1. European
2. Asian (India)

b) Calculating a quota for each group: Your manager confirms that in order to achieve the research objectives, 50 representatives from each group and the total sample size of 100 respondents would be appropriate.

c) Determining specific condition(s) to be met and quota in each group: Both genders, males and females need to be represented equally in your sample group. This is an important condition that needs to be satisfied. Accordingly, you recruit 25 males and 25 females from each group.

The application of quota sampling ensures that the sample group represents certain characteristics of the population chosen by the researcher. For the example above, an equal representation of both genders, males and females, has been chosen as an important characteristic of sampling.

3-Snowball sampling

This is a sampling technique, in which existing subjects provide referrals to recruit samples required for a research study. Identifying sample participants through a network or chain approach where the first participant would lead to the next and further on through referrals. Also called chain-referral sampling is defined as non-probability sampling technique in which the samples have traits that are rare to find.

Example,

If you are studying the level of customer satisfaction among the members of an elite country club which specializes in 'star gazing club', you will find it extremely difficult to collect primary data sources unless a member of the club agrees to have a direct conversation with you and provides the contact details of the other members of the club.

There are three different types of Snowball Sampling:

a) Linear Snowball Sampling: The formation of a sample group starts with one individual subject providing information about just one other subject, and then the chain continues with only one referral from one subject. This pattern is continued until enough number of subjects are available for the sample.

b) Exponential Non-Discriminative Snowball Sampling: In this type, the first subject is recruited, and then he/she provides multiple referrals. Each new referrals then provides with more data for referral and so on, until there is enough number of subjects for the sample.

c) Exponential Discriminative Snowball Sampling: In this technique, each subject gives multiple referrals. However, only one subject is recruited from each referral. The choice of a new subject depends on the nature of the research study.

4-Judgmental sampling

It is also called purposive sampling and authoritative sampling. The researcher chooses the sample based on whom they think would be appropriate for the study. In other words, where the researcher selects units to be sampled based on their knowledge and professional judgment. This is used primarily when there is a limited number of people that have expertise in the area being researched.

Example

In a study wherein a researcher wants to know what it takes to graduate summa cum laude (with the highest distinction) in college, the only people who can give the researcher first-hand advice are the individuals who graduated summa cum laude. With this very specific and very limited pool of individuals that can be considered as a subject, hence the researcher must use purposive sampling.

Exhibit 6: Categories of Non-Probability Sampling

Type of Sampling Technique	Description	Cost & Degree of Use	Advantages	Disadvantages	
Convenience Sampling	Using the most easy to reach, convenient samples.	Very low cost & very widely used	No preliminary lists of data required.	Samples chosen may be non-representative, random sampling error visible.	
Quota Sampling	Classifying the population on the basis of specific properties and fixing specific number of sample elements to be picked from each.	Moderate cost & extensively used	Includes stratification yet requires no previous data compilation records.	Includes scope of researcher's biasing . Non-random and so population mean can not be determined.	
Snowball Sampling	Selecting initial set of respondents and thereafter choosing subsequent respondents by way of references from the initial set and so on.	Low cost & used in special situations	Helps in identifying sample members in populations involving rare/ difficult to approach characteristics.	Open to huge biasing as sample units are purely linked to one another.	
Judgemental Sampling	Selecting the sample based on researcher judgement basis the presumption of a certain characteristic.	Moderate cost & average use	Can be used in specific forecasting situations to meet specific objectives.	Strong biasing due to researchers belief might exist. Sample may be non representative.	

Sample Size and Determination

In sampling analysis, the most ticklish question is: What should be the size of the sample or how large or small should be? If the sample size ('n') is too small, it may not serve to achieve the objectives, and if it is too large, we may incur huge cost and wastage of resources.

As a general rule, one can say that the sample must be of optimum size, i.e., it should neither be excessively large nor too small. Technically, the sample size should be large enough to give a confidence interval of the desired width, and as such, the size of the sample must be chosen by some logical process before the sample is taken from the universe.

Size of the sample should be determined by a researcher keeping in view the following points:

(i) **Nature of the universe:** Universe may be either homogenous or heterogeneous in nature. If the items of the universe are homogenous, a small sample can serve the purpose. But if the items are heterogenous, a large sample would be required. Technically, this can be termed as the dispersion factor.

(ii) **Number of classes proposed:** If many class-groups (groups and sub-groups) are to be formed, a large sample would be required because a small sample might not be able to give a reasonable number of items in each class group.

(iii) **Nature of study:** If items are to be intensively and continuously studied, the sample should be small. For a general survey, the size of the sample should be large, but a small sample is considered appropriate in technical surveys.

(iv) **Technique of sampling:** Sampling technique plays an important part in determining the size of the sample. A small random sample is apt to be much superior to a larger but badly selected sample.

(v) **Standard of accuracy and acceptable confidence level:** If the standard of accuracy or the level of precision is to be kept high, we shall require a relatively larger sample. For doubling the accuracy for a fixed significance level, the sample size has to be increased fourfold.

(vi) **Availability of finance:** In practice, the size of the sample depends upon the amount of money available for the study purposes. This factor should be kept in view while determining the size of the sample for large samples results in increasing the cost of sampling estimates.

(vii) **Other considerations:** Nature of units, size of the population, size of the questionnaire, availability of trained investigators, the conditions under which the sample is being conducted, the time available for completion of the study, are a few other considerations to which a researcher must pay attention while selecting the size of the sample.

There are two alternative approaches for determining the size of the sample. The first approach is 'to specify the precision of estimation desired and then to determine the sample size necessary to ensure it,' and the second approach uses Bayesian statistics 'to weigh the cost of additional information against the expected value of the additional information.'

The first approach is capable of giving a mathematical solution, and as such, is a frequently used technique of determining 'n'. The limitation of this technique is that it does not analyze the cost of gathering information vis-a-vis the expected value of information. The second approach is theoretically optimal, but it is seldom used because of the difficulty involved in measuring the value of information. Hence, we shall mainly concentrate here on the first approach.

Determination of sample size through the approach based on precision rate and confidence level

Whenever a sample study is made, there arises some sampling error that can be controlled by selecting a sample of adequate size. The researcher will have to specify the precision that he wants with respect to his estimates concerning the population parameters.

The process of sampling for every research would include the following decisions:

- **Defining the sample population:** The researcher must, in totality, understand the population on which the research is to be conducted. Although the research will actually involve only a small sample population, the results or outcomes, in general, are implied to the entire population. As such, it is important to establish the characteristics of the population, so they match up with those of the sample.
  Eg. In research intended to study causes of increased absenteeism in a graduation college, the population would be all the students of the college.
- **Understanding the sampling frame:** The preconditions or qualifying criterion for any element in the population to be selected as a part of the total sample must be clearly established.
  Eg. Continuing with the college example, setting up parameters for students to form a part of a sample (minimum percentage of classes attended, etc.)
- **Specifying the sampling method:** Making a preference for the sampling method from probability & non-probability techniques is specification of sampling method.
- **Selecting the sample size:** Finalizing the final count respondents to be covered in the sample. The sample size should be big enough to be able to represent the population as also small enough to be time & cost-effective
- **Sampling and data collecting:** This involves implementing the chosen sample collection technique and also applying the data collection instruments.

For instance, a researcher may like to estimate the mean of the universe within ± 3 of the true mean with 95 percent confidence. In this case, we will say that the desired precision is ±3, i.e., if the sample means is Rs 100, the true value of the mean will be no less than Rs 97 and no more than Rs 103. In other words, all this means that the acceptable error, 'e', is equal to 3. Keeping this in view, we can now explain the determination of sample size so that specified precision is ensured.

(a) Sample size when estimating a mean: The confidence interval for the universe means, μ, is given by

$$\bar{X} \pm z \frac{\sigma_p}{\sqrt{n}}$$

where x = sample mean;

z = the value of the standard variate at a given confidence level (to be read from the table giving the areas under the normal curve as shown in the formula section) and it is 1.96 for a 95% confidence level;

n = size of the sample;

s = standard deviation of the population (to be estimated from past experience or on the basis of a trial sample).

(b) Calculation of Sample Size: Prior to calculating the sample size, it is critical to establish a few things about the target population as also the needed sample:

- **Population Size:** Total number of people that fit the research demographics. Although the exact count may not be available, generally, an approximation for the population may be adopted.
- **The Margin of Error (Confidence Interval):** Since no samples will be perfect, pre-decide on how much will be allowed. The confidence interval sets limits on how high or low as compared to the population mean is acceptable to the researcher as the sample mean fluctuates. Most commonly accepted intervals range between +5% to − 5%.
- **Confidence Level:** What degree of confidence do you want to exercise on the actual mean falling within the said confidence interval? The most commonly adopted confidence intervals are 90%, 95%, and 99% level of confidence.
- **Standard of Deviation:** What amount of variance is expected in your responses?

Mathematical calculation of the needed sample size.

The confidence level relates to a z-score. This remains a constant value required for the equation. Given below are the z-scores for the most commonly used confidence levels:

- 90% z Score = 1.645
- 95% z Score = 1.96
- 99% z Score = 2.326

Substituting, z-score, Standard of Deviation, and Confidence interval into the equation:

Necessary Sample Size = (z-score)^2 * StdDev*(1-StdDev) / (margin of error)^2

$((1.96)^2$ x .5(.5)) / (.05)^2

(3.8416 x .25) / .0025

.9604 / .0025

384.16

385 respondents are needed

Standard Error

The standard error (S.E.) is the measured standard deviation of a sampling distribution. It is considered fundamental to sampling theory. The usefulness of standard error can be traced in the following reasons:

1. The standard error tests whether the difference between observed and expected frequencies is because of the element of chance. The most accepted criterion is that a difference less than three times the S.E., is supposed to exist as a matter of chance & if the difference is equal to or any more than three times the S.E., it is definitely not as per chance, and this is perceived as a significant difference. This criterion forms base in the foundation that at X ± 3 (S.E.), the normal curve covers an area of 99.73 percent. Sometimes the criterion of 2 S.E. may be replaced with 3 S.E.

The standard error, therefore, becomes an important measure in significance tests or in testing hypothesis. In the case of a calculated parameter differing from the calculated statistic by more than 1.96 times the S.E., this difference is taken as significant at a 5% level of significance. It, as such, means that the difference is beyond the limits, i.e., it lies in the 5 percent area (2.5 percent on both sides) outside the 95 percent area of the sampling distribution.

Hence we may conclude with 95 percent confidence that the said difference is not on account of sampling fluctuations. In such a situation, the hypothesis would be rejected at a 5 percent level of significance. But if the calculated difference is less than 1.96 times the S.E., then it may be considered not significant at 5 percent level, and we can say with 95 percent confidence that it is owing to sampling fluctuations. In such a situation, the null hypothesis holds true. 1.96 is the critical value at a 5 percent level.

The cumulated product of critical value calculated at a certain level of significance, and the S.E. is known as 'Sampling Error' at that specific level of significance. This can be tested at other levels of significance as well, depending upon the requirement.

2. The standard error gives an idea about the reliability and precision of a sample. The smaller the S.E., the greater the uniformity of sampling distribution, and hence, greater is the reliability of the sample. Conversely, the greater the S.E., the greater the difference

between observed and expected frequencies. In such a situation, the unreliability of the sample is greater. The size of S.E. depends upon the sample size to a great extent, and it varies inversely with the size of the sample. If double reliability is required, i.e., reducing S.E. to 1/2 of its existing magnitude, the sample size should be increased four-fold.

There are two broad sources of error

1 – **Sampling Error:** The principal source of sampling error are the sampling method applied and sample size. It's been said larger the sample more accurate is the research.

2 – **Non-Sampling Error:** Non-sampling error arises from a faulty research design or mistake in executing research. It can be due to respondent error or administrative error. When a respondent fails to provide correct information or gives inaccurate information or information that can be biased.

	SAMPLING ERROR	**NON SAMPLING ERROR**
Meaning	Sampling error arises due to the sampling technique used to draw a sample	Non-Sampling error is due to the reasons other than sampling techniques during a survey process
Sample Size	Sampling error decreases with increase in sample size	Non-sampling error increases with increase in sample size
Cause	Deviation between sample mean and population mean	Deficiency in analysis of data
Type	Random	Random or Non-Random
Occurs	Only when sample is selected	Both in sample and census

Recap & Review Section

SUMMARY Chapter 5

A sample is a subset of the population, and a complete survey of the population is called a census. If we compare the census with a sample, sampling is less expensive. Sampling methods are of two broad categories. These are probability sampling method and non-probability sampling. The size of the samples that needs to be collected from the population can be determined by various factors like time, funds, and the purpose of the study. The sample size depends on the nature of the analysis to be performed. For higher precision, higher confidence is used. Typical confidence levels are 95% and 99%. There are two major sources of error in survey research; these are sampling error and non-sampling error. Hence to minimize the error, researcher needs to focus on the design of the questionnaire, selection of appropriate sampling method, adequate sample size, employing trained investigators, and finally, care in the data processing.

Exhibit 7: Most Trusted Brand Survey

The Economic Times, Brand Equity – 25th March 2020, shared "THE MOST TRUSTED BRANDS 2020". Top 10 brands in order of ranking 1 to 10 (Cadbury tops the charts followed by WhatsApp, Good Day, Facebook, Colgate, Dettol, Amul, Parle-G, Horlicks, Fevicol). An official survey conducted among a sample size of 2200 respondents in four different states. The questionnaire prepared for different target groups, i.e., chief wage earner, homemaker, young & older males, and females.

Respondent was exposed to 392 brands divided into 20 categories.

Qualitative research was used through four parameters

Attribute 1 – Quality

Attribute 2 – Value for Money

Attribute 3 – Recommendation

Attribute 4 – Understanding customer's need

Likert scale was used for rating at 10 point scale where 10 stands for "perfect in every way" and 1 stand for "Extremely poor."

The score was calculated by using the Average weighted score.

Results were shared in descending order as "THE MOST TRUSTED BRAND."

Caselet 5 – Kiran Garments

Kiran has a chain of restaurants in many cities of northern India and was interested in diversifying her business. Her only son, Jai, never wanted to be in the hospitality line. To settle Jai into a line that would interest him, Kiran decided to venture into garment manufacturing. She gave this idea to her son, who liked it very much. Jai had already done a course in fashion designing and wanted to do something different for the consumers of this industry. An idea struck him that he should design garments for people who are very bulky but want a lean look on wearing readymade garments. The first thing that came to his mind was to have an estimate of people who wore large-sized shirts (42 sizes and above) and large-sized trousers (38 sizes and above).

A meeting of experts from the garment industry and a number of fashion designers was called to discuss how they should proceed. Many are wanting to estimate the size of such a market. Another issue that was bothering them was how to approach the respondents. It was believed that asking people about the size of their shirt or trouser may put them off and irritate them, and there may not be any worthwhile response. A suggestion that came up was that they should employ some observers at entrances of various malls and their job would be to look at people who walked into the malls and see whether the concerned person was wearing a big sized shirt or trouser. This would be a better way of approaching the respondents. This procedure would help them to estimate in a very simple way the proportion of people who wore big-sized garments.

Questions

1. Name the sampling design that is being used in the study.
2. What are the limitations of the design so chosen?
3. Can you suggest a better design?
4. What method of data collection is being employed?

Check Your Knowledge

CYK 1 Which ONE of the following is the advantage of simple random sampling?

a. Calculating the accuracy of the results.

b. The results are always representative.

c. Interviewers can choose respondents freely.

d. Respondents can refuse to participate.

Answer (a)

CYK 2 Which ONE of the following is the main disadvantage of using non-probability sampling techniques?

a. Expenses involved

b. Non representative results

c. Human judgment error

d. Respondents can refuse to participate.

Answer (c)

CYK 3 Multistage cluster sample is helpful when:

a. The population is widely dispersed geographically

b. Limited time and money availability

c. You want to use a probability sample in order to generalize the results

d. All of the above

Answer (d)

CYK 4 What is the effect of increasing the sample size upon the sampling error?

a. The sampling error gets reduced.

b. The sampling error gets increased.

c. No effect on the sampling error

d. None of the above

Answer (a)

CYK 5 Snowball sampling helps the researcher to:

a. Access deviant or hidden populations

b. Incorporate qualitative study

c. Overcome the problem of not having an accessible sampling frame

d. All of the above

Answer (d)

Questions

Q1. Under what circumstances may a sample be preferred over the census?

Q2. Suggest the least expensive and also the least time-consuming sampling techniques? What could be the primary limitations of this technique?

Q3. A manufacturer wants to conduct a survey on users to determine the demand potential for a new steel refurbishing machine. The new machine has a capacity of 200 tons and costs 30 Lakhs. It can be used for creating products from steel and can be used by automobile & appliance manufacturers.

a. Identify the population and sampling frame that could be used.

b. Describe how a simple random sample can be drawn using the identified sampling frame.

c. Which sampling technique would you recommend? Why?

Q4. How do probability sampling techniques differ from non-probability sampling techniques?

Q5. List the qualitative factors that must be considered in determining the sample size?

Q6. What is the relevance of drawing a sampling plan in research? Explain the factors which should be considered while selecting a sample.

Q7. What is the significance of the concept of standard error in a sampling analysis?

Q8. Discuss any three sampling techniques with their relative merits and demerits.

Application Question

Q1. To determine the effectiveness of the advertising campaign for a new mobile handset; the management would like to know what percentage of the population is aware of the new brand. The advertising agency thinks that this figure is as high as 70 percent. The management would like a 95 percent confidence interval and a margin of error not greater than plus or minus 2 percent.

(a) What sample size should be used for this study?

(b) Suppose that the management wanted a 99 percent confidence level with an error of plus or minus 3 percent, how would the sample size change?

(Given 95 percent area is covered, within ± 1.96 standard deviations in a normal distribution. Also, 99 percent area is covered with ± 2.58 standard deviation in a normal distribution).

Q2. A life insurance company wants to estimate from a sample, the proportion of its policyholders that intend to buy a new policy within the next six months. Define the sample size that is required to establish at 98 percent confidence, the sample proportion and true proportion will differ by less than 0.025?

Q3. Identify sampling methods used in each of the following statements.

(a) The population placed in alphabetical order. Starting with the 8th name, every 9th member thereafter was selected as a member of the sample. The sample, therefore, consisted of numbers 8, 17, 26, 35, and so on.

(b) Executives were subdivided into three groups, including MNC employees, industrial executives, and bank executives. Random samples were taken from each of these groups, and the sample results were weighted according to the number in the group relative to the total.

Measurement & Scaling Techniques

Keywords: *Nominal Scale, Ordinal scales, Interval Scale, Ratio Scale, Comparison Scale, Ranking Scale, Itemised rating Scale, Likert Scale, Semantic Differential Scale, Stapel Scale, Reliability, Validity*

Research as an integral feature involves respondents communicating their feelings, attitudes, and evaluations in specific and measurable forms. A range of scales has been developed to facilitate this feature. Each has its unique properties. It now becomes essential for the analyst to comprehend their widely varying measurement properties. While some scales are limited in their mathematical properties up to the extent of only being able to establish an association between variables, other scales incorporate many extensive mathematical properties. Some finally, may state the possibility of establishing a cause and effect relationships between the identified variables.

Levels of Measurement

One of the important research tools is the questionnaire. In order to develop a survey/questionnaire, first, the researcher should decide on how the data is to be measured. Scaling in measurement implies the construction of an instrument to gather data. There are a number of factors that must be considered in choosing an appropriate scaling method in a

Four scales of measurement:
- *Nominal*
- *Ordinal*
- *Interval*
- *Ratio*

questionnaire designing & data analysis. This chapter summarizes the different types of scaling methods in order to provide a guideline for the selection of scaling methods for survey/questionnaire.

Measurement is the assignment of numbers to characteristics of objects, which portray the object, according to a certain set of rules. Primarily all researches focus around four levels of measurement: nominal, ordinal, interval, and ratio scales. These scales are used to accumulate data through surveys and questionnaires.

I Nominal scales

Nominal scales are adopted for non-quantitative labeling variables, which are unique and different from one another. To elaborate, it is a system of classification without placing the entity along a continuum or priority list. It may involve a simple count of the frequency of cases allocated to the various categories. This scale is the most simple of all the variable measurement scales. This scale cannot be used for mathematical calculations as numerics used in the scale only indicates variables categories (for coding). If so desired, it is possible to nominally assign numbers to each label as suggested in the given an example:

An example of a nominal scale: (Please tick)

Types of Nominal Scales:

- *Dichotomous: A nominal scale that has only two labels is called 'dichotomous'; for example, Yes/No.*
- *Nominal with Order: The labels on a nominal scale arranged in an ascending or descending order is termed as 'nominal with order'; for example, Excellent, Good, Average, Poor, Worst.*
- *Nominal without Order: Such nominal scale which has no sequence, is called 'nominal without order'; for example, Black, White. It is also referred to as a categorical scale. This scale is most certainly the crudest of measurement scales. The scale classifies individuals, organizations, objects, brands, or any other entity into generalized categories with no order implication. Nominal scale is a naming scale, where variables are simply "named" or labeled, with no specific order.*

Which of the following toiletries do you buy online?					
Shampoo		Hair Oil		Conditioner	
Body Wash		Deodorant		Face-wash	

Numbers will come in later by specifying in totality, the number of 'ticks' to each product. The numbers here have no significant arithmetic property at all and act only as labels. The minimal measure of average, which may in use, is the 'mode' as this simply is a set of frequency counts.

There are also cases where this scale is used for the purpose of classification, the numbers here associated with variables are only tags for categorization or division with no mathematical relevance.

E.g., a customer survey asking "Which brand of laptops do you prefer?"

Options: 'Macbook'-1 , 'Dell'-2, 'Sony'-3, 'Acer'-4

In this question, the number holds only a coding relevance to the brand. The brands have been placed randomly with no specific order. The only relevance of numbers is for coding & eventually categorization.

II Ordinal scales

Ordinal scales consist of the ranking of individuals, brands, or even attitudes along the continuum of characteristics under scaling. Ranking here is done strictly in order of preference. For example, if a researcher has asked buyers to rank five brands of cars in order of preference, the responses would indicate the buyers' priority list, as suggested in the example given below.

E.g., An ordinal scale used to determine buyers' preferences among five brands of SUV.

Such tables reveal to the researcher the order of preference. However, limitations could be in the form of nothing being ascertained about how much more one brand is preferred over another, i.e., there are no statistics about the interval amongst the two brands.

This scales not only assigns values to the variables but also measures the rank or order of the variables, such as:

- Awareness
- Satisfaction
- Happiness

Degree of client satisfaction

- Very Unsatisfied
- Unsatisfied
- Neural
- Satisfied
- Very Satisfied

Ordinal Scale explains the descriptive values along a continuum but has no starting point or a measure of establishing the differences between two different orders. Thus, the distance between variables can't be calculated.

PARTICULAR	NOMINAL SCALE	ORDINAL SCALE	INTERVAL SCALE	RATIO SCALE
Characteristics	Description	Order	Distance	Description, Order, Distance and Origin
Sequential Arrangement	Not Applicable	Applicable	Applicable	Applicable
Fixed Zero Point	Not Applicable	Not Applicable	Not Applicable	Applicable
Multiplication and Division	Not Applicable	Not Applicable	Not Applicable	Applicable
Addition and Subtraction	Not Applicable	Not Applicable	Applicable	Applicable

Continued...

Difference between Variables	Non-Measurable	Non-Measurable	Measurable	Measurable
Mean	Not Applicable	Not Applicable	Applicable	Applicable
Median	Not Applicable	Applicable	Applicable	Applicable
Mode	Applicable	Applicable	Applicable	Applicable

III Interval scales

This scale overcomes the shortcoming of the ordinal scale by not only specifying the order of preference but also specifying the gaps between the preferred and the not so preferred options. The interval scale, also called the cardinal scale takes into account equal units of measurement, thereby making it possible to conclude not only the order of scale & scores but it also simultaneously measures the distance between them. However, an obvious observation is that the zero point (base level) on an interval scale is arbitrary and may not stand at a true zero.

We can safely say that two respondents at scale positions 1 and 2 are as far apart as two respondents at scale positions 4 and 5. On the contrary, a person with score 10 feels twice as strongly as one with score 5 is not a suggested implication. Temperature recording may involve an interval scale, being measured either in Centigrade or Fahrenheit. 40°F cannot be taken to being twice as hot as 20°F since the corresponding temperatures on the centigrade scale, 4.4°C and – 6.6°C, do not follow the ratio of 2:1. Interval scales can be both in numeric or semantic formats.

Examples of interval scales in numeric and semantic formats

Indicate your views on the following parameters, scoring them on a scale of 5 down to 1 (i.e., 5 = Excellent; 1 = Poor)					
Gold cot Apricots are:					Circle the appropriate score on each line
Succulent	5	4	3	2	1
Fresh in taste	5	4	3	2	1
Free of skin blemish	5	4	3	2	1
Value for money	5	4	3	2	1
Attractive packaging	5	4	3	2	1

Indicate your views on Gold cot Apricots by ticking the appropriate responses below:					
	Excellent	V.Good	Good	Fair	Poor
Succulent					
Fresh in taste					
Free of skin blemish					
Value for money					
Attractive packaging					

IV Ratio scales

Ratio Scale is the highest level of measurement, having the properties of both an interval scale as well as of a fixed origin or zero point scale. Ratio scale variables include weights, lengths, and times. Ratio scales allow the researcher to seek a comparative assessment between differences of scores and their relative magnitudes. For example, the difference between 5 and 10 minutes has the same implication as that between 10 and 15 minutes, while 10 minutes is empirically twice as long as 5 minutes.

Respondent	Style 1	Style 2	Style 3
A	95	98	85
B	98	89	85
C	90	100	76

Comparative analysis of the levels of measurement

Scale	Basic Characteristics	Examples	Permissible Statistics
Nominal	Numbers indicative of labeling and classifying objects.	India Cricket team, Religion, Educational background, Marital Status, etc.	Percentages, Mode, Chi-square, Contingency coefficient, Binomial test
Ordinal	Numbers indicating the relative order of the objects, however, the difference in the magnitude of the score cannot be known	Preference Ranking, Image Ranking, Social Class, etc.	Percentile, Quartiles, Median, Rank order Correlation, ANOVA
Interval	Difference between the objects can be known, however, the ratio of the scores has no meaning	Attitude, Opinion, Index Numbers	Product moment correlation coefficient, t-test, z-test, ANOVA, Regression Analysis, Factor Analysis
Ratio	Ratios of the score value have a meaningful interpretation	Age, Income, Market Share, Sales, Cost, etc.	Geometric means, Harmonic Means and Coefficient of variation

Alternative Categorization of Measurement Scales

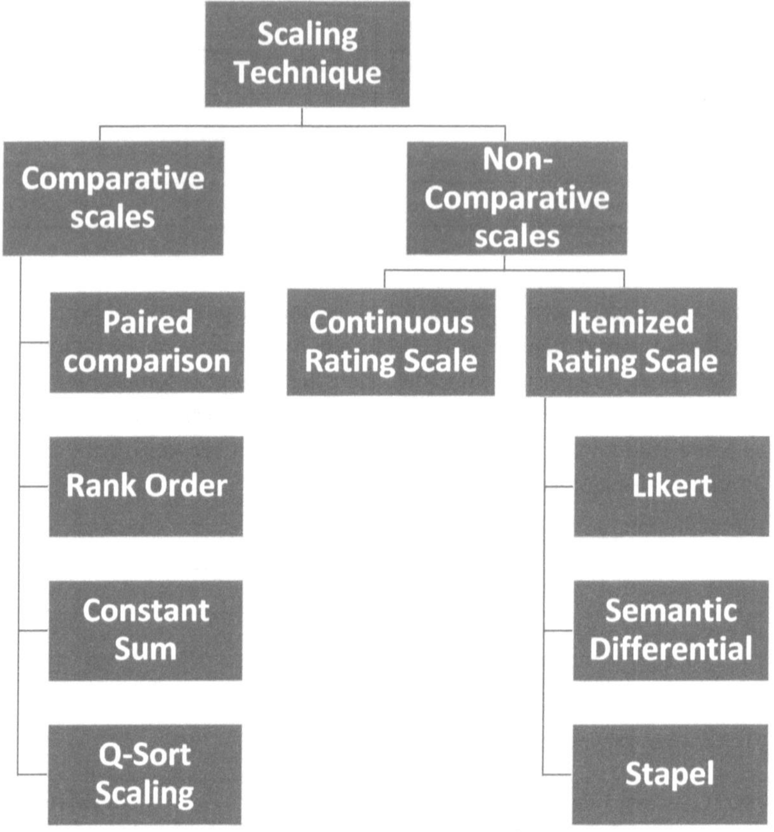

All types of scales that find application in research fall into two major categories: **comparative scales and non-comparative scales**.

Comparative scaling requires the respondent to compare one option against another. Non-comparative scaling, on the contrary, requires respondents to evaluate a single option. The evaluation, in this case, is independent of the other options under study.

I Comparative scales

Under this type of scaling, the respondent is asked to compare one brand/product/ service etc. against another. The evaluation here is dependent on other brands/products/ services under the same study. It is a direct comparison of stimulus object. For example, the respondent might be asked about his/her preference between the MacBook and Dell Laptop. The comparative data can only be interpreted in relative terms and possess the ordinal or rank-order properties.

SCALE	Description	Example
Paired Comparison	This scale symbolizes two variables from which one needs to selected. This technique is mostly implied in product testing, to give the consumers with a comparative analysis of the two major products in the market.	Coca-Cola VS PEPSI VS SAMSUNG
Rank Order	This scale involves ranking of objects in a specific order as per the preference of the respondent.	How useful did you find the following areas of the Careers Service? Please don't select more than 1 answer(s) per row. not at all useful / slightly useful / moderately useful / very useful / extremely useful Documentation Knowledge Advice
Constant Sum	Constant sum scale involves using a continual sum of units like rupees, points, marks etc. in describing features and attributes of a particular product or service.	How many hours of your day are spent participating in the following activities? Using Qualtrics products 5 Walking the dog 1 Relaxing while Qualtrics gathers data for you 18 Worrying about your next project 0 Total 24
Q-Sort	Q-Sort scale is used to sort out the most appropriate objects out of a large number of given variables. It focuses on the ranking of the given objects in descending order to form similar piles based on specific attributes.	Q-Sort Scaling Example High Efficiency / Moderate Efficiency / Low Efficiency

II Non-Comparative scales

Non-Comparative scales is called as monadic or metric scale. It is a scale in which each object is scaled independently of the other objects in the stimulus set under study. The resulting data are assumed to be an interval and ratio scale. For example, a respondent may be asked to rate their preference for the MacBook Laptop on a preference scale (1 = not at all preferred, 5 = greatly preferred). It can be categories in a continuous rating scale and itemized rating scale.

Commonly identified Sources of Error in Measurement

(a) Respondent: The reluctances& non-cooperative attitude of the respondent may cause major ambiguities in results. The respondent may especially be hesitant in revealing or voicing strong negative feelings or, quite possibly, may not have enough knowledge on the said area.

(b) Situation: Situational factors or environmental factors may also create or lead to misleading conclusions. Any situation which creates a strain on the interview process can have serious implications on the interviewer-respondent rapport and the consequent outcomes of the same.

(c) The researcher himself: The interviewer can, on his own, lead to distortion in responses on account of rewording questions or improper sequencing of questions. His behavior & conduct, physical appearance, style though seemingly insignificant, might dissuade fair responses from the respondents. Further, a careless approach in processing may additionally distort the findings.

(d) Instrument: Errors in findings may creep in because of the faulty measuring instrument used. Even the use of com-plicated terminologies, industrial jargon, or language beyond the comprehension of the respondent may lead to confusing results and create ambiguity in findings. Besides, other faults can be poor printing, not providing space for the respondent to answer, omissions in response choice.

SCALE	Description	Example
CONTINUOUS RATING SCALE	It is a graphical rating scale in which respondents are expected place the object at a position of their choice. It is done by selecting and marking a point along the vertical or horizontal line, which ranges between two extreme criteria.	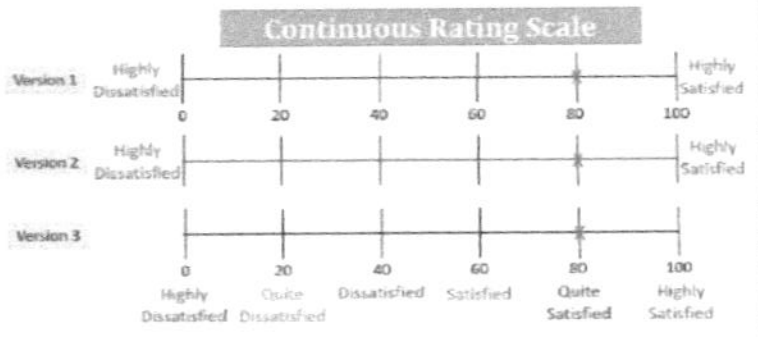
ITEMIZED RATING SCALE	This scales focuses on choosing a particular category among the various given categories. Each class is briefly defined by the researchers to facilitate such selection. The three most commonly used itemized rating scales are Likert scales, Semantic differential and Stapel scale.	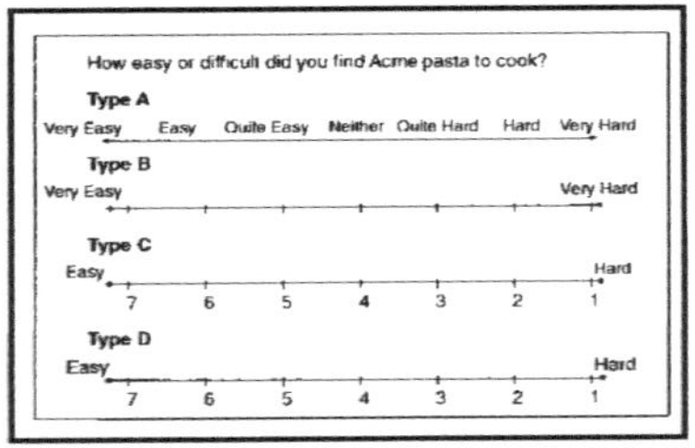
LIKERT SCALE	Likert scale comprises of the researcher providing some statements and asking the respondents to mark their level of agreement or disagreement over these statements by selecting any one of the options from the five given alternatives.	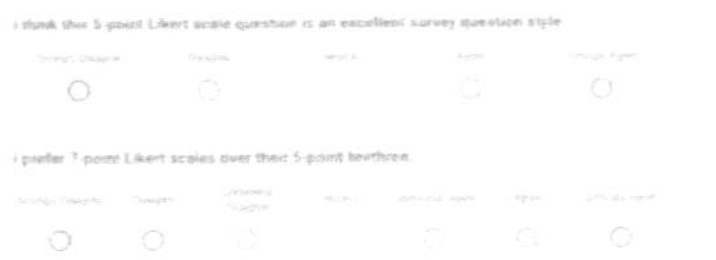
Semantic Differential Scale	Semantic differential is a bi-polar non-comparative rating scale requiring the respondent to mark on any of the points for each given attribute of the object as per personal choice.	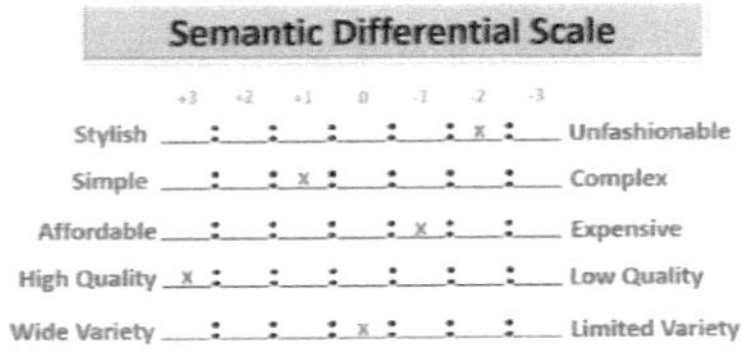

Continued…

Stapel Scale	Stapel scales measures the response, perception or attitude of the respondents against a particular object using a unipolar rating. E.g.The range of a Stapel scale is between – 5 to +5, eliminating 0, thus confining to 10 units.	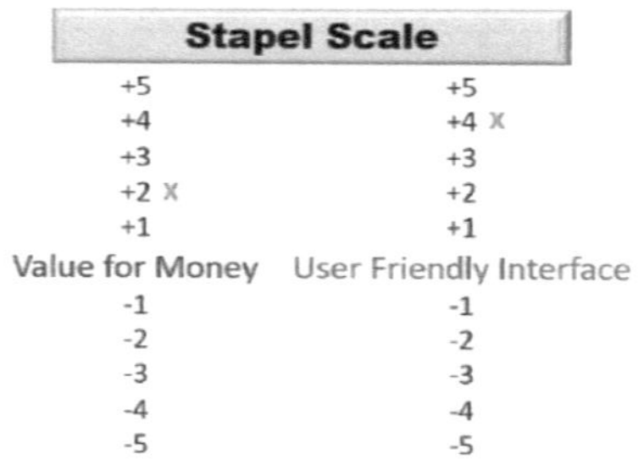Stapel Scale +5 +5 +4 +4 x +3 +3 +2 x +2 +1 +1 Value for Money User Friendly Interface -1 -1 -2 -2 -3 -3 -4 -4 -5 -5
Graphic Rating Scale	This scales offers the respondents a form of continuum on which provide a rating of an object according to a criterion.	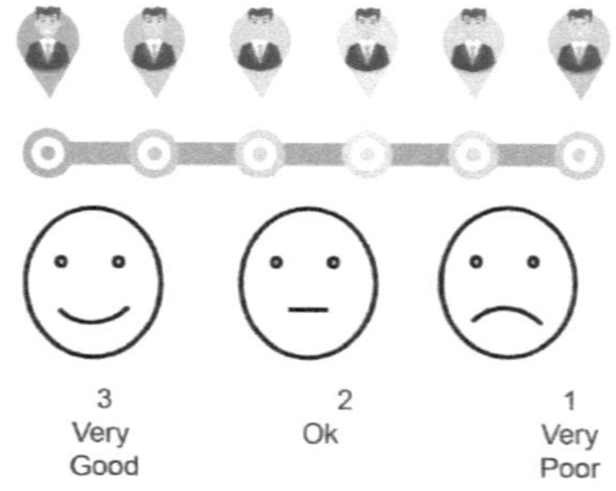3 Very Good 2 Ok 1 Very Poor

Establishing Criteria for Measurement Scale

Once the choice of scale has been made by the researcher, it is important to check that:

1. The chosen scales measure the unobservable construct that is intended to measure (i.e., the scales are 'valid'),
2. The scale measures the intended construct consistently and precisely (i.e., the scales are 'reliable')

Together, validity and reliability and, constitute the yardsticks against which the adequacy, accuracy, suitability & relevance of the measurement scales used in research can be established.

Reliability

Reliability measures the degree to which the measurement scale used is dependable. i.e. if we use this scale multiple times, do we get the same result every time.

e.g., The same weight of a product recorded from a weighing scale multiple times establishes its reliability. It is important, however to understand that reliability implies consistency and not accuracy. Measurement scales used must be tested for reliability.

There are four essential components of estimating reliability:

Inter-rater reliability – measuring consistency between two or more independent researchers for the same construct.

Test-retest reliability – measuring consistency between two tests conducted on the same construct, to the same sample at two different points in time.

Split-half reliability – measuring consistency between two halves of a construct under study.

Internal consistency reliability – measuring consistency between different items of the same construct.

Validity

Validity measures the extent to which a measure or scale devised actually measures the underlying construct that it is supposed to measure. E.g., Is a measure of loyalty really measuring loyalty?

Validity of an instrument can be measured both theoretically & empirically. Theoretical measure focuses on how well a theoretical idea can be converted into practical measurement instrument. This consists of two subtypes: face and content validity

* **Face validity** refers to an apparent and observable indicator of validity.
* **Content validity** refers to how well a set of scale items matches with the relevant construct issues under study.

Empirical assessment of validity, on the contrary, explains the degree to which a given measure relates to one or more external criterion, based on empirical observations.

This includes four sub-types: convergent, discriminant, concurrent, and predictive validity.

	Reliability	**Validity**
Definition	A parameter maintained to establish consistency across results.	A parameter maintained to measure the amount of connect between results & measuring instrument.
Objectives	To measure the dependability of a scale free from researches bias.	To measure the extent to which a scale measures what it claims to measure.
Types	Inter-rater reliability Test-retest reliability Split-half reliability Internal consistency reliability	Theoretical validity Empirical validity

Besides Reliability & Validity, the critical elements that form the prerequisites of a good measurement scale are sensitivity & accuracy in measuring variability in responses and the ease of using an instrument & its practicability.

Recap & Review Section

SUMMARY Chapter 6

Nominal, Ordinal, Interval, and Ratio are four levels of measurements. Nominal scale yields on category, Ordinal scale gives sequence; Interval scale begins to reveal the magnitude between points on sales, and Ratio scales explain both orders and absolute distance between any two points on the scales.

The measuring scale can be divided into three types: comparative, non-comparative, and semantic scales. The scaling techniques are available for the measurement of attitudes. There is no unique way to select particular scaling techniques for research.

Caselet 6 – Work from Home Under COVID-19 Lockdown

There is no clarity on exactly what proportion of the workforce was allowed to telecommunicate & clarify the changed way of working before COVID-19 struck. Huge number of businesses in the IT sector shifted to adopting a flexible workspace policy. Yet, definition of flexibility varies across organization, to some it can mean simply the ability to control your hours or manage your own workload.

Kumar, senior partner and regional lead for IT consultancy Sigma, believes India's lower home working rate is linked to traditional workplace culture. Majority IT companies still follow a top-down management approach which requires their employees besides other things, punch in and out for work, and their bonus and KPIs tied closely to attendance.

Arindam, a manager at a regional Bank, feels he has less control over his employees when they're not in the office. "Work-from-home makes things tougher, less efficient communication and employees affect efficiency," he says. I host daily virtual meets, just to ensure that all are on the same page, maintain consistency in thought. His thought behind daily reporting is trying to motivate, however, his team seems to be taking it in the spirit of increased obtrusion on privacy & doubting their integrity.

Requirements to check more is hitting some employees hard. "Before the lockout happened, it was not mandatory to report every day, but now everything done should be carefully recorded in daily reports and sent to the boss which is frustrating!" says Avika, a Tech firm employee.

You have been hired as a consultant to investigate the factors which relate to employee resistance to work from home. The objectives would be to discover the impacts of, Supervision, Daily reporting, Work culture, Non-adaptability, Improper communication & Impact of personal commitments at home.

A. Based on the objectives of your research suggest suitable data collection techniques that should be applied for this research.

B.   Design a questionnaire measuring each of the above using the different scaling techniques as discussed in the chapter.

C.   Further examine the questions as given here:

1. From the given list, tick the factors that as per you create a positive impact on productivity:

a. Less Supervision

b. Perks at workplace

c. Salary Hike

d. Recognition

e. Flexibility

f. Clarity in communication

2. Rank the following in order of their creating a positive impact on productivity:

a. Supervision

b. Perks at workplace

c. Salary Hike

d. Recognition

3. State your degree of agreeability in each of the statement given in the below table:

	Completey Disagree	Disagree	No opinion	Agree	Completely Agree
I rank recognition above all at my office					
The rude conduct of my coworkers keeps makes me avoid work					
Trust is an integral element in increasing my efficiency					
Biometrics for measuring productivity is a weird idea					
My performance indicators need to be well defined					

Indicate the type of measurement (nominal, ordinal, interval or ratio) which is being used in each of the above questions.

Check Your Knowledge

CYK 1 A business suffering from a high level of customer complaints about a product wants a detailed understanding of what is wrong. Which of the following methods of research would be the best in identifying the main cause of the complaints?

a. Collect press cuttings from many sources

b. Focus group

c. Telephone survey

d. Buy a detailed report analyzing the overall market place

Answer (c)

CYK 2 (a) A retail store operating in a relatively low socio-economic areas wants to ascertain consumer preference patterns towards specific store policies. The store involves a questionnaire using different practices on a scale of the best (+5) to worst (-5). The scale options are presented only in the numeric form. What type of scale does this correspond to?

a. Semantic differential scale

b. Likert scale

c. Graphic rating scale

d. Stapel scale

Answer (d)

(b) The same questionnaire is now administered to a group of illiterates, and numeric on ratings are now replaced with symbols or pictures. The new scale now is?

a. Semantic differential scale

b. Likert scale

c. Graphic rating scale

d. Stapel scale

Answer (c)

CYK 3 An inventor has developed a new device to sanitize toothbrushes. Each time they are placed on the device it uses steam and lab tests have proven it to be very effective in germ-killing. The inventor now wants to know how people would feel about his invention and also if toothbrush sanitation is actually a problem area or not. What methods of data collection could be most suited to gather relevant data to this end?

a. Questionnaire

b. Company literature

c. Projective techniques

d. Case study

Answer (a)

CYK 4 What sampling method involves selecting individuals in such a way that anyone in the total population has an equal chance of being chosen?
a. Quota sampling
b. Cluster sampling
c. Stratified sampling
d. Random sampling

Answer (d)

Questions

Q1. What are the basic characteristics of a scale?

Q2. What are the differences between

a) Stapel scale and the semantic differential

b) Comparative vs. non-comparative scales

c) Itemized vs non-itemized scale

d) Reliability vs.validity

e) Single-item and Multiple-item scale

Q3. How many scale categories should be used in an itemized rating scale? Elucidate.

Q4. Develop a Likert, a Semantic differential, and a Stapel scale for measuring preference towards a certain PVR.

Q5. 1. Ascertain the specific type of scale being used in each of the following.

a. I like to solve a number of games.

Disagree ———————————-Agree

1   2   3   4   5

b. How old are you? ____________________

c. Please rank the following activities in terms of your preference by assigning ranks 1 (most preferred) to 5 (least preferred).

i. Reading ____________________

ii. Net-streaming ____________________

iii. Socialising ____________________

iv. Shopping ____________________

v. Eating out ____________________

d. On an average weekday, how much time do you devote to social networking sites?

i. <15 minutes ____________________

ii. 15-30 minutes ____________________

iii. 31-60 minutes ____________________

iv. 61-120 minutes ____________________

v. >120 minutes____________________

Q6. What are the four key levels of measurement?

Q7. Discuss the major types of validity that concern a researcher.

Q8. What is the meaning of measurements in research? Give examples.

Q9. What is the error in measurement? Discuss various types of measurement accuracy and the methods to measure them.

Q10. 'The numeric used in the nominal scale carry no mathematical relevance'. Elucidate.

Application Questions

1. Indigo airlines wants to ascertain the image it has in the minds of its flyers. Construct a seven-item Likert and Semantic differential scale to measure the perceived image of the airline. Make sure that the items correspond to the same seven dimensions.

2. Indicate the type of measurement scale you would use for each of the following characteristics. Justify your choice and develop the appropriate question for each characteristic under the scale chosen.

(a) Occupation

(b) Brand loyalty

(c) Followership of a radio channel

(f) News channel

3. Indicate the type of scale (nominal, ordinal, interval, or ratio) that is being used in each of the following questions:

(a) How large is the market size for Fast-food?

(b) Which of the following functional areas of management would you want to take up in your Master's program?

(i) Data Analytics

(ii) Trade Finance

(iii) Organization Development

(iv) Entrepreneurship

(c) State the order of your preference for the following colors.

(i) Red (ii) White

4. Design a 5-item Likert scale to measure the opinion of the general public for what measures should be taken to spread awareness on COVID-19.

5. Develop a semantic differential scale to measure the image of two hospitals, Apollo Hospitals vs. Fortis Healthcare.

Descriptive & Inferential Statistics

> **Keywords:** *Descriptive statistics, Inferential statistics, Classification, Tabulation, Graphical Presentation, Diagrammatical Presentation, Central Tendency, Normal Distribution, Standard deviation, Skewness, Correlation, Regression*

Meaning

The word statistics has a different meaning to different people. For some, it is a one-number description of a dataset in terms of numbers used as measurements or counts. Mathematicians use statistics to describe data in one-word numbers, or it is a summary of an event for them. Number, 'n', is the statistic describing how big the set of numbers is and how many pieces of data are in the set.

Also, knowledge of statistics is applicable and used in day to day life in different ways. Statistics are used by people to make decisions about the problems based on different types of information available to them. However, in behavioral sciences, the word statistics mean something different; that is, its prime function is to draw statistical inference about the population based on both qualitative and quantitative information.

The word statistics is defined in both singular and the plural ways. In a singular sense, statistics refers to what is called statistical methods. When statistics is defined in plural sense, it refers to data.

We will use the term statistics in a singular sense. It refers to a branch of science which deals with the collection of data, data classification, analysis, and interpretations of statistical data.

The science of statistics is broadly divisible under two headings:

i) Descriptive Statistics, and (ii) Inferential Statistics

Descriptive Statistics

Most of the observations in this universe are subject to variability and especially observations related to human behavior. It is a well-known fact that attitude, intelligence, and personality differ from individual to individual. In order to make a sensible definition of the group regarding their observations/scores, it is necessary to express them in a correct and precise manner. For this purpose, observations make as a single estimate.

Inferential Statistics

Inferential statistics extracts data from a sample and uses it to draw inferences about its population. As inferential statistics aims at drawing conclusions from a sample and generalizing them to a population, it is essential to be sure that the sample accurately represents the population.

At a macro level, Inferential statistics involves:

- Defining the population under study.
- Drawing a representative sample from that population.
- Using analysis to incorporate the sampling error.

As the researcher does not get to choose a convenient sample, random sampling needs to be applied to gather the confidence that the sample is a true population representative.

Random sample is an integral method for identifying samples that represent the population on an average. It can be used to generalize from the sample to the entire population.

The tools used to conduct inferential statistics such as Hypothesis testing & ANOVA have been discussed at length in the coming chapter.

Differences

Descriptive statistics	Inferential Statistics
Concerned with describing the target population	Makes inferences from the sample and generalizes them to the population
Works with a smaller data set	Works with a larger data set
Error involved in usually less	Error involved is usually more
Organize, analyze, and present the data in a meaningful manner	Compares, test, and predicts future outcomes
Final results are shown in the form of charts, tables and graphs	Final result are the probability scores
Describes the data which is already known	Tries to make conclusions about the population that is beyond the data available
Tools-measures of central tendency (mean, median, mode), spread of data (range and standard deviation)	Tools-Hypothesis tests and Analysis of Variance

Descriptive statistics is a branch of statistics, which deals with descriptions of obtained data. Based on these descriptions, a particular group of the population defines a corresponding characteristic. The descriptive statistics include classification, tabulation, diagrammatic, and graphical presentation of data. It also includes measures of central tendency and variability. These measures enable researchers to know about the tendency of data, which further enhance the ease in describing the phenomena. Such single estimates of the series of data which summarizes the distribution are known as parameters of the distribution. These parameters define the distribution completely.

Descriptive statistics involves two operations:

(i)   Organization of data, and
(ii) Summarization of data.

Organization of Data

There are four primary statistical techniques for editing or organizing the data.

These are:

i.   Classification
ii.   Tabulation
iii. Graphical Presentation, and
iv.   Diagrammatical Presentation

Classification

Classification is the process of arranging data into sequences according to their common characteristics or separating them into different related parts. In other words, the arrangement of data in groups according to similarities or the process of arranging data into homogeneous (similar) groups according to their common characteristics. A classification comprises a summary of frequencies, individual scores or score ranges for a variable. In the most straightforward distribution, we have a value of variables as well as the number of persons who had each value.

Once data are collected, it needs arranging in a format from which meaningful conclusions can be drawn. Thus by classifying data, the investigators move a step ahead regarding making a decision. This arrangement of data helps researcher in comparison and analysis.

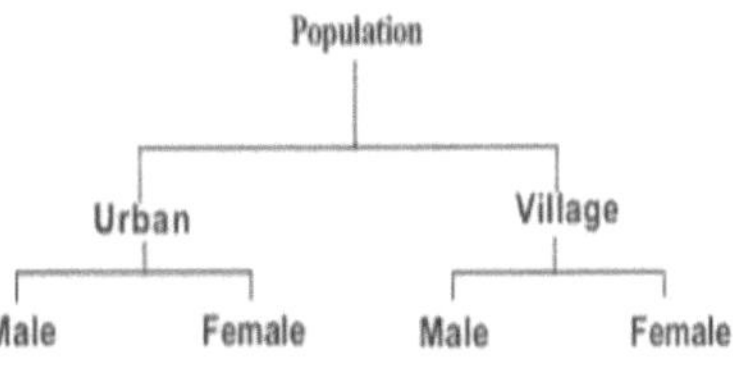

For example, the population of India can be grouped according to age or marital status etc.

A much clear picture of information of score emerges when the raw data are organized as a frequency distribution. A frequency distribution shows the number of cases falling within a given class interval or range of scores. A frequency distribution is a table that shows each

160   Fundamentals of Research

score as obtained by a group of individuals and how frequently each score occurs. There are four types of classification:

- Geographical classification (When data are classified on the basis of location or areas),
- Chronological classification (classification on the basis of time, like months, years),
- Qualitative classification (classified on the basis of some attributes or quality such as sex, color of hair, literacy),
- Quantitative classification (classification of data according to some characteristics, which can be measured such as height, weight, income etc.)

Tabulation

It is a systematic & logical presentation of numeric **data** in an engaging, easy to read, and coordinated manner in rows and columns, to facilitate comparison and statistical analysis. Tabulation is the process of presenting detailed data in the form of a table. A tabular presentation of data becomes more legible and fit for further statistical analysis. A table is a systematic arrangement of classified data in rows and columns with appropriate headings and sub-headings. Hence, a frequency distribution can be either in the form of a table or in the form of a graph. The main components of a table are:

Table Number.......................
Title ....
(Head Note, if any)

Stub **(Row heading)**	**Caption (Column Heading)**				**Total (Rows)**
	Sub- Head		**Sub- Head**		
	Column- **Head**	**Column-** **Head**	**Column-** **Head**	**Column-** **Head**	
Stub Entries **(Row Entries)**					
Total Columns					

Source Note:
Footnote:

i. Table number: When there is more than one table in a particular analysis, a table should need marking with a number for their reference and identification. The number needs writing in the center at the top of the table.

ii. Title of the table: Every table should have an appropriate title, which describes the content of the table. The title should be clear, brief, and self-explanatory. It can be placed either centrally, on top of the table, or just below or after the table number.

iii. Caption: Captions are brief and self-explanatory headings for columns. Captions may involve headings and sub-headings. The captions require placement in the middle of the columns. For example, we can divide students of a class into males and females, rural and urban.

iv. Stub: Stubs stand for brief and self-explanatory headings for rows.

v. Body of the table: This is the real table that contains numerical information or data in different cells. This arrangement of data remains according to the description of captions and stubs.

vi. Headnote: This is written below the title and explains the unit of measurements used in the table body.

vii. Source of data: Researcher needs to specify the sources from which data is taken at the end of the table.

viii. Footnote: This is a qualifying statement that is to be written below the table explaining specific points related to the data which have not been covered in the title, caption, and stubs.

Graphical Presentation of Data

The purpose of preparing a frequency distribution is to provide a systematic way of looking at and understanding data. The information contained in a frequency distribution often is displayed in graphic and diagrammatic forms. In the graphical presentation of frequency distribution, frequencies are plotted on a pictorial platform formed of horizontal and vertical lines known as a graph.

A graph indicating appropriate scales on two mutually perpendicular lines called the X and Y axis are to be created. The horizontal line is called the abscissa and vertical the ordinate. Like different kinds of frequency distributions, there are many kinds of graphs too, which enhance the scientific understanding of the reader.

Commonly used graphs are Histogram, Frequency polygon, Frequency curve.

The essential types of graphical patterns used in statistics are:

i. Histogram:

It is one of the most popular methods for presenting continuous frequency distribution in the form of a graph. In this type of distribution, the upper limit of a class is the lower limit of the following class. A histogram consists of a series of rectangles, with its width equal to the class interval of variables on the horizontal axis and the corresponding frequency on the vertical axis as its heights.

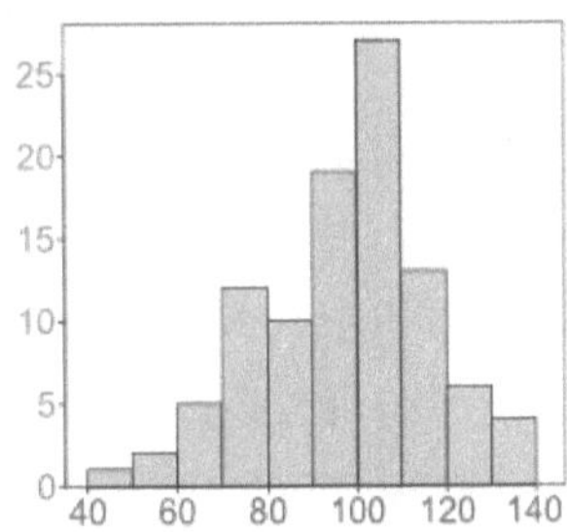

ii. Frequency polygon:

Prepare an abscissa originating from and ending at X. Again, construct the ordinate starting from and ending at Y. Now label the class-intervals on abscissa stating the exact limits or midpoints of the class-intervals. We can also add one extra limit keeping zero frequency on both sides of the class-interval range. The size of the measurement of small squares on graph paper depends upon the number of classes to be plotted. The next step is to plot the frequencies on ordinate using the most comfortable measurement of small squares depending on the range of whole distribution. To plot

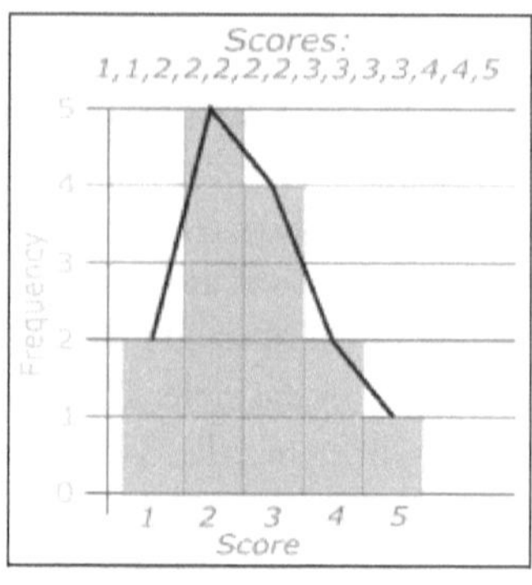

a frequency polygon, we have to mark each frequency against its concerned class on the height of its respective ordinate. After putting all frequency marks, draw a line joining the points. This is called a polygon

iii. Frequency curve:

A frequency curve is a smooth, freehand curve drawn through frequency polygon. The objective of smoothing the frequency polygon is to eliminate as far as possible the random or erratic fluctuations that are present in the data.

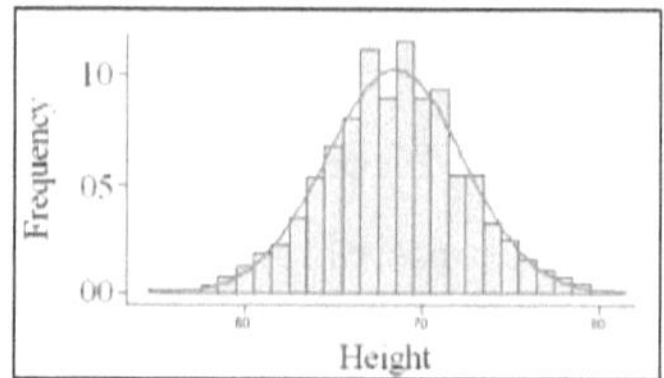

Diagrammatic Presentation of Data

Diagram is a visual form for the presentation of statistical data. It represents the data in a simple, readily comprehensible form. Diagrammatic presentation is used only for the presentation of the data in visual form, whereas the graphic presentation of the data can be used for further analysis. There are different forms of diagrams, e.g., Bar diagram, Sub-divided bar diagram, Multiple bar diagram, Pie diagram.

i. Bar diagram:

The bar diagram is most useful for categorical data and defined as a thick line. The bar diagram is drawn from the frequency distribution table representing the variable on the horizontal axis and the frequency on the vertical axis. The height of each bar will be corresponding to the frequency or value of the variable.

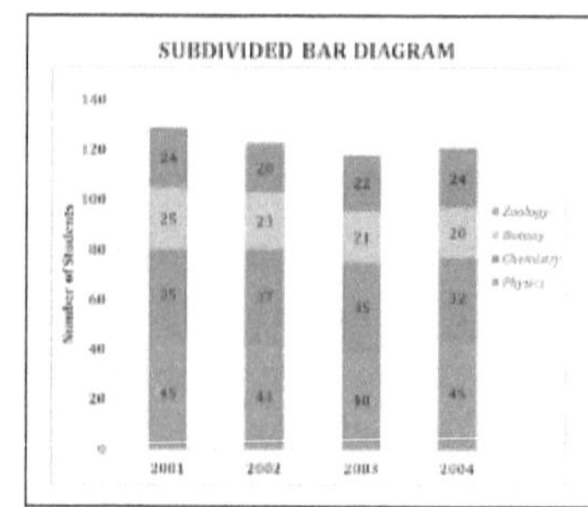

ii. Sub-divided bar diagram:

The study of sub-classification of a phenomenon can be done by using a sub-divided bar diagram. Corresponding to each sub-category of the data, the bar is divided and shaded.

There will be as many shades as there will sub-portion in a group of data. The portion of the bar occupied by each sub-class reflects its proportion in the total.

iii. Multiple Bar diagram:

This diagram is used when comparisons are shown between two or more sets of interrelated phenomena or variables. A set of bars for person, place, or related phenomena are drawn side by side without any gap. To distinguish between the different bars in a set, different colors or shades are used.

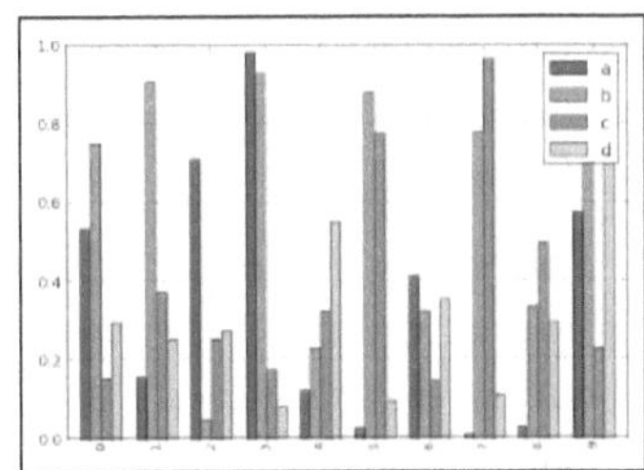

iv. Pie diagram:

It is also known as an angular diagram. A pie chart or diagram is a circle divided into component sectors corresponding to the frequencies of the variables in the distribution. Each sector will be proportional to the frequency of the variable in the group. A circle represents 360 degrees. So 360-degree angles are divided in proportion to percentages. The degrees represented by the various parts of a given magnitude can be obtained by using this formula.

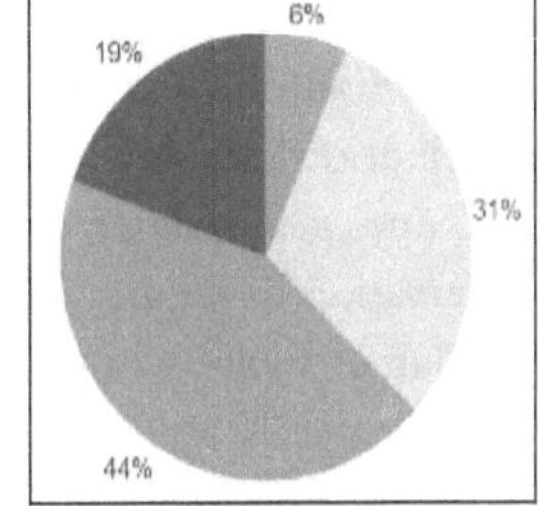

Summarization of Data

Descriptive Statistics provide simple summaries about the sample via graphs and numbers, mainly measures of center tendency, frequency distribution, and variation. Also, the frequency distribution of obtained data may differ in two ways, first in measures of central tendency, and second, to the extent to which scores are spread over the central value. Both types of differences are the components of summary statistics.

Central Tendency

It is the middle point of distribution. Tabulated data provides the data in a systematic order and enhances its understanding. Generally, in any distribution, values of the variables tend to cluster around a central value of the distribution. This tendency of the distribution is known as the central tendency, and measures devised to consider this tendency are known as measures of central tendency. Central tendency measure may be useful if it accurately represents the distribution of scores on which it is based. A good measure of central tendency must possess the following characteristics:

- It should be clearly defined-The definition of a measure of central tendency should be clear and unambiguous so that it leads to one and only one information.
- It should be readily comprehensible and easy to compute.
- It should be based on all observations-A good measure of central tendency should be based on all the values of the distribution of scores.

Commonly used measures for a central tendency are:

- Arithmetic Mean
- Median
- Mode
- Geometric Mean
- Harmonic Mean

i. Arithmetic Mean: The arithmetic mean is the most popular and widely used measure of central tendency. Whenever we refer to the average of data, it means we are talking about its arithmetic mean. This is calculated by dividing the sum of the values of the variable by the total number of values. It is also a useful measure for further statistics and comparisons among different data sets. One of the major limitations of arithmetic mean is that it cannot be computed for open-ended class-intervals.

ii. Median: Median is the middlemost value in a data distribution. It divides the distribution into two equal parts so that exactly one-half of the observations are below and one half is above that point. Since the median clearly denotes the position of an observation in an array, it is also called a position average. Thus, more technically, the median of an array of numbers arranged in order of their magnitude is either the middle value or the arithmetic mean of the two middle values. It is not affected by extreme values in the distribution.

Name & Meaning	Formula / Example	Used for
Arithmetic Mean [average]	$\dfrac{sum}{size} = \dfrac{a+b+c}{3}$	Most situations ("average item")
Median [middle value]	Middle of sorted list (2 middles? Average 'em)	Wildly varying samples (houses, incomes)
Mode [most popular]	Most popular value	No compromises (winner takes all)
Geometric Mean [average factor]	$\sqrt[3]{abc}$	Investments, growth, area, volume
Harmonic Mean [average rate]	$\dfrac{3}{\dfrac{1}{a}+\dfrac{1}{b}+\dfrac{1}{c}}$	Speed, production, cost

iii. Mode: Mode is the value in a distribution that corresponds to the maximum concentration of frequencies. In more simple words, the mode is the point in the distribution comprising maximum frequencies therein.

iv. Geometric Mean: The geometric mean is a type of average usually used for growth rates, like population growth or interest rates. While the arithmetic mean **adds** items, the geometric mean **multiplies** items. Also, you can only get the geometric mean for positive numbers. It is the average growth of an investment computed by multiplying **n** variables and then taking the **n**[th]–root.

v. Harmonic Mean: Harmonic mean is a type of average that is calculated by dividing the number of values in the data series by the sum of reciprocals of each value in the data series. It is often used to calculate the average of the ratios or rates and is the most appropriate measure. It equalizes the weights of each data point.

For any set of data wherever computation is possible, the following inequality holds, Average mean>GM>HM

Normal Distribution

The bell-shaped curve is technically known as the Normal Probability Curve or simply Normal Curve. The corresponding frequency distribution of scores, having just the same values of all three measures of central tendency (Mean, Median, and Mode), is known as Normal Distribution.

Many variables in the physical (e.g., height, weight, temperature) biological (e.g., age, longevity, blood sugar level), behavioral (e.g., Intelligence; Achievement; Adjustment; Anxiety; Socio-Economic-Status) and sciences are normally-distributed in nature. Hence to measure such behavioral aspects, the Normal Probability Curve in simple terms Normal Curve works as a reference curve, and the unit of measurement is described as (Sigma).

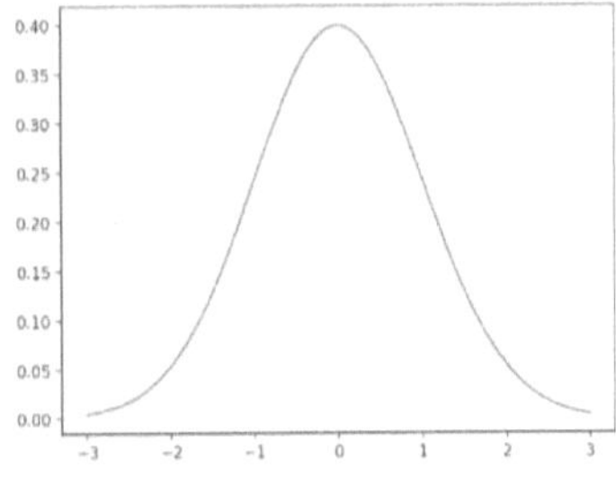

The characteristics of the normal probability curve are:

The Normal Curve is Symmetrical: The normal probability curve is symmetrical around its vertical axis called ordinate. The symmetry about the ordinate at the central point of the curve implies that the size, shape, and slope of the curve on one side is identical to that of the other. In other words, the left and right halves to the central middle point are mirror images.

The Normal Curve is Unimodel: Since there is only one maximum point in the curve, thus the normal probability curve is unimodal,i.e., it has only one mode.

Application of Normal Distribution

There are a number of applications of the normal curve in various field. These are:

i.   To determine the percentage of cases (in a normal distribution) within given limits or scores.

ii.   To determine the percentage of cases that are above or below a given score or reference point.

iii. To determine the limits of scores, which include a given percentage of cases to determine the percentile rank of an individual or a student in his own group.

iv.   To find out the percentile value of an individual on the basis of his percentile rank.

v.   Dividing a group into sub-groups according to certain abilities and assigning the grades.

vi.   To compare the two distributions in terms of overlapping.

vii. To determine the relative difficulty of test items.

The normal probability curve table is generally limited to the areas under unit normal curve with N = 1, ss = 1. In case, when the values of N and s are different from these, the measurements or scores should be converted into sigma scores (also referred to as standard scores or z scores). The process is as follows: $z = \dfrac{X - M}{\sigma}$ or $z = \dfrac{x}{\sigma}$

In which: z = Standard Score X = Raw Score M = Mean of X Scores, s = Standard Deviation of X Scores

Dispersion

In the previous section, we have discussed measures of central tendency. By knowing only the mean, median, or mode, it is not possible to have a complete picture of a set of data. Average does not tell us about how the score or measurements are arranged in relation to the center. It is possible that two sets of data with equal mean or median may differ in terms of their variability. Therefore, it is essential to know how far these observations are scattered from each other or from the mean. Measures of these variations are known as the measures of dispersion. The most commonly used measures of dispersion are range, average deviation, quartile deviation, variance, and standard deviation.

i) Range

The range is one of the simplest measures of dispersion. It is designated by R. The range is defined as the difference between the largest score and the smallest score in the distribution. It gives the two extreme values of the variable. A large value of range indicates greater dispersion, while a smaller value indicates lesser dispersion among the scores. The range can be a good measure if the distribution is not much skewed.

ii) Average deviation

Average deviation refers to the arithmetic mean of the differences between each score and the mean. It is always better to find the deviation of the individual observations with reference to a certain value in the series of observations and then take an average of these deviations. This deviation is usually measured from the mean or median. Mean, however, is more commonly used for this measurement. The advantage of using average deviation is that it is less affected by extreme values as compared to the standard deviation. It provides a better measure for comparison of the formation of different distributions.

iii) Standard deviation

Standard deviation is the most stable index of variability. In standard deviation, instead of the actual values of the deviations, we consider the squares of deviations, and the outcome is known as a variance. Further, the square root of this variance is known as standard deviation and designated as SD. Thus, the standard deviation is the square root of the mean of the squared deviations of individual observations from the mean. Standard deviation from a sample (n) and population denoted by (N), respectively. If all the scores have an identical value in a sample, the SD will be 0 (zero). The advantage of using standard deviation is that it is based on all observations. It is amenable to further mathematical treatments. Of all measures of dispersion, the standard deviation is least affected by the fluctuation of sampling.

$$\text{Standard Deviation} = \sqrt{\frac{\sum(x - \bar{x})^2}{n - 1}}$$

Skewness and Kurtosis

There are two other important characteristics of a frequency distribution that provide useful information about its nature. They are known as Skewness and Kurtosis.

i) Skewness

Skewness is the degree of asymmetry of the distribution. In some frequency distributions, scores are more concentrated at one end of the scale. Such a distribution is called a skewed distribution. A distribution is said to be "skewed" when the mean and median fall at different points in the distribution and the balance i.e., the point of center of gravity is shifted to one side or the other to left or right. In a normal distribution, the mean equals the median exactly and the

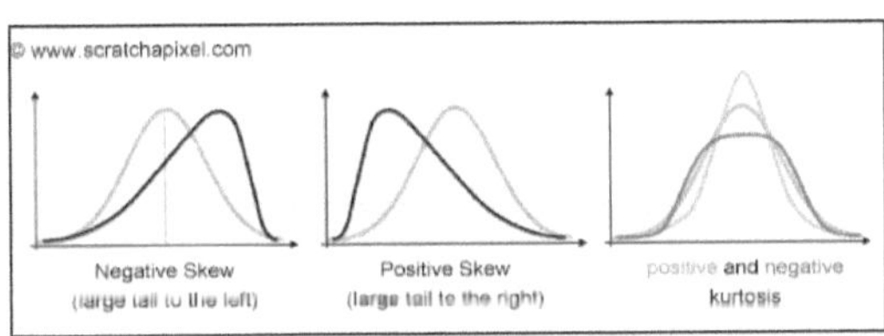

skewness is, zero (Sk =0). Thus, skewness refers to the extent to which a distribution of data points is concentrated at one end or the other. Skewness and variability are usually related; the more the skewness, the greater the variability.

ii) Kurtosis

The term kurtosis refers to (the divergence) in the height of the curve, especially in the peakness or flatness of a frequency distribution curve when compared with the normal distribution curve. The kurtosis of a distribution is the peakedness of the graph. If a distribution is more peaked than normal, it is said to be Leptokurtic. This kind of

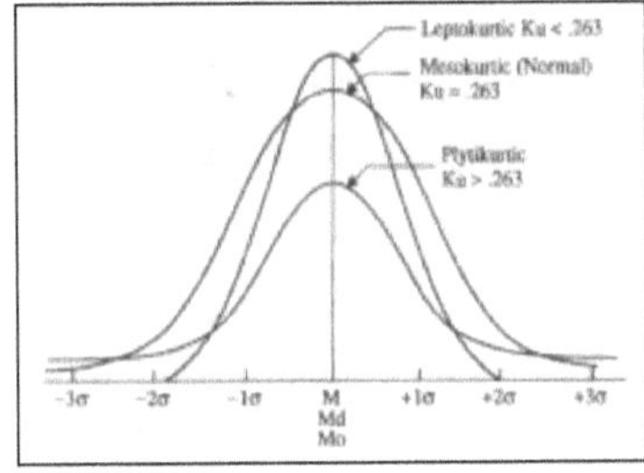

peakedness implies a thin distribution. On the other hand, if a distribution is flatter than the normal distribution, it is known as Platykurtic distribution. A normal curve is known as Mesokurtic.

Difference Between Dispersion and Skewness

Dispersion	Skewness
Shows the spread of values from the central value i.e., It measures the tendency of a data set distributed over a range in statistical analysis	Shows whether series is symmetrical or asymmetrical i.e., it measures the asymmetry in a statistical distribution from the normal distribution
Study of the Variability	Study of concentration in lower and higher variable
Cannot be presented by means of diagrams & graphs. Range, standard deviation and average deviation are most common way to calculate dispersion	Skewness can be presented by diagram as it is calculated in the form of positive and negative skewness. Mean, Median, mode are the common ways to calculate skewness
It determines the degree of variation in the set of data	It determines the extent of variation in terms of lower and higher value
It is used for other statistical methods such as regression analysis	It can be used for economical analysis for e.g. finance or investing

Correlation

Correlation is a measure of association between two variables. Typically, one variable is denoted as X, and the other variable is denoted as Y. The relationship between these variables is assessed by the correlation coefficient. Following statements are an example of correlations:

i.   As the intelligence (IQ) increases, the marks obtained increase. As introversion increases, the number of friends decrease.

ii. More the anxiety a person experiences, the weaker the adjustment with the stress.

iii. As the score on openness to experience increases, scores on creativity tests also increase.

iv. On a reasoning task, as the accuracy increases, the speed decreases.

v.   When the cost increases, the sales decrease.

vi. As the age of the child increases, the problems solving capacity increase.

vii. More the practice, better the performance.

Broadly correlation is classified as linear and nonlinear. When all the points on the scatter diagram tend to lie near a line which looks like a straight line, the **correlation** is said to be **linear. Correlation** is said to be **non-linear** if the ratio of change is not constant.

One of the basic forms of relationship is a linear relationship. A linear relationship can be expressed as a relationship between two variables that can be plotted as a straight line. The linear relationship can be expressed in the following equation:

$Y = a + bX$

- Y is a dependent variable (variable on y-axis),
- á(alpha)is a constant or Y intercept of straight line,
- b(beta)is slope of the line and
- X is independent variable (variable on x-axis).

The direction of the relationship can be positive or negative, is an important aspect of the description of the relationship. If the two variables are correlated, then the relationship is either positive or negative. The absence of a relationship indicates zero correlation. Let us look at the positive, negative, and zero correlation.

> *Correlations is a statistical tool that defines the relationship between two variables. For, e.g. the relationship between the price of a mobile and its quantity demanded.*
>
> *Correlation coefficients are used to measure the strength of the relationship between two variables.*
>
> *Positive correlation is a relationship between two variables in which both variables move in tandem—that is, in the same direction.*
>
> *Negative correlation or inverse correlation is a relationship between two variables whereby they move in opposite directions.*
>
> *DEGREE OF CORRELATION*
>
> *+1 Perfect Positive*
>
> *-1 Perfect Negative*
>
> *Positive or Negative, if the value of 'r' is 0.50, it is called moderate correlation.*
>
> *When it lies between 0.50 and 0.75, the degree of correlation is high and when it lies between 0.25 and 0.50, the degree of correlation is low.*

Positive Correlation

The positive correlation indicates that as the values of one variable increase, the values of other variables should also increase. Further, as the values of one variable decreases, that of the other variable should also decrease. This establishes that both variables progress in the same direction.

For example,

a) When the intelligence quotient (IQ) increases, the marks obtained increase.

b) When income increases, the expenditure also increase.

Negative Correlation

The Negative correlation indicates that when the values of one variable increase, that of the other decrease. Further, as the value of one variable decreases, that of the other increases. This means that two variables move in the opposite direction. For example,

a) As the intelligence (IQ) increases, the errors on reasoning tasks decrease.

b) As hope increases, depression decreases.

No Relationship

Apart from positive and negative correlations, it is also possible that there is no relationship between x and y. That is, the two variables do not share any relationship. If they do not share any relationship (technically, the correlation coefficient is zero), then, obviously, the direction of the correlation is neither positive nor negative. It is often called a zero correlation or no correlation.

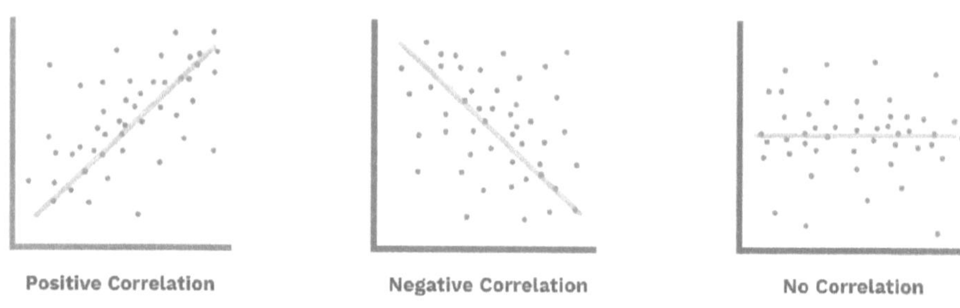

Measurements of Correlation Coefficient

The correlation coefficient can be calculated in various ways. The correlation coefficient is a description of the association between two variables in the sample. So it is descriptive statistics. **Correlation coefficients** are used in statistics to measure how strong a relationship is between two variables. There are several types of correlation coefficient: Pearson's correlation (also called Pearson's **R**) commonly used in linear regression.

The most commonly used approach is Pearson's correlation coefficient formula.

FORMULA: Pearson correlation coefficient.

rxy = Pearson r correlation coefficient between x and y

n = number of observations

xi = value of x (for ith observation)

yi = value of y (for ith observation)

Two other formulas are commonly used: the sample correlation coefficient and the population correlation coefficient.

Sample correlation coefficient

Sx and sy are the sample standard deviations, and sxy is the sample covariance.

Population correlation coefficient

$$\rho_{xy} = \frac{\sigma_{xy}}{\sigma_x \sigma_y}$$

The population correlation coefficient uses sx and sy as the population standard deviations, and sxy as the population covariance.

Regression

The simplest form of the regression is simple linear regression (at times, also called bivariate regression). Carl Frederick Gauss discovered a method of least squares (1809) and later on developed Gauss-Markov theorem (1821). Sir Francis Galton contributed to the method of regression and also gave the name.

Regression goes one step beyond correlation in identifying the relationship between two variables. It creates an equation so that values can be predicted within the range framed by the data. That is if you know X you can predict Y and if you know Y you can predict X. This is done by an equation called regression equation. When we have a scatter plot you have learnt that the correlation between X and Y are scattered in the graph and we can draw a straight line covering the entire data. This line is called the regression line.

The **y** variable is often termed the criterion variable and the **x** variable the predictor variable. The slope is often called the regression coefficient and the intercept the regression constant.

The slope can also be expressed compactly as ß = r × s y /s x

Normally we then predict values for **y** based on values of **x**. This still does not mean that y is caused by x. It is still imperative for the researcher to understand the variables under study and the context they operate under before making such an interpretation.

Simple algebra also allows one to calculate x values for a given value of y.

To obtain regression equation we use the following equation:

b = {N * Σxy} − {Σy2*Σy} / {(N * Σx2) − (Σy2)}

Regression equation can also be written including error component '**ẻ**'

The regression equation can be written as

$$Y = a + bX + e$$

Where,

Y = the scores on Y variable

X = scores on X variable

a = the Y-intercept of the regression line for the sample or regression constant in sample

b = the slope of the regression line or regression coefficient in sample

e = error in prediction of the scores on Y variable, or residual

Multiple Regression

We have data on two variables (Y and X), and we create an equation, called regression equation, which later on helps us in predicting the score of one variable (Y) by simply using the scores on another variable (X). Regression analysis tries to predict the Y variable from the X variable. In the general form, it tries to predict Y from an X1, X2, ..., Xk, where k is the number of predictor variables.

When we have multiple predictors rather than a single predictor variable, the regression carried out is called multiple regression. The multiple correlation coefficient denoting a correlation of one variable with multiple other variables. The multiple correlation coefficient is denots as RABCD. k which denotes that A is correlated with B, C, D, up to k variables.

The Multiple R can be calculated for two predictor variable as follows. Where,

RA.BC = is multiple correlation between A and linear combination of B and C.

rAB= is correlation between A and B

rAC= is correlation between A and C

rBC= is correlation between B and C

Recap & Review Section

SUMMARY Chapter 7

In this chapter, we have learned about a measure of central tendency around which data is clustered. The chapter discusses how we can develop a meaningful and useful conclusion from data collected, analyzed with the help of statistical derivatives like mean, median, mode test it against the data. The concept of variation, skewness are useful in describing data more meaningfully. We also learnt the interesting procedures of computing the correlations, regression and multiple regression especially, when we are interested in controlling for one or more variables.

Caselet 7 – Chocolate Shop

Meher has recently taken over her family business of making home chocolates. She is still exploring the nuances of the new trade and wishes to carry forward the past legacy which has been in her family for over a decade. Currently, their shop deals primarily in chocolate favours like Milk chocolate, Hazelnut, Butterscotch, Bitter, Almond, Rum-n-raisin, and Fruit & Nut.

New to the business, Meher is curious to see which flavours are the most popular, amount of money a typical customer spends, and how the customers would rate the flavours on taste, product selection, and service. She decides to track the primary flavours purchased and the amount customers spend. In addition, she asks these customers to rate the tastiness of the chocolates, selection, and service on a scale from 1 to 5 with 5 being the highest and 1 the lowest.

Table 1: Total amount spent by customer

Chocolate flavour purchased	Total amount spent by customer	Rating of Taste	Rating for selection of product	Rating of service
Milk chocolate	21.99	5	4	2
Hazelnut	18.13	3	2	4
Butterscotch	25.43	4	3	3
Bitter	1.99 4	5	4	4
Almond	17.19	4	5	4
Rum-n-raisin	15.19	3	4	3
Fruit & Nut	25.21	2	4	5

In addition, Meher would like to know how her chocolates compare with others. She contacts her cousin, Jas, who runs a similar chocolate store in another city. Jas, sends her customer data that is grouped. However, Meher can find estimates for measures such as the mean and standard deviation. Table 2 contains the frequency distribution of the total amount spent by customers. For example, 15 customers spent between 30.00 to 39.99.

Table2 : Frequency distribution of the total amount spent by customers

Class	Frequency
0.00 to 9.99	4
10.00 to 19.99	18
20.00 to 29.99	20
30.00 to 39.99	15
40.00 to 49.99	4
50.00 to 59.99	5
60.00 to 69.99	5
70.00 to 79.99	2
80.00 to 89.99	1
90.00 to 99.99	1

Now that Meher has all this data, she needs some help organizing and analyzing it. She would like the following to be included in the report:

1) Total amount spent by customer (Table 1)
- Construct a frequency distribution and relative frequency distribution for the data.
- Construct a bar graph and pie chart.
- Discuss the results of the tables and charts.

2) Frequency distribution of the total amount spent by customers (Table 2)
- Construct a frequency distribution and relative frequency distribution for the data.
- Construct a histogram.

Check Your Knowledge

CYK1 What does a significant test statistic reveal?
a. The importance of the effect.
b. It indicates that the test statistic is larger than expected when there is no effect on the population.
c. The null hypothesis is rejected.
d. All of the above.

Answer (b)

CYK 2 Which of the given statements is true?

a. Standard error is calculated exclusively from sample attributes.

b. Standard deviation is calculated exclusively from sample attributes.

c. Standard error measures central tendency.

d. All of the above.

Answer (a)

CYK 3 Which of the following sentences are true about descriptive statistics?

a. Descriptive statistics enables decisions about your data.

b. Descriptive statistics describes data.

c. Descriptive statistics enables drawing inferences data

d. All of the above.

Answer (b)

CYK 4 10 respondents have been asked to record their weight. The average weight of all is 69 kg. The conclusion that 69 kg is the average weight of all respondents is an example of:

a. Descriptive statistics

b. Inferential statistics

c. A parameter

d. A population

Answer (b)

CYK 5. Which of the following does not constitute a goal of descriptive statistics?

a. Data Summarisation

b. Displaying findings about collected data

c. Reporting numerical findings

d. Estimating characteristics of the population

Answer (d)

CYK 6 Assuming data is collected on the yearly average temperature at Delhi International Airport from 1900 to 2000, and researcher is interested in presenting change over time, what is the most effective graphical display?

a. Histogram

b. Scatter plot

c. Pie chart

d. Line chart

Answer (d)

CYK 7 The following values depict the number of chocolates sold by a vendor per day over a two-week period: 13, 14, 17, 17, 24, 26, 28, 29, 29, 31, 32, 38, 45, 57. The distribution of chocolate sales can be described as:

a. Bi-modal and positively skewed
b. Uni-modal and negatively skewed
c. Bi-modal and negatively skewed
d. Uni-modal and positively skewed

Answer (d)

CYK 8 MOTZEN is assumed to the highest market share amongst cellphone users in Dubai. A random sample of 250 cellphone users were asked about then network they subscribe to. What type of data collection is this & what is the most suited graphical technique to highlight the various market shares, amongst those listed below?
a. Quantitative data to be represented in a pie chart
b. Qualitative data to be represented in a histogram
c. Quantitative data to be represented in a bar chart
d. Qualitative data to be represented in a pie chart

Answer (d)

CYK 9 Graphical representation of a cumulative relative frequency distribution is termed as?
a. Histogram
b. Pie chart
c. Box plot
d. None of the above

Answer (d)

CYK 10 Histogram is a graphical representation of which of the following:
a. An ogive
b. A frequency distribution
c. A cumulative relative frequency distribution
d. A stem and leaf plot

Answer (b)

CYK 11 A frequency distribution represents:
a. Table of the individual observations taken from a sample
b. Individual listing of the random values taken from a data set
c. Listing of the individual observations arranged in ascending
d. Table classifying the number of data values into classes with counts of the number of data values that fall into each of the classes

Answer (d)

CYK 12 The difference between a histogram and a bar chart is
a. Histogram reflects qualitative data while the bar chart represents quantitative data
b. Adjacent rectangles in a histogram show a gap while those for a bar chart do not

c. Histogram reflects both qualitative and quantitative data and bar chart represents only quantitative data

d. Adjacent rectangles in a bar chart have a gap while those for a histogram do not.

Answer (d)

CYK 13 Data on the heights of five students has been collected.On the basis of this information conclusion is drawn that the average height of students all in the batch is 170 cm. This is an example of:

a. Descriptive statistics

b. Statistical inference

c. A parameter

d. A population

Answer (b)

Questions

Q1. Distinguish between

a) Cross-tabulation and Frequency distribution

b) Skewness and Kurtosis

c) Correlation and regression

Q2. How is the relative flatness or peakedness of a distribution measured? What indications about a population may be drawn from the degree of Kurtosis in a Normal distribution curve?

Q3. Describe the procedure for calculating frequencies. Suggest the most suited measure of Dispersion used in statistical analysis.

Q4. What is central tendency. Discuss the limitations of various measures of central tendency? What is the significance of calculating mode? Illustrate with examples.

Q5. What are Scatter diagrams & how may they be used in Regression analysis?

Q6. What do you understand by regression? Explain its significance in decision making.

Applied Question

Q1. Assuming a bus moves covers a specified measurable distance in two parts. It covers the first half of the distance at the speed of 50km/hr and remaining second half at the speed of 70km/her. Compute the athematic, geometric and harmonic means for the given distance & explain the degree of variability amongst the three estimates.

Q2. The monthly salaries (in rupees) of 12 staff members of a McDonald officers are:

5000, 5500, 5100, 5400, 10000, 5100, 5300, 5450, 5250, 5700, 5100, 5520

Calculate the mean, median& the mode among the given salaries.

As an HR head of McDonalds, which among the three calculated measures would you consider as the best representative of central tendency for the above data set and why?

Hypothesis Testing

> **Keywords:** *Null hypothesis, Alternative hypothesis, Confidence limit, One-tail & two-tail test, Type I & Type II Error, Parametric & Non parametric tests.*

Research begins with a problem and aims to find a solution. The research should propose a set of suggested solutions that the study intends to solve. Such tentative solutions formulated as propositions are called a hypotheses.

Hypothesis therefore is:

'It is a proposition that can be put to the test to determine validity' by (Goode and Hatt).

'A hypothesis is a question put in such a way that an answer of some kind can be forthcoming' (Rummel and Ballaine).

Hypothesis Testing

A statistical hypothesis is defined as a statement, which may or may not be true about the population parameter or about the probability distribution of the parameter that we wish to validate based on sample information.

Inferential statistics tie up the logic of hypothesis testing. In hypothesis testing, we have a particular value in mind. We hypothesize that this value characterizes the population of observations. The question is whether that hypothesis is reasonable in the light of the evidence from the sample.

Hypothesis testing is one of the essential areas of statistical analyses. Sometimes hypothesis testing is referred to as the statistical decision-making process. In day-to-day situations, we make decisions about the population based on sample information. Most times, experiments are performed with random samples instead of the entire population, and inferences drawn from the observed results are then generalized over to the population as the whole. Before drawing inferences about the population, we should realize the fact that the observed results might have come due to chance factors. Accuracy or preciseness of inference increases if the chance factor is ruled out.

Hypothesis can be broadly categorized as Null and Alternative Hypothesis. Null Hypothesis (H0) examines the probability of chance occurrence of the observed results. The null hypothesis is a statement of no differences. The other way to state the Null Hypothesis is that the two samples come from the same population. Here, we assume that the population follows a normal distribution, and both groups have equal means and standard deviations. Since the null hypothesis is a testable proposition, there is a counter proposition to it known as an Alternative Hypothesis and denoted by H1. In contrast to the null hypothesis, the Alternative Hypothesis (H1) proposes that:

i. the two samples belong to two different populations,
ii. their means are estimates of two different parametric means of the respective population, and
iii. there is a significant difference between their sample means.

The alternative hypothesis (H1) is not directly tested statistically; instead, its acceptance or rejection is determined by the rejection or retention of the null hypothesis. A statistical test assesses the probability 'p' of the null hypothesis is correct. If probability 'p' is too low, H0 is rejected, and H1 is accepted. It is inferred that the observed difference is significant. If probability 'p' is high, H0 is accepted, and it is inferred that the difference is due to the chance factor and not due to the variable factor.

Confidence Limit and Significance

The limits (or range) within which the hypothesis should lie with specified probabilities are called the confidence limits or fiduciary limits. It is customary to take these limits at 5% or 1% levels of significance. If the sample value lies between the confidence limits, the hypothesis is accepted; if it does not, the hypothesis is rejected at the specified level of significance. Experimenters and researchers have selected some arbitrary standards called levels of significance to serve as the cut-off points or critical points along the probability scale, to separate the significant difference from the non-significant difference between the two statistics, like means or standard deviations.

Generally, the .05 and .01 levels of significance are the most popular in social sciences research. The level of significance decides the confidence with which a researcher accepts or rejects a null hypothesis. These may, hence, sometime, be termed as levels of confidence. Their meanings may be clear from the following:

Level	Amount of confidence	Interpretation
0.05	95%	If the experiment is repeated a 100 times, only on five occasions the obtained mean will fall outside the limited $\mu \pm 1.96\,SE$
0.01	99%	If the experiment is repeated a 100 times, only on one occasions the obtained mean will fall outside the limited $\mu \pm 2.58\,SE$

The values 1.96 and 2.58 have been taken from the 't' tables keeping large samples in view. The .01 level is more rigorous and a higher standard as compared to the .05 level and would require a larger value of the critical ratio for the rejection of the Ho. Hence if

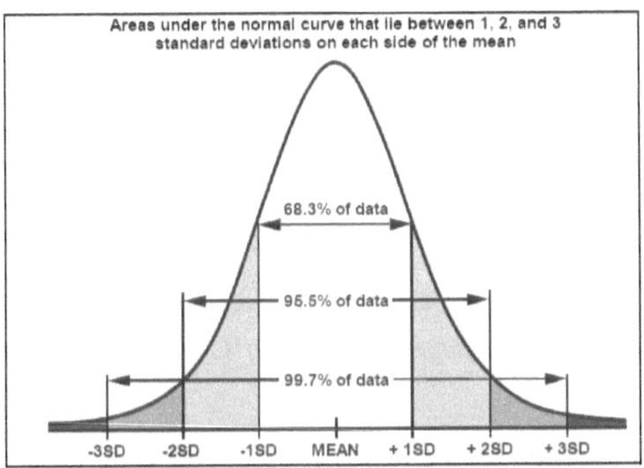

an obtained value of 't' is significant at .01 levels, it is automatically significant at .05 level, but the reverse is not always true. The level of significance (p<.05) is that probability of chance occurrence of observed results upto and below which the probability 'p' of the null hypothesis being correct is considered too low and the results of the experiment are considered significant.

On the other hand, if p exceeds, the null hypothesis (H0) cannot be rejected because the probability of it being correct is considered quite high. In such cases, observed results are not considered significant (p >0.5).

The selection of the level of significance depends on the choice of the researcher. Generally level of significance is taken to be 5% or 1% (i.e., = .05 or = .01). If the null hypothesis is rejected at .05 level, it means that the results are considered significant so long as the probability 'p' of getting it by mere chance of random sampling works out to be 0.05 or less (p< .05). In other words, the results are considered significant if out of 100 such trials only five or less number of the times the observed results may arise from the accidental choice in the particular sample by random sampling.

Errors in Hypothesis Testing

In hypothesis testing, there would be no errors in decision making as long as a null hypothesis is rejected when it is false. Also, a null hypothesis is accepted when it is true. But the decision to accept or reject the null hypothesis is based on sample data. No testing procedure will ensure a correct decision based on sampled data. There are two types of errors regarding the choice to accept or to reject a null hypothesis.

Types of Errors in testing Hypothesis

Type I Error

When the null hypothesis is true, a decision to reject it is an error, and this kind of error is known as Type I error in statistics. The probability of making a Type I error is denoted as 'a' (read as alpha). The null hypothesis is rejected if the probability 'p', of its being correct does not exceed 'p'. The higher the chosen level of 'p' for considering the null hypothesis, the higher is the probability of Type I error.

Type II Error

When the null hypothesis is false, a decision to accept it is known as Type II error. The probability of making a Type II error is denoted as 'b'(read as beta). The lower the chosen

REAL SITUATION	Statistical decision based on sample	
	Ho Accepted	Ho Rejected
Ho True	Right Decision	Type 1 error
Ho False	Type II error	Right decision

i.e.,level of significance 'p' for rejecting the null hypothesis, the higher is the probability of the Type II error.

With a lowering of 'p', the rejection region, as well as the probability of the Type I error declines, and the acceptance region (1-p) widens correspondingly. The goodness of a statistical test is measured by the probability of making a Type I or Type II error. For a fixed sample size 'n', 'a' and 'b' are so related that the reduction in one causes an increase in the other. Therefore, simultaneous decreases in 'a' and 'b' are not possible.

Procedure for Testing Hypothesis

Step 1. Set up a null hypothesis suitable to the problem.

Step 2. Define the alternative hypothesis.

Step 3. Calculate the suitable test statistics.

Step 4. Define the degrees of freedom for the test situation.

Step 5. Find the probability level 'p' corresponding to the calculated value of the test statistics and its degree of freedom. This value is given in the relevant tables.

Step 6. Reject or accept the null hypothesis based on tabulated value and calculated value at a practical probability level.

There are some situations in which inferential statistics is carried out to test the hypothesis and draw a conclusion about the population, for example (i) Test of hypothesis about a population mean (Z test), (ii) Testing hypothesis about a population mean (small sample t-test).

One-tail and Two-tail Test

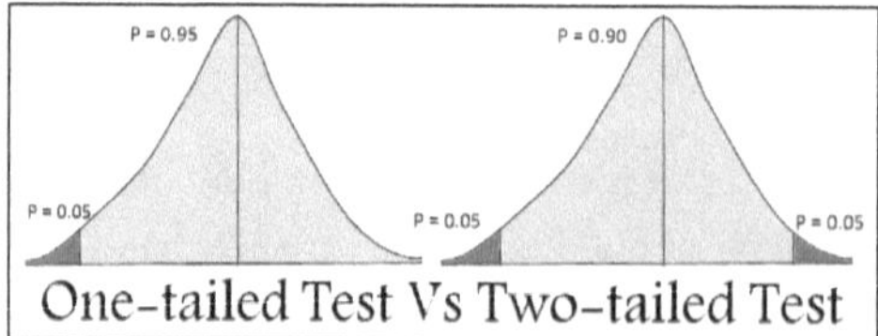

A statistical test finds its basis on two competing hypotheses: the null hypothesis H0 and the alternative hypothesis H1. The type of alternative hypothesis H1 defines if a test is one-tailed or two-tailed.

Depending upon the statement in alternative hypothesis (H1), either a one-tail or two-tail test is chosen to test the statistical significance.

A one-tail test is a directional test. It is formulated to find the significance of both the magnitude and the direction (algebraic sign) of the observed difference between the two statistics. Thus, in two-tailed tests researcher is interested in testing whether one sample mean is significantly higher (alternatively lower) than the other sample mean. Simply, test is called one-sided (or one-tailed) only if the null hypothesis gets rejected when a value of the test statistic falls in one specified tail of the distribution. Further, the test is called two-sided (or two-tailed) if the null hypothesis gets rejected when a value of the test statistic falls in either one or the other of the two tails of its sampling distribution.

Choosing whether to perform a one-tailed or a two-tailed hypothesis test is one of the methodology decisions that needs to be considered prior to conducting statistical analysis. Before we cover in detail about this test, it's essential to know that hypothesis tests take all of the sample data and convert it to a single value, which is known as a test statistic. Some of the commonly used test statistics are t-tests, z tests, F tests, ANOVA. These test statistics follow a sampling distribution. Probability distribution plots display the probabilities of obtaining test statistic values when the null hypothesis is correct. On a probability distribution plot, the portion of the shaded area under the curve represents the probability that a value will fall within that range.

The graph displays a sampling distribution for t-values. The two shaded regions cover the two-tails of the distribution. Keep in mind that this t-distribution assumes that the null hypothesis is correct for the population. Consequently, the peak (most likely value) of the distribution occurs at t=0, which represents the null hypothesis in a t-test. Typically, the null hypothesis states that there is no effect.

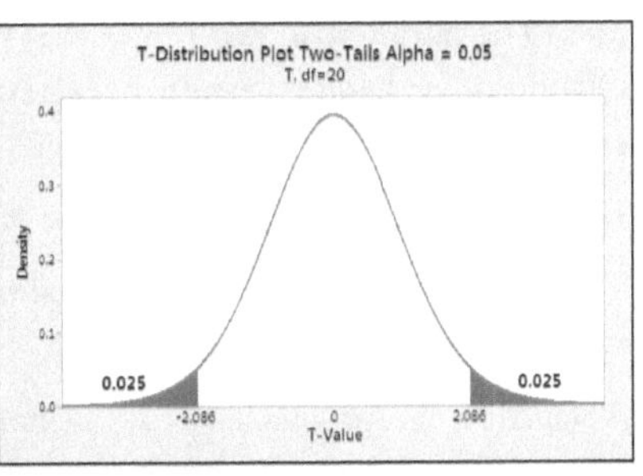

As t-values move further away from zero, it represents larger effect sizes. When the null hypothesis is true for the population, obtaining samples that Exhibit a large apparent effect becomes less likely, which is why the probabilities taper off for t-values further from zero.

A Two-tailed test is associated with an alternative hypothesis for which the sign of the potential difference is unknown. For example, suppose we wish to compare the averages of two samples A and B. Before setting up the experiment and running the test, we expect that if a difference between the two averages is highlighted, we do not know whether A would be higher than B or the opposite. This situation drives us to choose a two-tailed test, associated with the following alternative hypothesis: H1: average(A) ≠ average(B). Two-tailed tests are by far the most commonly used tests.

A one-tailed test is associated with an alternative hypothesis for which the sign of the potential difference is known before running the experiment and the test. In the example

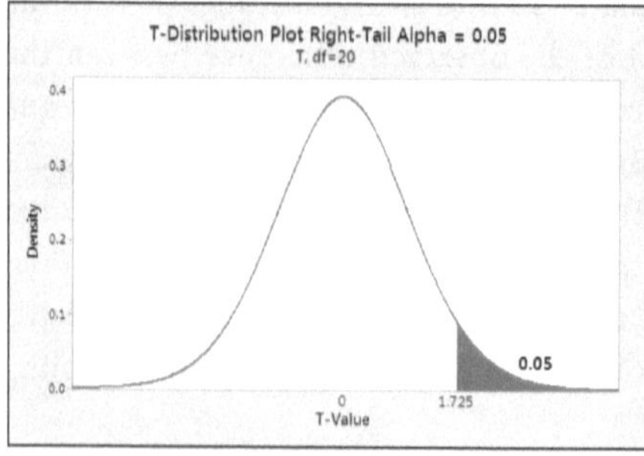

described above, the alternative hypothesis related to a one-tailed test could be written as follows:

average(A) < average(B) or average(A) > average(B), depending on the expected direction of the difference.

One-tailed hypothesis tests are also known as directional and one-sided tests because the test can have effects only in one direction.

When one-tailed test is performed, the entire significance level percentage goes into the extreme end of one tail of the distribution.

Types of Hypothesis Testing

The generalization of the findings to the population from the sample is made through statistical tests. A statistical test is a formal technique that relies on the probability distribution for concluding the reasonableness of the hypothesis.

The hypothesis testing related to differences is classified as parametric and non-parametric tests. The **parametric test** is one that has information about the population parameter. On the other hand, the **non-parametric test** is one where the researcher has no idea regarding the population parameter.

Difference Between Parametric and Non-parametric Tests

The fundamental differences between parametric and non-parametric tests are discussed in the following points:

A statistical test, in which specific assumptions are made about the population parameter is known as the parametric test. A statistical test used in the case of non-metric independent variables is called a non-parametric test.

In the parametric test, the test statistic is based on distribution. On the other hand, the test statistic is arbitrary in the case of the non-parametric test.

In the parametric test, it is assumed that the measurement of variables of interest is done on an interval or ratio level. In the non-parametric test, wherein the variable of interest is measured on a nominal or ordinal scale.

In general, the measure of central tendency in the parametric test is mean, while in the case of the non-parametric test is median.

In the parametric test, there is complete information about the population. Conversely, in the non-parametric test, there is no information about the population.

The applicability of the parametric test is for variables only, whereas the non-parametric test applies to both variables and attributes.

For measuring the degree of association between two quantitative variables, Pearson's coefficient of correlation is used in the parametric test, while Spearman's rank correlation in the non-parametric test

Exhibit 8: Hypothesis Test* Hierarchy

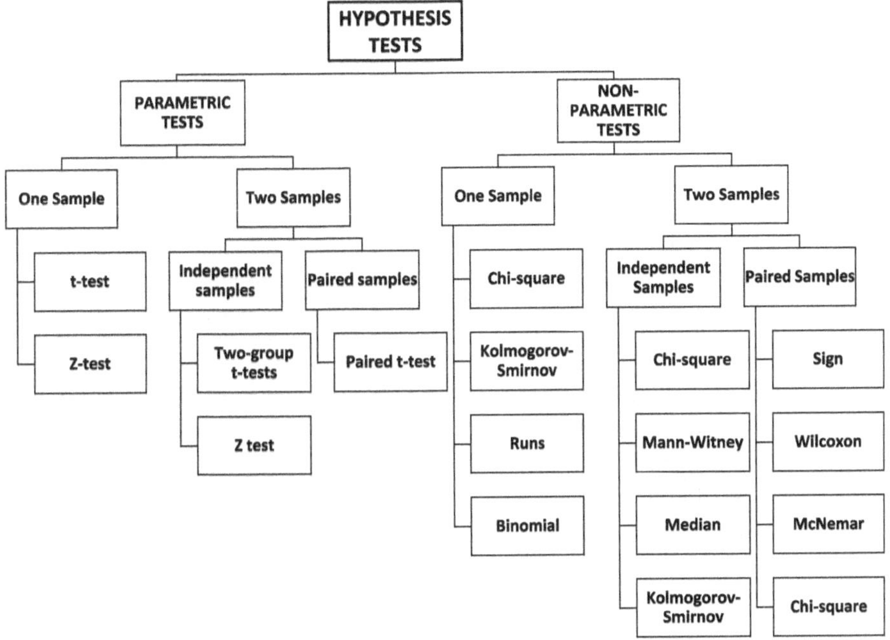

1. Parametric Test

The parametric test is the hypothesis test, which provides generalizations for making statements about the mean of the parent population. A t-test based on Students t-statistic, is often used in this regard.

The t-statistic rests on the underlying assumption that there is a normal distribution of a variable, and the mean is either known or at least assumed to be known. The population variance is calculated for the sample. It is assumed that the variables of interest in the population are measured on an interval scale.

The nature of quantitative data and various descriptive statistical measures that are in use in the analysis of data include measures of central tendency, variability, relative position, and relationships of normal probability curve, etc. There are two classes of parametric statistical tests: descriptive and inferential. Descriptive tests will reveal the shape of data in

---

** (Authors Disclaimer: The text covers the commonly used parameter in Hypotheses testing, Extensive research of all parameters/test was beyond the scope of this book)

the sense of how the values of a variable are distributed. Inferential tests will suggest results from a sample about a population.

The distinction is also made between the number of variables considered about each other:

Univariate analysis: analyses the qualities of one variable at a time. Only descriptive tests can be used in this type of analysis.

Bivariate analysis: considers the properties of two variables in relation to each other. Inferences can be drawn from this type of analysis.

Multivariate analysis: looks at the relationships between more than two variables. Again, inferences can be drawn from results.

For making inferences about various population values (parameters), we generally make use of parametric and non-parametric tests. The concept and assumptions of parametric tests are explainable with the inference regarding the means and correlations of large and small samples and the significance of the difference between the means and correlations in large and small independent samples.

A parametric statistical test specifies certain conditions such as the data to be normally distributed etc. The non-parametric statistics does not require the terms of parametric statistics. In the use of parametric tests for making statistical inferences, we need to take into account certain assumptions about the nature of the population distribution, and also the type of measurement scale used to quantify the data.

Parametric tests normally involve data expressed in absolute numbers or values rather than ranks; an example is the Students t-test.

The parametric statistical test operates under certain conditions. Since these conditions are not ordinarily tested, they are assumed to hold valid. The meaningfulness of the results of a parametric test depends on the validity of the assumption. Proper interpretation of parametric test based on normal distribution also assumes that the scene being analyzed results from measurement, atleast an interval scale.

Let us try to understand the term population. Population refers to the entire group of people which a researcher intends to follow regarding a phenomenon. The study is generally conducted on a sample of the said population, and obtained results are then applied to the larger population from which the sample was selected.

Assumption For Parametric Testing

Parametric tests like, t and f tests may be in use for analyzing the data which satisfy the following conditions:

- The population from which the sample is drawn should be normally distributed.
- Normal Distributions refer to frequency distribution following a normal curve, which is infinite at both the ends.

- The variables involved must have been measured on an interval or ratio scale.
- Variable and its types (Dependent and Independent), a characteristic that can have different values.
- The observation must be independent. The inclusion or exclusion of any case in the sample should not unduly affect the results of the study.
- These populations must have the same variance or, in individual cases, must have a known ratio of variance. This exception is homoscedasticity. The samples have equal or nearly equal variances. This condition is known as equality or homogeneity of variances and is particularly important to determine when the samples are small.
- The observations are independent. The selection of one case in the sample is not dependent upon the selection of any other case.

Tests like t, z are called parametrical statistical tests. The next part describes the test of the hypothesis about a population mean in the case of a single population and the difference between the two means for two populations. One of the crucial things that have to be kept in mind is the use of an appropriate test statistic. In case the sample size is large (n > 30), the Z statistic would be used. For a small sample size (n < 30), a further question regarding the knowledge of population standard deviation (a) is asked. If the population standard deviation a is known, a Z statistic can be used. However, if a is unknown and is estimated using sample data, a t-test with appropriate degrees of freedom is used under the assumption that the sample is drawn from a normal population. It is assumed that the readers have the knowledge of Z and t-distribution from the course on statistics. The table summarizes the appropriateness of the test statistic for conducting a test of hypothesis regarding the population means.

Sample Size	Standard deviation of population	
	Known	Unknown
Large n>30	Z	Z
Small n<=30	Z	T

Case of Single Population

Case of Small Sample t-Test

In case the sample size is small (n<30) and is drawn from a population having a normal population with unknown standard deviation a, a t-test is used to conduct the hypothesis for the test of the mean. The t-distribution is a symmetrical distribution, just like the normal one. However, t-distribution is higher at the tail and lower at the peak. The t-distribution is flatter then the normal distribution. With an increase in the sample size

$$t = \frac{\bar{x} - \mu_0}{s/\sqrt{n}}$$

(and hence degrees of freedom), t-distribution loses its flatness and approaches the normal distribution whenever n > 30.

The procedure for testing the hypothesis of a mean is similar to what is explained for a large sample. The test statistic used in this case is:

$$t_{n-1} = \frac{\overline{X} - \mu_{H_0}}{\hat{\sigma}_{\overline{X}}}$$

$$\text{where, } \hat{\sigma}_{\overline{X}} = \frac{s}{\sqrt{n}}$$

(wheres σ = Sample standard deviation)

n-1 = degrees of freedom

The objective of any statistical test is to determine the likelihood of a value in a sample, given that the null hypothesis is true. A t-test is typically used in the case of small samples and when the test statistic of the population follows a normal distribution.

A t-test is when the test statistic follows a t-distribution, and use to understand whether the null hypothesis is true statistically. It was initially developed by W.S.Gossett in 1908 to monitor the stout quality while working in a brewery. A t-test (also known as Student's t-test) is often used to test if two samples are statistically different from each other. A t-test does this by comparing the means of both samples.

A t-test is widely in use, where we have only small samples available. Further, where population variance is unknown and needs estimation from the sample itself, the t-test may be most appropriate.

There are two types of t-tests: **one sample and two samples.** The one-sample t-test is used to test the null hypothesis that the mean of the population is equal to a specific value, while the two-sample t-test is used to compare the mean values of both samples. The two-sample t-tests may be conducted on independent samples, paired-samples, or overlapping samples. Most test statistics have the form t =Z/s, where Z and s are functions of the data. Z may be sensitive to the alternative hypothesis (i.e., its magnitude tends to be larger when the alternative hypothesis is true). In contrast, 's' is a scaling parameter that allows the distribution of 't' to be determined.

$$t = \frac{Z}{s} = \frac{\overline{X} - \mu}{\hat{\sigma}/\sqrt{n}}$$

Case of Large Sample z-test. As mentioned earlier, in case the sample size n is large or small, but the value of the population standard deviation is known, a Z-test is appropriate. There can be alternate cases of two – tailed and one-tailed tests of hypotheses. The test statistic is given by,

$$Z = \frac{\overline{X} - \mu_{H_0}}{\dfrac{\sigma}{\sqrt{n}}}$$

where,

x = Sample mean

s = Population standard deviation

$\mu H0$ = The value of μ under the assumption that the null hypothesis is true

n = Size of sample

In alternative Hypothesis

Alternative Hypothesis $\mu < \mu0$	Reject the Null Hypothesis if $Z < - Za$	Accept the Null Hypothesis if $Z \geq - Za$
$\mu \neq \mu0$	$Z < - Za/2$ Or $Z > Za/2$	$- Za/2 \leq Z \leq Za/2$

Tests For Difference Between Two Population Means

The test of the significance of the difference between two population means using t and z-tests.

Case of Small Sample

If the size of both the samples is less than 30 and the population standard deviation is unknown, the procedure described above to discuss the equality of two population means is not applicable and in that case t-test would be applicable under the assumptions:

1. Two population variances are equal.
2. Two population variances are not equal.

1. Population variances are equal

If the two population variances are equal, it implies that their respective unbiased estimates are also equal. In such a case, the expression becomes:

$$\sqrt{\frac{\hat{\sigma}_1^2}{n_1} + \frac{\hat{\sigma}_2^2}{n_2}} = \sqrt{\frac{\hat{\sigma}^2}{n_1} + \frac{\hat{\sigma}^2}{n_2}} = \hat{\sigma}\sqrt{\frac{1}{n_1} + \frac{1}{n_2}}$$

$$(\text{Assuming } \hat{\sigma}_1^2 = \hat{\sigma}_2^2 = \hat{\sigma}^2)$$

2. When population variances are not equal

In case population variances are not equal, the test statistic for testing the equality of two population means when the size of samples is small is given by:

$$t = \frac{(X_1 - X_2) - (\mu_1 - \mu_2)H_0}{\sqrt{\frac{\hat{\sigma}_1^2}{n_1} + \frac{\hat{\sigma}_2^2}{n_2}}}$$

The degrees of freedom in such a case is given by the expression:

$$\text{d.f.} = \frac{\left(\dfrac{s_1^2}{n_1} + \dfrac{s_2^2}{n_2}\right)^2}{\dfrac{1}{n_1 - 1}\left(\dfrac{s_1^2}{n_1}\right)^2 + \dfrac{1}{n_2 - 1}\left(\dfrac{s_2^2}{n_2}\right)^2}$$

Case of Large Sample

In case both the sample sizes are greater than 30, a Z-test is used. The hypothesis to be tested may be written as:

H0 : $\mu 1 = \mu 2$

H1 : $\mu 1 \ne \mu 2$

where,

$\mu 1$ = Mean of population 1

$\mu 2$ = Mean of population 2

$$Z = \frac{(\overline{X}_1 - \overline{X}_2) - (\mu_1 - \mu_2)H_0}{\sqrt{\dfrac{\sigma_1^2}{n_1} + \dfrac{\sigma_2^2}{n_2}}}$$

The above is a case of two-tailed test. The test statistic used is:

x 1 = Mean of sample drawn from population 1

x 2 = Mean of sample drawn from population 2

n1 = Size of sample drawn from population 1

n2 = Size of sample drawn from population 2

Tests Concerning Population Proportion

In the tests about proportion, one is interested in examining whether the respondents possess a particular attribute or not. For example, the interest could be in the proportion of students who are drinkers or the proportion of consumers who use a particular brand of product or the percentage of skilled employees in a company who are not satisfied with their present job.

Case of Single Population Proportion

Suppose we want to test the hypotheses

H0 : $p = p0$

H1 : $p \ne p0$

For large sample, the appropriate test statistic would be:

$$Z = \frac{\bar{p} - P_{H_0}}{\sigma_{\bar{p}}}$$

where,

$\bar{p}$ = sample proportion

P_{H_0} = the value of p under the assumption that null hypothesis is true

$\sigma_{\bar{p}}$ = Standard error of sample proportion

The value of $\sigma_{\bar{p}}$ is computed by using the following formula:

$$\sigma_{\bar{p}} = \sqrt{\frac{P_{H_0}\, q_{H_0}}{n}}$$

where,

$q_{H_0} = 1 - P_{H_0}$

n = Sample size

Two Population Proportions

Here, the interest is to test whether the two population proportions are equal or not. The hypothesis under investigation is:

$$Z = \frac{\bar{p}_1 - \bar{p}_2 - (p_1 - p_2)\, H_0}{\sigma_{\bar{p}_1 - \bar{p}_2}}$$

where,

$\bar{p}_1$ = Sample proportion possessing a particular attribute from population 1

$\bar{p}_2$ = Sample proportion possessing a particular attribute from population 2

$\sigma_{\bar{p}_1 - \bar{p}_2}$ = Standard error of difference between proportions.

$(p_1 - p_2)_{H_0}$ = Value of difference between population proportion under the assumption that the null hypothesis is true.

H0 : p1 = p2 Þ p1 – p2 = 0

H1 : p1 ≠ p2 Þ p1 – p2 ≠ 0

The alternative hypothesis assumed is two-sided. It could as well have been one-sided. The test statistic is given by:

ANOVA

Structure of results:

Source	SS	df	MS	F	Sig.
Between	SS_b	k-1	MS_b	MS_b/MS_w	p value
Within	SS_w	N-k	MS_w		
Total	$SS_b + SS_w$	N-1			

The last section discussed the test of hypothesis concerning both the Z and t-tests for the equality of two population means. However, if there are more than two populations, the test for the equality of means could be difficult; hence we use the analysis of variance (ANOVA) technique. The technique helps in performing this test in one go. **R.A.Fisher** developed the theory concerning ANOVA. The basic principle underlying the technique is that the total variation in the dependent variable is broken into two parts, one which can be attributed to some specific causes and the other that may be attributed to chance and other which is attributed to the specific causes is called the variation between samples, and the one which is attributed to chance is termed as the variation within samples. Therefore, in ANOVA, the total variance may be decomposed into various components corresponding to the sources of the variation.

Analysis of variance (ANOVA) has two types:

One way analysis

A one-way ANOVA is a type of statistical test that compares the variance in the group means within a sample whilst considering only one independent variable or factor. It is a hypothesis-based test, meaning that it aims to evaluate multiple mutually exclusive theories about our data and we are comparing more than three groups based on the one-factor variable, then it said to be a one-way analysis of variance (ANOVA). For example, if we want to compare whether or not the mean output of three workers is the same based on the working hours of the three workers.

Before we can generate a hypothesis, we need to have a question about our data that we want an answer to. For example, adventurous researchers studying a population of walruses might ask "Do our walruses weigh more in early or late mating season?" Here, the independent variable or factor (the two terms mean the same thing) is "month of mating season". In an ANOVA, our independent variables are organised in categorical groups. The one-way ANOVA compares the means between the groups you are interested in and determines whether any of those means are statistically significantly different from each other. Specifically, it tests the null hypothesis:

where μ = group mean and k = number of groups. If, however, the one-way ANOVA reports statistically significant result, we accept the alternative hypothesis (H_1), which is that there are at least two groups. This means that are statistically significantly different from each other. Use SPSS to solve your data. The results of a one-way ANOVA mentioned below:

An example:

Source	SS	df	MS	F	Sig.
Between	91.476	2	45.733	4.467	.021
Within	276.400	27	10.237		
Total	367.867	29			

This will be reported as follows:

There was a statistically significant difference between groups determined by one-way ANOVA ($F_{(2,27)}$ = 4.467, p = .021). This is all you will need to write for the one-way ANOVA per se. However, in reality, it is also important to report means ± standard deviations for your groups, as well as follow up a statistically significant result with a post hoc test. If SPSS Statistics used, these descriptive statistics will be reported in the output along with the result from the one-way ANOVA. The general form of writing the result of a one-way ANOVA is as follows:

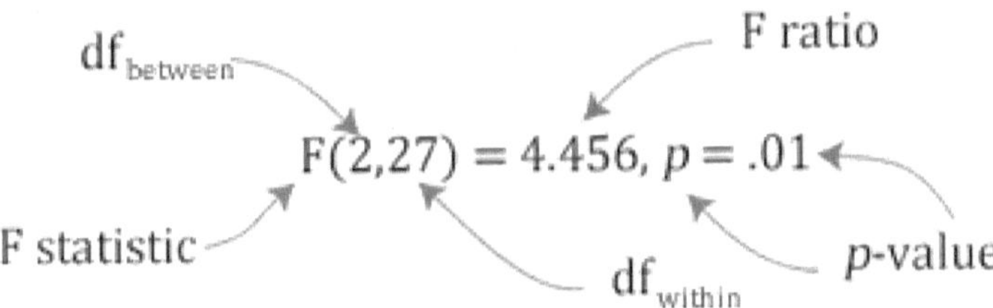

where df = degrees of freedom.

The result should not be reported as "significant difference," but instead reported as a "statistically significant difference." This is because of the decision as to whether the result is significant or not, should not be based solely on the statistical test.

In a one-way ANOVA, there are two possible hypotheses.

The null hypothesis (H0) stating that there is no difference between the groups & equality between means. (Walruses weigh the same in different months)

The alternative hypothesis (H1) states that there is a difference between the means and groups. (Pandas have different weights in different months)

Two-way analysis

The two-way analysis of variance is an extension to the one-way analysis of and is a hypothesis-based test. In the two-way ANOVA each sample is defined in two ways, and resultingly put into two categorical groups. Thinking again of our walruses, researchers might use a two-way ANOVA if their question is: "Are walruses heavier in early or late mating season and does that depend on the gender of the walrus?" In this example, both "month in mating season" and "gender of walrus" are factors – meaning in total, there are two factors. Once again, each factor's number of groups must be considered – for "gender" there will only two groups "male" and "female".

When factor variables are more than two, then it is said to be a two-way analysis of variance (ANOVA).

Assumptions

- The populations from which the samples were obtained must be normally or approximately normally distributed.
- The samples must be independent.
- The variances of the populations must be equal.
- The groups must have the same sample size.

When to use two-way Anova: Two-way ANOVA (also known as a factorial ANOVA, with two factors) when there are one measurement variable and two nominal variables. The nominal variables (often called "factors" or "main effects") are found in all possible combinations.

Because the two-way ANOVA considers the effect of two categorical factors, and the effect of the categorical factors on each other, there are three pairs of null or alternative hypotheses for the two-way ANOVA. Consider the example of the walrus experiment, where the month of mating season and gender are the two independent variables.

H0: The means of all month groups are equal
H1: The mean of at least one month group is different

H0: The means of the gender groups are equal
H1: The means of the gender groups are different

H0: There is no interaction between the month and gender
H1: There is interaction between the month and gender

Difference between One way Anova and Two Way Anova

	One-Way ANOVA	**Two-Way ANOVA**
Definition	A test that allows one to make comparisons between the means of three or more groups of data considering one independent variables.	A test that allows one to make comparisons between the means of three or more groups of data, where two independent variables are considered.
Number of Independent Variables	One	Two

What is Being Compared?	The means of three or more groups of an independent variable on a dependent variable.	The effect of multiple groups of two independent variables on a dependent variable and on each other.
Number of Groups of Samples	Three or more	Each variable should have multiple samples

2. Non-Parametric Test

Non-parametric tests are known as distribution-free tests. They are defined as the hypothesis test, which is are not based on underlying assumptions i.e., they do not require the population's distribution to be denoted by specific parameters. These tests are mainly based on differences in medians. Hence, they are alternately known as the distribution-free test. These test assumes that variables measured are on a different scale, whether on a nominal or ordinal level.

The use and application of several non-parametric tests involve unrelated and related samples. These would include the Chi-square test, Median test, Mann-Whitney U test, Sign test, and Wilcoxon-matched-pairs signed-ranks test.

Statistical tests built around discovering the means, standard deviations, etc. of the typical characteristics of a Gaussian curve are inappropriate for analyzing non-parametric data that do not follow this pattern. Hence, non-parametric data cannot be statistically tested in the above ways.

Non-parametric statistical tests are used when:

- the sample size is very small;
- few assumptions can be made about the data;
- data are rank-ordered or nominal;
- samples are taken from several different populations.

The levels of measurement of the variables, the number of samples, whether they are related or independent, are all factors that determine which tests are appropriate. In order to avoid producing reams of impressive looking, though meaningless, analytical output, it is up to the researcher to ensure that the tests are appropriate for the type of data you have.

Some of the tests that that may come across in testing are:

- Kolmogorov-Smirnov (used to test a two-sample case with independent samples, the values of which are ordinal),
- Kruskal-Wallis (an equivalent of the analysis of variance on independent samples, with variables measured on the ordinal scale),
- Cramer coefficient (gives measures of association of variables with nominal categories) and

- Spearman and Kendall (which provide a range of tests to measures association such as rank-order correlation coefficient, coefficient of concordance and agreement for variables measured at the ordinal or interval levels).

Assumption of Non-Parametric Testing

1. The researcher might face a situation that do not need the assumptions and conditions and thus cannot use parametric statistical procedures. In such a situation, non-parametric statistics must be applied.
2. If the sample is in the form of nominal or ordinal scale and the distribution of the sample is not normally distributed, and also the sample size is very small, it is always advisable to make use of the non-parametric tests for comparing samples and to make inferences or test the significance or trustworthiness of the computed statistics. In other words, the use of non-parametric tests is recommended in the following situations:

Where the sample size is quite small. If the size of the sample is as small as N=5 or N=6, the only alternative is to make use of non-parametric tests.

When assumptions like the normality of the distribution of scores in the population are doubtful, we use non-parametric tests.

When the measurement of data is available either in the form of ordinal or nominal scales or when the data can be expressed in the form of ranks or in the shape of + signs or − signs and classification like 'good-bad', etc., we use non-parametric statistics.

The first meaning of non-parametric covers techniques that do not rely on data belonging to any particular distribution. These include, among others:

- Distribution free methods: This means that there are no assumptions that the data have been drawn from a normally distributed population. This consists of non-parametric statistical models, inference, and statistical tests.
- Non-parametric statistics: In this, the statistics are based on the ranks of observations and do not depend on any distribution of the population.
- No assumption of a structure of a model: In non-parametric statistics, the techniques do not assume that the structure of a model is fixed. In this, the individual variables are typically assumed to belong to parametric distributions, and assumptions about the types of connections among variables are also made.
- The assumptions of classical or standard tests are not applied to non-parametric tests.
- If the sample size is very small, there may be no alternative except to use a non − parametric statistical test.
- Non-parametric tests typically make fewer assumptions about the data and may be relevant to a particular situation.
- The hypothesis tested by the non-parametric test may be more appropriate for research investigation.

Non-parametric Tests Used for Inference

The most frequently used non-parametric tests for drawing statistical inferences in case of unrelated or independent samples are:

1) Chi-square test;
2) Median test; and
3) Mann-Whitney 'U' test.

The Chi-Square (x2) Test

The Chi-square test is applied only to discrete data meaning the data that is counted rather than measured. It is a test of independence and is used to estimate the likelihood that some factor other than chance accounts for the observed relationship.

The Chi-square (a^2) does not measure the degree of relationship between variables under study. It is a test that measures how expectations compare to actual observed data (or model results). The data used in calculating a chi-square statistic must be random, raw, mutually exclusive, drawn from independent variables, and drawn from a large enough sample. For example, the results of tossing a coin 100 times meet these criteria.

The Chi-square test merely evaluates the probability that the observed relationship results from chance. The basic assumption, as in case of other statistical significance, is that the sample observations have been randomly selected. The formula for chi-square (X2) is:

$$\chi_c^2 = \sum \frac{(O_i - E_i)^2}{E_i}$$

In which c=degrees of freedom, O=observed value(s), E=expected value(s)

The Median Test

The Median test is used for testing whether two independent samples differ in central tendencies. It gives information as to whether it is likely that two independent samples have been drawn from populations with the same median. It is particularly useful when even the measurements for the two samples are expressed on an ordinal scale. In using the median test, we first calculate the combined median for all measures (scores) in both samples. Then both sets of scores at the combined median are dichotomized, and the data are set in a 2 x 2 table with two rows, one containing below the median and the other row containing above the median. On the column side, we have two columns, one containing the sample 1 and the other column containing sample 2.

The Mann-Whitney U Test

The Mann-Whitney U test is more useful than the Median test. It is one of the most useful alternatives to the parametric t-test when the parametric assumptions cannot be met and when the measurements are expressed in ordinal scale values. Hence, the Mann–Whitney U test is the true non-parametric counterpart of the t-test and gives the most accurate estimates of significance, especially when sample sizes are small and/or when the data do not approximate a normal distribution.

The Sign Test

The Sign test is the simplest test of significance in the category of non-parametric tests. It makes use of plus and minus signs rather than quantitative measures as its data. It is particularly useful in situations in which quantitative measurement is impossible or inconvenient, but on the basis of superior or inferior performance, it is possible to rank with respect to each other, the two members of each pair.

The sign test is used either in the case of a single sample from which observations are obtained under two experimental conditions. The researcher wants to establish that the two conditions are different.

The use of this test does not make any assumption about the form of the distribution of differences. The only assumption underlying this test is that the variable under investigation has a continuous distribution.

The Wilcoxon Matched Pairs Signed Ranks Test

The Wilcoxon matched-pairs signed-ranks test is more powerful than the sign test because it tests not only direction but also the magnitude of differences within pairs of matched groups.

This test, like the sign test, deals with dependent groups made up of matched pairs of individuals and is not applicable to independent groups. The null hypothesis would assume that the direction and magnitude of the pair difference would be about the same.

Equivalent Test & Difference

Difference Between Z-test and T-test

1. Z-test is a statistical hypothesis test that follows a normal distribution while T-test follows a Students T-distribution.
2. A T-test is appropriate when you are handling small samples (n < 30) while a Z-test is appropriate when you are handling moderate to large samples (n > 30).
3. T-test is more adaptable than Z-test since Z-test will often require certain conditions to be reliable. Additionally, the T-test has many methods that will suit any need.
4. T-tests are more commonly used than Z-tests.
5. Z-tests are preferred than T-tests when standard deviations are known.

PARAMETRIC TEST	NON-PARAMETRIC TEST
Independent Sample t Test	Mann-Whitney test
Paired samples t test	Wilcoxon signed Rank test
One way Analysis of Variance (ANOVA)	Kruskal Wallis Test
One way repeated measures Analysis of Variance	Friedman's ANOVA

Recap & Review Section

SUMMARY Chapter 8

A hypothesis is a statement about a parameter. There are two types of hypotheses: null and alternative hypotheses. Important concepts involved in the process of hypothesis testing i.e., level of significance, one tail test, two tail test, Type I error, Type II error are explained. A general procedure for hypothesis testing is also given. Hypothesis testing considers the probability that the result of a study could have come about even if the experimental procedure had no effect. If this probability is low, the scenario of no effect is rejected, and the theory behind the experimental procedure is supported.

The expectation of an effect is the research hypothesis, and the hypothetical situation of no effect is the null hypothesis. When a result (that is, a sample score) is so extreme that the result would be very unlikely if the null hypothesis were true, the null hypothesis is rejected, and the research hypothesis supported. If the result is not that extreme, the null hypothesis is not rejected, and the study is inconclusive.

Psychologists usually consider a result too extreme if it is less likely than 5% (that is, a significance level of .05) to have come about if the null hypothesis were true. Psychologists sometimes use a more stringent 1% (.01 significance level), or even .01% (.001) significance level), cutoff.

The cutoff percentage is the probability of the result being extreme in a predicted direction in a directional or one-tailed test. The cutoff percentages are the probability of the result being extreme in either direction in a non-directional or two-tailed test.

There are two kinds of decision errors one can make in hypothesis testing. A Type I error is when a researcher rejects the null hypothesis, but the null hypothesis is actually true. A Type II error is when a researcher does not reject the null hypothesis, but the null hypothesis is actually false.

There has been much controversy about significance tests, including critiques of the basic logic and, especially, that they are often misused. One major way significance tests is misused when researchers interpret not rejecting the null hypothesis as demonstrating that the null hypothesis is true.

Research articles typically report the results of hypothesis testing by saying a result was or was not significant and giving the probability level cutoff (usually 5% or 1%) the decision was based on.

Parametric and non-parametric tests are important for students, especially researchers working in any field. Parametric tests include all methods of statistics when the sample size is large, whereas, in non-parametric tests, the sample size is small. There are some advantages and disadvantages to both the tests. In this unit, we discussed the statistical inference based on parametric tests. A parametric test is a test that assumes certain parameters and distributions are known about a population, contrary to the non-parametric one. The parametric test uses a mean value, while the non-parametric one uses a median value. The parametric approach requires previous knowledge about the population, contrary to the non-parametric approach.

Caselet 8 – Pace Two-Wheelers

Pace Ltd is a manufacturer of scooters and motorcycles. As a part of its operating policy, the executives wished to determine whether the customers' and dealers' satisfaction depended upon warranty cards or not. To test this, the company has withdrawn the warranty cards from the market. Pace Ltd's marketing research department developed a questionnaire in a summated scale form to collect data for customer satisfaction with and without the warranty cards. The department mailed a questionnaire to a random sample of customers when they have warranty cards. After that, it sent the same questionnaire to the same set of customers, when they did not have warranty cards. The company also sent the questionnaire to dealers who have provided marks out of 100 for their satisfaction levels. The data collected by the research department is as follows.

No. of observation	Customer's satisfaction when they have warranty cards	Customer's satisfaction when they do not have warranty cards	Dealers
1	74	43	92
2	81	23	42
3	35	88	54
4	59	55	59
5	90	67	83
6	33	53	30
7	82	85	34
8	68	70	54
9	56	30	39
10	46	75	65

Questions

1. Find out the effect of warranty cards on the satisfaction of customers from the above given data. Use 5% as the level of significance to test the hypothesis.
2. Determine the difference between the dealers and customers satisfaction with and without the warranty cards. Use 5% as the level of significance to test the hypothesis.
3. What should the organization do to overcome this problem?

Check Your Knowledge

CYK 1. A statement whose validity is tested by a sample is termed as ?
a. Null Hypothesis
b. Statistical Hypothesis
c. Simple Hypothesis
d. Composite Hypothesis

Answer: (b)

CYK 2. The rejection probability of Null Hypothesis tested true is termed as ?
a. Level of Confidence
b. Level of Significance
c. Level of Margin
d. Level of Rejection

Answer (b)

CYK 3. The critical region being evenly distributed the test is termed as?
a. Two tailed
b. One tailed
c. Three tailed
d. Zero tailed

Answer (a)

CYK 4. Type 1 error occurs when?
a. Rejecting H0 if it is True
b. Rejecting H0 if it is False
c. Accepting H0 if it is True
d. Accepting H0 if it is False

Answer (a)

CYK 5. A hypothesis when rejected at 0.01 level of significance:
a. Must be rejected at any level
b. Must be rejected at the 0.01 Level
c. Must not be rejected at the 0.01 Level
d. May or may not be rejected at the 0.01 Level

Answer (d)

CYK 6. What is the underlying assumption when we use the t-distribution to perform a hypothesis test?
a. That the underlying distribution has more then one modal class
b. That the underlying population has a constant variance
c. That the underlying population has a non-symmetrical distribution
d. That the underlying population follows Normal distribution

Answer (d)

CYK 7. Which of the following statements about hypothesis testing is true?
a. If the p-value is greater than the significance level, we fail to reject Ho
b. A Type II error is rejecting the null when it is actually true
c. If the alternative hypothesis is that the population mean is greater than a specified value, then the test is a two-tailed test
d. None of the above statements are true

Answer (a)

CYK 8. Green sea turtles have normally distributed weights, measured in kilograms, with a mean of 134.5 and a variance of 49.0. A particular green sea turtle's weight has a z-score of – 2.4. What is the weight of this green sea turtle? Round to the nearest whole number.

a. 17 kg

b. 151 kg

c. 118 kg

d. 252 kg

Answer (c)

CYK 9. Which of the following exam scores is better relative to other students enrolled in the course?

- A psychology exam grade of 85; the mean grade for the psychology exam is 92 with a standard deviation of 3.5
- An economics exam grade of 67; the mean grade for the economics exam is 79 with a standard deviation of 8
- A chemistry exam grade of 62; the mean grade for the chemistry exam is 62 with a standard deviation of 5

a. The psychology exam score is relatively better

b. The economics exam score is relatively better

c. The chemistry exam score is relatively better

d. All of the exam scores are relatively equivalent

Answer (c)

Questions

Q1. Explain the procedure for testing a statistical hypothesis

Q2. Differentiate between

a) Null Hypothesis Vs. Alternative Hypothesis

b) Type 1 error vs. Type 2 error

c) Parametric vs Non-parametric testing

d) t-test vs. z-test

e) One Way Anova vs. Two Way Anova

Q3. List out different types of Hypothesis

Q4. What is the Hypothesis and characteristics of good Hypothesis

Q5. How do you test a hypothesis?

Application Question

1. The company ABC manufacturing bulbs hypothesizes that the life of its bulbs is 150 hours with a known standard deviation of 20 hours. A random sample of 25 bulbs gave a mean life of 110 hours. Using a 0.05 level of significance, can the company conclude that the mean life of bulbs is less than the 150 hours?

2. The manager of a bank is trying to decide which of the two supposedly equally good ATM machines to install, tests each machine 500 times, and finds that machine I fail to work 30 times, and machine II fails to work 12 times. Using a 0.05 level of significance, can he conclude that two machines are not equally good?

3. If 56 out of a random sample of 200 boys consume protein supplement, while 31 out of a random sample of 100 girls consume protein supplement, can we conclude at the 0.05 level of significance that the proportion of male supplement taker is higher than that of female supplement taker?

4. The Movie/cinema experience in India has taken a new upswing with the business booming for the newly established multiplexes. And it is no different in the state of Maharashtra either. Families go to the malls and multiplexes to have a wholesome experience. A study in a particular city of Maharastra (Nasik) tried to find out if the movie experience is diverse in 4 different multiplexes of the city, whether according to the multiplexes experience or according to the movies screened in them. These four popular malls are screening four latest Hindi movies in their multiplexes. The following are the footfalls recorded (in thousands) per week.

	Multiplex #1	Multiplex #2	Multiplex #3	Multiplex #4
Movie #1	40	36	45	30
Movie #2	38	42	50	41
Movie #3	36	30	48	35
Movie #4	46	47	52	44

Using ANOVA, find out:

a. Is there a significant difference in the viewership of the four movies?

b. Is there a considerable disparity in the footfalls amongst the four multiplexes?

Interpretation and Report Writing

Keywords: *Report Layout, Executive Summary, Bibliography, Appendices/Appendix, Glossary, Ethics, Plagiarism, Grammarly, Urkund, Turnitin Copyrights, Intellectual Property, Data Confidentiality, Data Anonymity.*

After the data is collected through various techniques or methods of research, the researcher tries to find out a solution to a problem. Such solutions or conclusions can be reached with the help of analyzing or evaluating the data systematically. After the data is collected through multiple forms already discussed in previous chapters, data needs to be evaluated, interpreted and presented in a meaningful form.

Evaluation and interpretation provides an in-depth understanding of the data collected, and also provides an answer to the aims and objectives of the study. These elements in research aim at understanding the reasons, justifying, or predicting particular objects, behaviors, incidents, or practices in the real world.

Steps in Analysing of Data

Systematic steps have to be followed for the process of evaluating the collected information or the data supports. The researcher tries to organize and give meaning to the collected information. It is used in such a way so that there is less chance of bias or confusion. With the help of systematic evaluation of data, several answers can be found by the researcher and also attempt to uncover the various facts of the variables, events, and behavior.

Steps involved in the evaluation of data:

i. **Review of the collected data:** This step involves an overview of the data collected from multiple sources i.e., interviews, videotapes, audiotapes, observation, etc. The aim of this review is to gather as much information as is required pertaining to the variables under study.

ii. **Categorizing the collected data:** From the collected information, the researcher or the analysts sorts relevant information, which may have an effect, direct or indirect on the behavior, objects, events, or practices selected for the study. After sorting the data, the researcher categorizes similar information under various categories or themes, e.g., the researcher may categorize the information into concerns, suggestions, strengths, weaknesses, similar experiences, program inputs, recommendations, outputs, and outcome indicators.

iii. **Naming/labeling the categories:** This step in the evaluation process comprises of labeling the sorted and categorized themes, e.g., collating all suggestions under the category of propositions.

iv. **Identifying causal relationships:** With the help of categorizing and labeling information, researcher gets an idea of the direction and flow of information. This enables the researcher identifying patterns, associations and causal relationships. E.g., if most people of the sample under study belong to the same geographic area, we may state that people if living in that area may have a specific problem. Alternatively, most people of the sample under study belong to the same income bracket; then, we would state that because they all have the same income, they are not adequately motivated. These patterns or associations of the themes are made on the basis of the experience of respondents in the sample and the experience of the researcher during the study.

v. **Recording/filing the data:** Once the patterns of relationships are analyzed, the researcher needs to keep a track of the same. These records or files serve as a guide for future reference, while a similar sample is being studied.

Significance & Structuring of Research Report

Excellent writing & communication are vital skills for successful research. Effective communication is required at every stage of the project, but the main writing tasks are to be focussed at the beginning and end of the research project. The beginning explains what needs to be done along the research, and the end explains what has been done. The task is enabled with the help of word processing packages, which provide simple ways to record, store, edit, expand, and condense text and to present it in an attractive fashion.

Preparing a report on findings of the research conducted, is the ultimate challenge to the researcher/analyst. Reporting of data refers to the interpretations and conclusions backed by relevant support of the literature review and the reasons supporting such findings.

While preparing the final report of the research conducted, the researcher needs to be very cautious and least biased. The reports can be represented in an organized way by following the given step.

(i) Preparation of the content of the report

Even before starting the procedure of writing down the report, the researcher needs to formulate the findings according to the need and requirements of those for whom the report is intended. For example, the researcher has to create the scope and content of research on the basis of the funders/bankers, employees, clients, customers, the public, etc. for whom the research was conducted.

(ii) Review and discussion of the report

The researcher then needs to review and also discuss the interpretations and results with the people on whom the research was conducted.

(iii) Preparation of the executive summary

The researcher then prepares an executive summary (that is, a summing up of the conclusions and recommendations). The brief may contain the description of the organization's people, events, and practices under study. It also includes an explanation of the research goals, methods, and analysis procedures; listing of conclusions and recommendations; and any relevant attachments. If required, the summary may also include the details of questionnaires, interview guides that have been used by the researcher.

(iv) Scope of future the research

Based on the overall research conducted, the researcher also prepares a list of areas that may be studied further. The scope acts as a research plan to guide future research in similar areas.

Steps in Report Writing

The research reports are a descriptive summary and act as a guide for future research in similar areas. The documentation of the research report is very crucial and sensitive because the report records information for easy understanding and follow up. There are several ways in which the contents of a report is prepared. Stepwise report writing is discussed as follows:

1) Title Page

This is the first page of the report and it contains the details of the topic of the research. It should include the name of the organization/product/service/program, that is being researched. It should also contain date, institution and researcher mentor brief.

2) Table of Contents

The list of contents as prepared by researchers indicates the specific page number where the component of research work has been covered.

3) Executive Summary

Executive summary or abstract of the research, is usually a one-page, precise/concise overview of the findings and recommendations of the research conducted.

Report Writing	
1	Tile Page
2	Table of contents
3	Executive Summary
4	Purpose
5	Background
6	Methodology
7	Results & Findings
8	Conclusion
9	Limitation
10	Recommendation
11	Refrences
12	Appendices

4) Purpose of the Report

The purpose of the report reflects the aims, objectives, and significance of the research. It also covers the detailing of the research types (qualitative or quantitative) that was used.

5) Background of the research

This topic shows a background of the people/event/ practice/program/organization under study. It focusses on the problem that needs to be studied and also the overall goals of the research. It covers the questions being answered in the research and also the relevant literature review on which the research is based.

6) Methodology

This section includes measures and procedures involved in the research. It contains information related to sampling, scale, data collection techniques etc.

7) Results and findings: This section covers results compiled on the basis of the data analysis. It discusses the results and findings of the research.

8) Conclusion and Interpretation: This section deals with interpretation and discussion of the findings. Conclusion are arrived at, on the basis of the interpretations. This section indicates the significant of the results, and the extent to it is helpful for future researches.

9) Limitations: This section is a compilation of limitations, experienced during the research. It reflects under what conditions the results may be generalized.

10) Recommendations and implications: The researcher put forward and recommends suggestions & implications of the study conducted.

11) References: This part of the report acknowledges the authors, books, studies, and journals, which were referred to in the literature review for the research conducted.

12) Appendices: It is the last section and contains the various sources (like questionnaire, company forms, case studies, data in tabular format, testimonials), which are analyzed and used by the researcher.

Precautions in Report Writing

Research report writing is ideally one of the most critical and important aspects of your academics. Researching is an investigative process that involves searching for new knowledge to expound on exiting knowledge. Finding new knowledge is never easy, especially in a field that has been overly researched. While evaluating, analyzing, and reporting the data, the researchers need to observe/avoid the following consideration:

Description	✓ ✗
1) The researcher should be clear and specific in describing the sample populations	✓
2) Should code the data for convenience in processing.	✓
3) Should frequently use diagrams and flow charts for convenient summarization.	✓
4) Should draw a conclusion on the basis of the present and other related studies in a similar field.	✓
5) Should develop policies for evaluating the qualitative data to prove the validity.	✓
6) Should select a suitable research topic.	✓
7) Should specify the focus of research (neither too broad, not too narrow and supported by relevant arguments).	✓
8) Should collect relevant data, organize it and collate it logically.	✓
9) Should substantiate claims by supporting facts.	✓
10) Should depend entirely upon the research design assuming that the design is perfect.	✗
11) Should only depend upon questionnaires, as the exclusive data source.	✗
12) Should ignore **plagiarism** and ethics in the research	✗
13) Should not add new points to the conclusion, leaving no scope for future study.	✗
14) Should ignore citations to augment the research.	✗
15) Should ignore the bibliography section of the research	✗

Research Ethics

"Ethics" refers to the norms for conduct that draw a line between acceptable behavior and unacceptable behavior. Research ethics is a set of principles defining how researchers and research organizations should conduct themselves when dealing with research participants, other researchers, colleagues, the users of their research, and society in general. Ethics may also be defined as an approach, procedure, or perspective for making decisions on how to act and for drawing analysis of complex problems.

Research holds value only when carried out in all honesty. The results of research become doubtful if the researcher integrity is challenged. While taking short cuts or resorting to cheating might seems tempting options, it is really not worth it. Not only does it discredit the research, but can also bring penalties and humiliation to the researcher. It is a simple rule stated in clear guidelines in the citation that prevent the research from copying another research and letting it pass as original work. This is called plagiarism (Several **Plagiarism** softwares like; Grammarly, Urkund, Turnitin are available to check duplication in work and guide originality). While it is important to refer to other research works, to form a background of the study, the research work may not be quoted, as such, in new research work.

Involving human participants in the research brings forth ethical issues about treatment inflicted. Respondents need to be respected, made aware of the implications of how you will be using in the research and the data confidentiality & privacy maintained.

All researches whether or not involving human intervention in the form of respondent data must adhere to honesty in data collection, analysis, and interpretation. The clarity in explanation at every step of the research process helps to avoid acquisitions or false reasoning. There are two main aspects relating to ethics and research.

- Values of the researcher pertaining to honesty, integrity, and candid approach.
- Respondent treatment in terms of information, consent, confidentiality, anonymity, and courtesy.

Principles/Ethical Code of Conduct

The principles involving the ethical Code of conduct are: **The principle of voluntary participation:** It indicates that people would not be forced or, in any way, pressurized into becoming a part of the research. Avoiding coercion, so participants voluntarily give their unbiased, precise, and clear inputs.

Ethics code of conduct:
- *The principle of voluntary participation*
- *The principle of informed consent*
- *The principle of confidentiality*
- *The principle of anonymity*

The principle of informed consent: The principle of informed consent applies that prospective research subjects must be totally informed about procedures and risks which may be involved in the research, and their consent to participate must be sought.

Ethical norms also as a pre-requisite maintain that researchers and participants are not in a situation in which they might at risk and physical and psychological harm.

The principle of confidentiality: Under this principle the participants are assured that information revealed will not be made accessible to anyone who is directly not a part of the study.

The principle of anonymity: This principles advocates that the participants' identity will be maintained anonymous throughout the research – even to the researchers themselves. Identity may be sought if the research objectives so demand but, in such a case it becomes imperative to seek the participant's consent. Once the principles have been defined it becomes important to understand why they are mandatory in conducting research (The principles put together constitutes the framework for the ethical code of conduct).

- The code of conduct fosters the aims of the research, such as cognition, truth, integrity, and avoidance of error. For example, avoiding false and misrepresentation of data, promoting truth, and avoiding error etc.
- The code of ethics provides values that are imperative to working in collaboration, involving trust, accountability & mutual respect. For example, ethical norms of research, like guidelines for copyright and patenting policies, sharing secondary data policies, and maintaining confidentiality rules, are designed so as to protect intellectual property while at the same time encouraging collaboration.

On having clearly established relevance of the ethical code of conduct, the next logical step would be, prescribing norms that would offer guidelines to be observed by the researcher during the process of research. These include:

Discuss intellectual property (Data security & Stewardship): In order to cover all discrepancies regarding stewardship and data consent, it would be a good idea to discuss 'who gets the credit' at the very beginning. The most appropriate approach would be to avoid disagreements about who gets the credit and in what sequence or order of priority. This would prevent many communication barriers and later complications and must be sorted even when many people would feel uncomfortable about the discussion on such topics. Honoring patents, copyrights, and all other forms of intellectual property reduces complexities of unpublished data, methods, or results that should be refrained from, especially without permission.

Avoiding plagiarism and maintaining authenticity in research findings: This involves working on primary data and avoiding duplicity. Secondary data, wherever used, must be acknowledged. In order to be able to furnish answers to questions relating to the study, authenticity and allowing others to re-look & re-analyze the results, researchers should preserve & archive primary data as also all the accompanying records. Storing data would allow the researcher to answer challenges if any, posed on the authenticity of the research.

Follow the rule of informed consent: When appropriately ensured, the process of consent guarantees that individuals are voluntarily participating in the research with complete knowledge of related risks and gains. Researchers should inform participants about the purpose & objectives of the research, expected time duration, and procedures involved.

Participants have the right to decline or say 'no' to participate and also to withdraw from the study even when it has started. However, the anticipated consequences of such withdrawals must also be announced.

Reasonably predictable factors that may influence the respondents' willingness to participate, like potential risks, lack of comfort, or adverse effects.

Incentives & Deterrent for participation: Especially for experimental research, all participants must be made aware of the nature of the treatment & these treatments will not available to the control groups. Also, explanation of how participants would be assigned to the two groups, treatment and control groups should be clearly elaborated. Finally, the available treatment alternatives and compensation on each or monetary cost of participation must be declared.

If research participants are not capable enough to evaluate the pros & cons of participation themselves (e.g., minors or people with cognitive disabilities), then the guardian or the person who is awarding the permission must be given access to the information.

The study of the factors regarding a job or organizational effectiveness should be conducted in an organizational setting involving no risk to participants' employability, and further, the confidentiality has to be protected.

Respect confidentiality and privacy: It becomes absolutely essential to respect the privacy of the respondent. For example, unique ways need to be devised to ask participants about their willingness to talk about topics that may be sensitive, without creating awkward or embarrassing situations. It could be a great idea to conduct detailed informal interviews to put the respondent at ease and stop at any apparent awkwardness. The data once collected, must be personally stored in a way that there is no scope of leak out. Protecting the privacy of the respondent becomes the critical duty of the researcher.

Discuss the limits of confidentiality, informing participants about how the data collected will be used, what would be done with the case materials, including photos and audio-visual recordings, and secure their consent. It also again becomes crucial to understand the legal norms in terms of confidentiality to avoid any complications which might prop in at a later stage.

Use of Internet: The use of web technology might be beneficial, yet it could be the most common source of a data leak. It is a good idea to consult a professional when the researcher himself is not very net-savvy. Otherwise, intruders may tap into data that you thought was thoroughly protected.

Respect Honest & Fair Practices: Maintaining honesty in all communications, whether formal or informal. Honesty in reporting data, results, methods, and procedures used, and even in the publication status. Trying to avoid fabrication, falsification, and misrepresentation of data.

Avoiding Biasing and maintaining objectivity: The researcher should try as much as possible to avoid biasing in experimental design, data analysis & interpretation. Also, activities like peer review, grant writing, expert testimonials, that forms integral aspects of research, hold it critical to maintain objectivity. Avoiding or minimizing biasness or self-deception seems the only approach.

Maintain your Integrity: Stick to your promises and agreements; conduct research with sincerity; aim at the consistency of both thought and action. The goal of the researcher should be to attain reliable & valid results, and care must be exercised to avoid deviations from the set goals.

Ensuring a carefully planned approach: Avoiding careless errors on account of negligence and carefully and thoroughly examining your own work as well as that of the peer groups becomes exceptionally crucial. Keeping schematic records on research activities, from data collection to research design and moving on to corresponding with agencies or research journals.

Terminal Items

Terminal items are the section that follows the text. It starts with APPENDICES, BIBLIOGRAPHY, followed by GLOSSARY. All the words are separate sections and appear in 'capital letters'.

All reference section pages are numbered in Arabic numerals. It should appear in continuation with the page numbers of text.

Appendices

Appendices is a plural form of 'appendix'. It contains supplementary material that is not an essential part of the text itself. It helps the author to authenticate the thesis or report and help the reader to check the data. All appendices are listed in TOC (Table of Contents)

1. Materials used
2. Original Data
3. Tables
4. Quotations
5. Legal decision
6. Questionnaire
7. Letters
8. Forms used in collecting data
9. Transcripts of Interviews
10. Case Studies

Biblographies

Bibliography is a list of the written sources of information on a researched subject. It appears as a list at the end of a book or article after appendices. It reflects what works the author used/consulted in writing the article or book. We may list works that a reader might find useful. The bibliographical information must be given with the following inputs: Authors, Title, Place of Publication, Publisher, Date of Publication, DOI (Digital Object Identifier).

There are different styles which format the information differently. The descriptions of each citation style shared below. A citation is a way of giving credit to the individuals for their creative and intellectual works. The work can be utilized to support the research. There are different ways of citing resources depending on the academic discipline you are involved in.

For example:

- APA (American Psychological Association) is used by Education, Psychology, and Sciences.
- MLA (Modern Language Association) style is used by the Humanities.
- Chicago/Turabian style is generally used by Business, History, and Fine Arts.

** For more detailed guidance, try one of the following websites:
http://www.usq.edu.au/library/referencing/apa-referencing-guide
www.purdueowl.com they provide online guidance for many of the standard writing styles.

Bibliography APA STYLE SIXTH EDITION

Kellerman. (2007). What every leader needs to know about followers. Harvard Business Review, 84-91.

Walia, A. (2015, April). Relationship between leadership styles and followership styles. International Journal of Advanced Research in Management and Social Sciences, 4(4), 171-180. Retrieved from www.garph.co.uk

Walia, A. M. (2019, December). Relationship between Followership styles and Performance in Service Sector. Think India Journal, 22(14), 719-727. doi:10.26643

Azam, M. K., & Uppal, M. K. (2019). "The Evolving Paradigms Of Customer Relationship Management – A Review Based paper". Think India Journal, 22(3), 294-305. Retrieved from https://journals.eduindex.org/index.php/think-india/article/view/8234

Bibliography CHICAGO STYLE

Kellerman. "What every leader needs to know about followers." Harvard Business Review, 2007: 84-91.

Walia, Anubha Maurya. "Relationship between Followership styles and Performance in Service Sector." Think India Journal 22, no. 14 (December 2019): 719-727.

Walia, Anubha. " Relationship between leadership styles and followership styles" International Journal of Advanced Research in Management and Social Sciences (Greenfield Advance Research Publishing House) 4, no. 4 (April 2015): 171-180.

Azam, M. Khalid, and Manpreet Kaur Uppal. 2019. 'The Evolving Paradigms Of Customer Relationship Management – A Review Based paper'. Think India Journal 22 (3), 294-305. https://journals.eduindex.org/index.php/think-india/article/view/8234.

Bibliography HARVARD STYLE

Kellerman, 2007. What every leader needs to know about followers. Harvard Business Review, pp. 84-91.

Walia, A., 2015. Relationship between leadership styles and followership styles. International Journal of Advanced Research in Management and Social Sciences, April, 4(4), pp. 171-180.

Walia, A. M., 2019. Relationship between Followership styles and Performance in Service Sector. Think India Journal, December, 22(14), pp. 719-727.

Azam, M. K. and Uppal, M. K. (2019) 'The Evolving Paradigms Of Customer Relationship Management – A Review Based paper', Think India Journal, 22(3), pp. 294-305. Available at: https://journals.eduindex.org/index.php/think-india/article/view/8234 (Accessed: 17March2020).

Bibliography IEEE 2006 STYLE

[1] A. M. Walia, "Relationship between Followership styles and Performance in Service Sector," Think India Journal, vol. 22, no. 14, pp. 719-727, December 2019.

[2] A. Walia, "Relationship between leadership styles and followership styles," International Journal of Advanced Research in Management and Social Sciences, vol. 4, no. 4, pp. 171-180, April 2015.

[3] Kellerman, "What every leader needs to know about followers," Harvard Business Review, pp. 84-91, 2007.

[4] M. K. Azam and M. K. Uppal, "The Evolving Paradigms Of Customer Relationship Management – A Review Based paper", think-india, vol. 22, no. 3, pp. 294-305, Sep. 2019.

Bibliography GOST NAME SORT STYLE

Kellerman What every leader needs to know about followers [Journal] // Harvard Business Review. – 2007. – pp. 84-91.

Walia Anubha Maurya Relationship between Followership styles and Performance in Service Sector [Journal] //Think India Journal. – December 2019. – 14 : Vol. 22. – pp. 719-727. – 0971-1260.

Walia Anubha Relationship between leadership styles and followership styles[Journal] // International Journal of Advanced Research in Management and Social Sciences. – [s.l.] : Greenfield Advance Research Publishing House, April 2015. – 4 : Vol. 4. – pp. 171-180. – 0973-9335.

Bibliography GB7714-2005 STYLE

Relationship between Followership styles and Performance in Service Sector. **Walia, Anubha Maurya. 2019.** 14, December 2019, Think India Journal, Vol. 22, pp. 719-727. 0971-1260.

Relationship between leadership styles and followership styles. **Walia, Anubha. 2015.** 4, s.l. : Greenfield Advance Research Publishing House, April 2015, International Journal of Advanced Research in Management and Social Sciences, Vol. 4, pp. 171-180. 0973-9335.

What every leader needs to know about followers. **Kellerman. 2007.** 2007, Harvard Business Review, pp. 84-91.

Bibliography ISO 690 – First element

Relationship between Followership styles and Performance in Service Sector. **Walia, Anubha Maurya. 2019.** 14, December 2019, Think India Journal, Vol. 22, pp. 719-727. 0971-1260.

Relationship between leadership styles and followership styles. **Walia, Anubha. 2015.** 4, s.l. : Greenfield Advance Research Publishing House, April 2015, International Journal of Advanced Research in Management and Social Sciences, Vol. 4, pp. 171-180. 0973-9335.

What every leader needs to know about followers. **Kellerman. 2007.** 2007, Harvard Business Review, pp. 84-91.

Bibliography TURABIAR STYLE

Kellerman. "What every leader needs to know about followers." Harvard Business Review, 2007: 84-91.

Walia, Anubha Maurya. "Relationship between Followership styles and Performance in Service Sector." Think India Journal 22, no. 14 (December 2019): 719-727.

Walia, Anubha. "Relationship between leadership styles and followership styles." International Journal of Advanced Research in Management and Social Sciences (Greenfield Advance Research Publishing House) 4, no. 4 (April 2015): 171-180.

Azam, M. Khalid, and Manpreet Kaur Uppal. 'The Evolving Paradigms Of Customer Relationship Management – A Review Based paper'. Think India Journal 22, no. 3 (September 26, 2019): 294-305. Accessed March 17, 2020. https://journals.eduindex. org/index.php/think-india/article/view/8234.

Bibliography MLA STYLE

Kellerman. "What every leader needs to know about followers." Harvard Business Review (2007): 84-91.

Walia, Anubha Maurya. "Relationship between Followership styles and Performance in Service Sector." Think India Journal 22.14 (2019): 719-727. <journals.eduindex.org/ index.php/think-india>.

Walia, Anubha. "Relationship between leadership styles and followership styles." International Journal of Advanced Research in Management and Social Sciences 4.4 (2015): 171-180. <www.garph.co.uk>.

Azam, M. K., and M. K. Uppal. 'The Evolving Paradigms Of Customer Relationship Management – A Review Based paper'. Think India Journal, Vol. 22, no. 3, Sept. 2019, pp. 294-05, https://journals.eduindex.org/index.php/think-india/article/view/8234.

Glossary

It is a short dictionary, an alphabetical list of words relating to a specific subject, text, or dialect, with explanations. A glossary appears after the bibliography. The position of Glossary can also appear on the introductory page of a book.

Recap & Review Section

Summary Chapter 9

A researcher having collected and analyzed data has to draw inferences and explains their significance. The process of explaining data after the analysis is called an interpretation of data. While in interpretation, certain precautions have to be taken, such as maintaining objectivity, ethics, avoiding biases, maintaining integrity. The final stage is report writing, which has to pass through a number of stages such as understanding the subject and its analysis, preparation of outline, creating a rough draft, and report finalization. The structure is diced in the preliminary part, text/body part, and terminal part. After report preparation, it must be thoroughly checked to satisfy that everything is order.

Check Your Knowledge

CYK1 A specific research was conducted on the sensitive issue of life mapping involving personal revelations. The privacy of the respondent here is a crucial concern. As such, the participants are not revealed to anyone but the researcher and staff. Under what principle of ethics would you advocate this:

a. Confidentiality

b. Anonymity

c. Ethics

d. Discretion

Answer (a)

CYK2. _________ means that the participant's approval is sought before using his responses as a part of the research. This is termed as:

a. Anonymity

b. Confidentiality

c. Consent

Answer (c)

CYK3 Which of the following is not true?

a. Misrepresenting and creating fraudulent data is dishonest.

b. Seeking consent prior to information sharing is critical.

c. Plagiarism in research is not appreciated.

d. Breaking confidentiality is not a problem.

Answer (d)

Questions

Q1. Explain the need, meaning, and essentials of interpretation.

Q2. Write short notes on

a) Bibliography b) Appendices c) Glossary d) Characteristics of good report

Q3. Define research ethics? Discuss in detail the steps a researcher needs to follow in formulating & presenting a good research report?

Q4. What is the structure of the research report? Elaborate the sequential steps involved in its layout.

Q5. Enumerate the guidelines for effective report writing? Support your answer with suitable examples.

Q6. What guidelines must a researcher adhere to for graphical and tabular representation of the research results?

Application Questions

1. Select a business report and map the contents of the report against the guidelines specified. Identify the deviations & discuss the reasons for the same.

2. Examine online reports and evaluate the process of adopted by them. Critically evaluate & suggest changes, if any, required.

3. Compare and compile data on government stand on lockdown under COVID-19 from three published sources. Present your findings in a structured report layout complete with all the terminal items.

Sample Report

Confidential

<table>
<tr><td align="center">

Marketing of flowers in the Delhi market

Prepared
by
Radhika Maurya
ABC Corporation
June 2019

XYZ Research Services
Safdarjung Enclave, New Delhi

</td></tr>
</table>

Only for limited circulation

Flowers more in demand as compared to the other products. X brand has maximum sale and close to it is Y. Retailing is not done professionally. Flower consumption is confined to rich people only as it is quite expensive. xxxxxxxxxxxxxxxxxxxxxxxxxxxxxxxxxxxxxxxxxxxxxx
xxxxxxxxxxxxxxxxxxxxxxxxxxxxxxxxxxxxxxxxxxxxxxxxxxxxxxxxxxxxxxxxxx

Introduction

The present study focuses on marketing of flowers and related products. With growing aesthetic concern xxxxxxxxxxxxxxxxxxxxxxxxxxxxxxxxxxxxxxxxxxxxxxxxxxxxxxxxxxxxxxxxxxxx xxxxxxxxxxxxxxxxxxxxxxxxxxxxxxxxxxxxxxxx research is confined to the Delhi NCR region.

Objectives and Scope of the Study

To study the existing flower market: This would involve categorizing the flowers available in Delhi into aesthetic defined spaces, estimating the demand pattern for each of the categories and to understand the marketing strategies adopted by different players for promoting and propagating.

Consumer diagnostic research: This would entail studying the existing consumer profile, i.e., perception and attitudes t.

Methodology

Information areas as relevant for the study are discussed as follows:

Flowers & Flower products: What is formally defined as FFP, what are the; certification procedures, what are the production estimates, and what is the nature of government and private support.

Market Analysis: An analysis of the major players in the NCR

Consumers: With reference to their demographic profile, lifestyle patterns, attitudes towards health and importance of nutrition, awareness, and perception

Sample

The consumers were also divided into three strata. The consumers were from the NCR, i.e., Delhi, Noida, and Gurgaon. The sample was more biased towards Delhi as the researchers felt that the availability of flowers was more in Delhi than in the suburbs. Focus group discussions were conducted for OCs. A total of 100 OCs were interviewed through a questionnaire for a quantitative data collection.

The Questionnaire

The questionnaire begins with the identification details of the respondent. It is divided into four parts.

Part A consists of 23 statements about the respondent's lifestyle and attitude. All statements are on a 5 point Likert scale.

Part B has Questions 1-6 related to grocery purchase behavior. Question 7 ascertains the respondent's attitude toward groceries. Question 8 is a product vs. type, brand, frequency, and quantity of purchase. Questions 1-6 are multiple-choice questions, while 7 is on a semantic differential scale. Question 8 is ratio scaled.

Part C measures awareness of products.

Part D consists of 29 statements about the respondent's post-consumption perception of flowers.

Study findings

Though awareness about aesthetic flowers in Delhi is increasing, supply is often sporadic and there is no systematic data bank xxxxxxxxxxxxxxxxxxxxxxxxxxxxxxxxxxxxxxxxxxxxxxxxxxx xxxxxxxxxxxxxxxxxxxxxxxxxxxxxxxxxxxxxxxxxxxxxxxxxxxxxxxxxxxxxxxxxxxxxxxxxxxxxxxx

Conclusions

The current research conducted in the NCR conveyed some significant findings:

Majority of the market players are xxxxxxxxxxxxxxxxxxxxxxxxxxxxxxxxxxxxxxxxxxxxxxxxxxxxxx xxxxxxxxxxxxxxxxxxxxxxxxxxxxxxxxxxxxxxxxxxxxxxxxxxxxxxxxxxxxxxxxxxxxxxxxxxxxxxxx

Analytics in Research

Keywords: *Descriptive Analytics, Predictive Analytics, Prescriptive Analytics, Analytical tools in research*

Information collected and expressed in quantitative form for a specific purpose is called data. Data is required to make a decision. Hence data should be obtainable, accurate, and adequate. We all are living among rich data availability and data-driven world. Data is revolutionizing business. Data is getting recorded, re-recorded, stored, and used 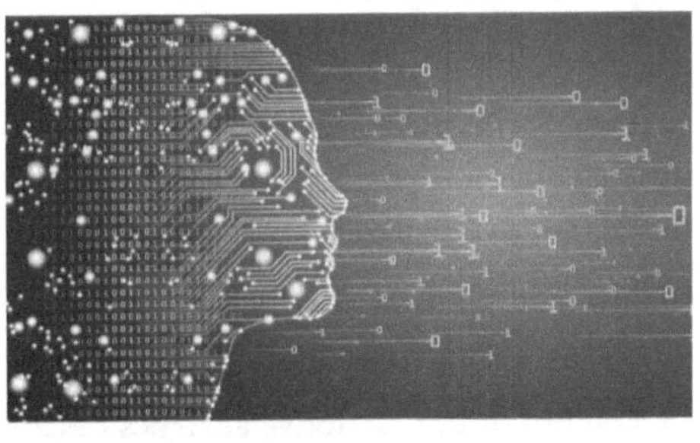 for various information retrieval and analysis. Presently all kinds of organizations are using data for multiple purposes, i.e., understanding the internal and external customers, the future scope of a business, expected changes, new growth or product opportunities, making human resource decisions, or managing budgets. Data is also impacting our day to day life. Companies from Health care, travel, technology, banks, BFSI, education.... the list is endless are working with data. Experts predict there will be a 4300% plus increase in annual data by 2021.

The journey of data and analysis will grow manifold by creating millions of IT jobs worldwide. Even though we heard about Data and Data Analytics, many still do not understand these buzz words.

What is Analytics

Analytics means a simple exploration for predicting what to target and what not to target. The analysis of data implies drawing hidden or concealed insights to aid decision making.

In 'Competing on Analytics,' Thomas Davenport defines analytics as, 'the extensive use of data, statistical and quantitative analysis, exploratory, predictive models, and fact-based management to drive decisions and actions.'

Analytics is an integral part of various businesses and corporates and it is an essential skill, which has been used in the past, is being used in the present and will find application in the future. Applications of analytics not only includes the study of business data using statistical analysis, which has been shared in previous chapters to understand historical patterns and improving business performance in the future by predicting with data, but also predict future aspect.

A sales manager analyses his team's performance data for business or sales optimization. Human Resource managers use employee data to predict performance or attrition or absenteeism. Marketers use Return of investment data to decide the budget. In today's workplace, senior professionals and contributors are leveraging analytics for a better outcome.

Types of Analytics

There are three kinds of analytics

1) Descriptive analytics
2) Predictive analytics.
3) Prescriptive analytics.

Mainly, two kinds of analytical models are used, descriptive and predictive (Kantardzic, 2011) by the organization.

In simple words, descriptive analytics describes what has happened in the past, whereas predictive analytics predicts what will happen in the future.

Descriptive models produce patterns that explain or generalize the intrinsic structure, relations, and interconnectedness of the mined data (Peng, Kou, Shi & Chen, 2008). Predictive models frequently apply supervised learning functions to estimate dependent variables based on the features of related independent variables (Hand et al., 2001). For example, a sales report of a company, say Samsung Mobile. This report will tell you how many handsets of Samsung mobile were sold, where they were sold, and at what price and maybe other information related to models, colors, location-wise, and so on. All such information will come from the data. All you are doing is slicing and dicing the data, observing and look at it from different angles and dimensions, etc. and interpret it. You do not need to be statistical expert, as minimal statistics are involved in descriptive analytics, although it is a potent tool because it provides information about the past. In contrast, a business owner's/professional/corporates primary concern is the future. If I run an institution, I want to predict how many students will be joining, and which course would be preferred. If I am a hotelier, I want to know how many bookings I will make in the holiday season. This is where predictive analytics comes in.

When we are identifying patterns in historical data, it is called Predictive analytics. Once data is analyzed, then using statistics helps in making inferences about the future.

Prescriptive analytics helps to answer questions, what should be done i.e, what prescription should be given. Data-driven decisions can be made by using insights from predictive analytics. In the face of uncertainty, it would allow businesses to make informed decisions. Prescriptive analytics techniques rely on various machine learning strategies. It finds patterns in large datasets by analyzing past decisions and events; the likelihood of different outcomes can be estimated.

Application in Industries

Today Analytics is used across industry verticals for strategic, operational, and tactical decision making. Best of the Industries are using analytics in there business like E-commerce, Retail, Banking, Finance, BFSI, Hotels, Telecom, Manufacturing, Retail, etc. Analytics is fast gaining pace using and finding its usage to drive revenue, reduce churn and improve network performance, operational efficiencies, supplies, forecasting, demand planning, productivity measurement, inventory status, talent acquisition, attrition, headcount management.

Retail

Today's customer is impatient and wants instant gratification and solution with excellent customer service. In order to stay ahead, Retail analytics helps businesses get deep insights into customer behavior by understanding customer's requirements and getting the right customers. Analytics helps in giving information on how to increase Margins at a product-level, Customer profile with Market Basket analysis, ROI of marketing spend, Store wise product-mix, Stock strategy, etc.

E-commerce

Amazon, Flipkart, Alibaba are known name in e-commerce businesses involving the sale of goods and services via electronic means. E-commerce analytics helps organizations convert data to insights, leading to better decision making used for maximizing revenue and profitability.

They create a wealth of information about their website, visitors, and usability to find new customers and increase conversions. They primarily use analytics to understand: Acquisition, Shopping, Purchasing behavior, and Economic Performance.

Healthcare

Analytics has a significant impact on essential business functions. It is used by hospitals and healthcare industry in analyzing medical care, predicting outbreaks of diseases (e.g., COVID Virus effect) and reducing hospital operating costs.

Your approach towards analytics is the key to find real success, and experts say that the best decisions are found in an integrated data environment. The seamless assimilation of relevant internal and external data sources and applications helps relevant internal and external, structured and unstructured, data sources that can be used to deliver insights for strengthening the company in the long term, while also improving customer delight, performance, and profitability with employee satisfaction.

Analytics is not a tool or a technology; rather it is **a** way of thinking and acting. Most organization use analytics in various sub function like Marketing Analytics, Finance Analytics, HR Analytics, Supply chain analytics etc. It not only helps in quick problem resolution but also facilitates decision making at a day-to-day level.

Analytics Tools

There are various free tools and some paid tools available, used by the organization for growth.

Paid tools are SAS, WPS, MS EXCEL, Tableau, Pentaho, Statistica, Qlikview, KISSmetrics, Weka, BigML.

Free Tools are Google Analytics, R, Python, Spotfire.

Recap & Review Section

SUMMARY Chapter 10

The applications of data analytics are endless. Because of Big Data, more and more data is being collected every day and brings new opportunities to apply data analytics. Statistical analysis is the core and heart of data analytics as insights are created from data. For analyzing data, both statistics and machine learning techniques are used. For example, Statistical programming languages such as R or Python are used for data analysis. There are three types of analytics: Descriptive analytics helps answer questions about what happened, Predictive analytics helps in providing an answer to questions about what will happen in the future, and Prescriptive analytics helps answer questions about what should be done. Businesses need to make efficient and effective decisions by using data analytics. Its used in combination to provide a well-rounded understanding of a companies needs and opportunities.

Exhibit 9-Amazon: Using Big Data to Understand Customers

Amazon has thrived by adopting an "everything under one roof" model. However, when faced with such a huge range of options, customers can often feel overwhelmed. They effectively become data-rich, with tons of options, but insight-poor, with little idea about what would be the best purchasing decision for them.

To combat this, Amazon uses Big Data gathered from customers while they browse to build and fine-tune its recommendation engine. The more Amazon knows about you, the better it can predict what you want to buy. And, once the retailer knows what you might want, it can streamline the process of persuading you to buy it for example, by recommending various products instead of making you search through the whole catalogue.

Amazon's recommendation technology is based on collaborative filtering, which means it decides what it thinks you want by building up a picture of who you are, then offering you products that people with similar profiles have purchased.

Amazon gathers data on every one of its customers while they use the site. As well as what you buy, the company monitors what you look at, your shipping address (Amazon can take a surprisingly good guess at your income level based on where you live), and whether you leave reviews/feedback.

This mountain of data is used to build up a "360-degree view" of you as an individual customer. Amazon can then find other people who fit into the same precise customer niche (employed males between 18 and 45, living in a rented house with an income of over $30,000 who enjoy foreign films, for example) and make recommendations based on what those other customers like.

The technical details

Amazon collects data from users as they navigate the site, such as the time spent browsing each page. The retailer also makes use of external datasets, such as census data for gathering demographic details.

Amazon's core business is handled in its central data warehouse, which consists of Hewlett-Packard servers running Oracle on Linux.

Ideas and insights you can steal

Too much choice and too little guidance can overwhelm customers and put them off making purchasing decisions. Recommendation engines simplify the task of predicting what a customer wants, by profiling them and looking what people who fit into similar niches buy. In this way, developing a 360-degree view of your customers as individuals is the foundation of Big Data-driven marketing and customer service.

Multiple Choice Question

SET 1

1) The Process of drawing a numerical description of the extent to which a person or object possesses some characteristics
a. Measurement b. Scaling c. Questionnaire d. Interview

2) The measurement that involves monitoring a respondent's involuntary responses to marketing stimuli via the use of electrodes and other equipment is called:
a. Projective Techniques b. Physiological measures c. Depth Interviews d. Multi-dimensional Scales

3) Validity that reflects whether a scale performs as expected in relation to other variables selected as meaningful criteria
a. Criterion-related Validity b. Content Validity. c. Construct validity d. Convergent Validity

4) Scale that indicates the relative position of two or more objects or some characteristics is called:
a. Ranking Scale b. Ordinal Scale c. Arbitrary Scale d. Ratio Scale

5) The method that involves the selection of items by a panel of judges based on their relevance, the potential for ambiguity, and the level of the attitude they represent
a. Cumulative scale b. Arbitrary Scale c. Item Analysis d. Consensus Scaling

6) Even numbered non-verbal rating scale using single adjectives instead of bipolar opposites is called _______________
a. Semantic Differential b. Multi-dimensional scaling c. Stapel Scale d. Standardised Instruments

7) Instrument's ability to accurately measure variability in stimuli or response is known as
a. Sensitivity b. Practicality c. Generalisability d. Economy

8) 7-point rating scale with end-points having bipolar labels with the semantic meaning is
a. Semantic differential scale b. Constant Sum Scale c. Graphic Rating Scale d. Likert Scale

9) Scale in which the respondent directly compares two or more objects and makes choices among them is
a. Ranking Scale b. Rating Scale c. Graphic Scale d. None of these

10) Scales where the respondent is asked to rate an item in comparison with another item or a group of items with each other based on a common criterion is
a. Method of paired comparison b. Forced Ranking c. Constant Sum Scale d. All of the above

11) Original source from which the researcher directly collects the data that has not been previously collected
a. Primary data b. Secondary Data c. Tertiary Data d. None of these

12) The technique in which the respondents and/or the clients communicate and/or observe by use of the internet
a. Online Ethnography b. Online Interview c. Online Questionnaire d. Online Focus Group

13) The issue to be considered for the secondary data include which of the following:
a. Sufficiency b. Reliability c. Suitability d. All of the above

14) The method that comprises of recording the behavioral pattern of people, things & events contained in a systematic manner to derive information about the area of interest

a. Observation b. Online Survey c. Schedules d. Warranty Cards

15) A technique that allows several members of a hiring company to interview a job candidate at the same time is

a. Panel Interview b. Self-administered interview c. Mail Interview d. Electronic Interview

Ans:

1)a 2)b 3)a 4)b 5)d 6)c 7)a 8)a 9)d 10)b 11)a 12)d 13)d 14)a 15)a

SET 2

1) Which analysis is related to descriptive analysis?
a. Univariate Analysis b. Bivariate Analysis c. Multivariate Analysis d. All of the above

2) Involves the orderly and systematic representation of numerical data in a form designed to elucidate the problem under consideration
a. Coding b. Classification c. Editing d. Tabulation

3) Which frequency expresses the number of items in an interval as a proportion or fraction of the total number of items in the data set?
a. Relative frequency b. Percentage Frequency c. Cumulative frequency d. None of the above

4) Which steps are involved in processing operations of data after collection of data?
a. Coding b. Classification c. Editing d. Tabulation

5) Which is a type of frequency distribution?
a. Continuous or grouped frequency distribution b. Discrete or ungrouped frequency distribution
c. Cumulative Frequency Distribution d. All of the above

6) A distribution where measurements are only approximate and expressed in class intervals ie, within certain defined limits is
a. Continuous Frequency Distribution b. Discrete Frequency Distribution c. Cumulative Frequency Distribution d. All of the above

7) In which Graphical Representation, way of preparing a two-dimensional diagram is in the form of circles?
a. Pie Chart b. Histogram c. Candle Stick d. None of the above

8) In which analysis, when there is a single measurement of each of the n sample objects or where there are several measurements of each of the n observations, but each variable is analyzed in isolation?
a. Univariate Analysis b. Bivariate Analysis c. Multivariate Analysis d. None of these

9) If a group of 'N' observations is arranged in ascending or descending order of magnitude, then the middle value is called
a. Mean b. Median c. Mode d. None of these

10) Which is the type of correlation on the basis of the number of variables?
a. Positive correlation b. Multiple correlation c. Linear Correlation d. Non-linear Correlation

11) Which characteristics come under Karl Pearson's Coefficient of Correlation?
a. Does not tell anything about the cause-and-effect relationship b. Independent of change of origin and scale c) Varies between − 1 and +1 d) All of the above

12) If one knows that the yield and rainfall are closely related, then one wants to know the amount of rain required to achieve a certain production. For this purpose we use analysis
a. Regression Analysis b. Coefficient of Correlation. c. Scatter Plots/Diagram d. None of these

13) When two attributes are present or absent together in the data, and the actual frequency is more than the expected frequency is called
a. Positive Association b. Negative Association c. Independent Association d. None of these

14) Which is not a type of test of significance for small samples?

a. t-test b. z-test c. F-test d. Q-test

15) Which test is the part of the parametric test?

a. Sign Test b. Run Test for Randomness c. Kruskal-Willis Test d. z-test

Ans:

1)d 2)d 3)a 4)c 5)d 6)a 7)a 8)a 9)b 10)b 11)d 12)a 13)a 14)d 15)d

SET 3

1. Define the correct sequence in the stage of sampling:

A	i) Sampling method selection ii) Population definition iii) Sampling frame development iv) Sampling unit specification v) Sample size determination
B	i) Population definition ii) Sampling frame development iii) Sampling unit specification iv) Sampling method selection v) Sample size determination
C	i) Sampling method selection ii) Sampling unit specification iii) Sample size determination iv)Population definition v) Sampling frame development
D	i) Sample size determination ii) Population definition iii) Sampling frame development iv)Sampling unit specification v) Sampling method selection

2) What are the two types of sampling methods?

a. Random or probability sampling and non-probability sampling b. Probability sampling and random sampling c. Probability sampling and non-random sampling d. All of the above

3) A non-probability method applied when the desired sample characteristic is less common:

a. Panel Sampling b. Snowball sampling c. Convenience sampling d. Purposive Sampling

4) The university book shop selects 200 of its more than 8000 customers to participate in a study on service quality in the shop. The book Shop has established a _________ for use in its research.

a. Population b. Field setting c. Dependent grouping d. Sample

5) A good sampling frame must be

a. Relevant b. Complete c. Precise d. All of the above

6) In hypothesis testing, the hypothesis which is tentatively is assumed to be true is called

a. Correct hypothesis b. Null Hypothesis c. Alternative Hypothesis d. Level of Significance

7) When sample size increases, which of the following is correct?

a. The standard error remains unchanged b. The standard error increases c. The standard error declines d. None of the above

8) In case the population has a normal distribution, then the sampling distribution of the mean

a. Has a mean equal to the population mean b. Has normal distribution c. Both a and b d. None of these

9) In which of the following sample designs, maps rather than lists or registers are used as the sampling frame?

a. Simple random sample b. Cluster sample c. Area Sample d. None of these

10) People who are available, volunteer, or can be easily recruited are used in the sampling method called ______.

a. Convenience sampling b. Simple random sampling c. Cluster sampling d. Systematic sampling

11) Selection of a number of participants for research in a way that this number represents the larger total group from which they have been picked up:

a. Research Design b. Sampling c. Data collection d. Random assignment

12) Identify which of the following does not form a random sampling technique?

a. Purposive sampling b. Stratified Sampling c. Cluster sampling d. Systematic sampling

13) Which analysis is the simultaneous analysis of two variables?

a. Univariate Analysis b. Bivariate Analysis c. Multivariate Analysis   d. None of these

14) Which of the following is a probability sampling method?

a. Snow-ball b. Stratified sampling c. Convenience d. Quota sampling

15) Among the following methods, which is the non-probability sampling method?

a. Systematic sampling b. Stratified sampling c. Cluster sampling d. Quota sampling

Ans:

1)b 2)a 3)b 4)d 5)d 6)b 7)c 8)c 9)c 10)a 11)b 12)a 13)b 14)a 15)d

Comprehensive Case Study – Tango Salad Cream

Across the world, the Salad Dressing market is expected to grow at a significant Compound annual growth rate (CAGR) because of the scope and its applications. Consumers have a wide variety of options, and their eating habits are making the food manufacturing industry becoming increasingly competitive.

With growth trends, various organization stakeholders are conducting a SWOT analysis, i.e., Strength, Weakness, Opportunities, and Threat and PORTER's Model for there organization. Various factors manufacturers have identified for customer loyalty, i.e., Choice and price competition.

Description:

There are various dressings available and used by consumers, which include herbs, veggies, fermented foods (vinegar, soy sauce), dry fruits & nuts, and fresh fruit. Various condiments, like cream or ketchup for salads, spices like chilies, and sweets like sugar and molasses, are also used. The blend of yogurt, dill, cucumber, and lemon juice is also used to dress simple salads in various parts of countries based on their culture.

Salad dressing and mayonnaise are consumed by a considerable amount of customers and form the highest consumed category of food dressing worldwide.

A segment of Salad dressing market covers:

- Salad dressing
- Creams
- Sauces (Ketchup, BBQ, Soy, Fish, Chilli, Worcestershire, Mustard)
- Mayonnaise

Food scientists use different kinds of salad dressings and mayonnaise for food preparations. Marketing salad dressing as a finishing sauce or is another trend in the market, and therefore Salad Dressing Market Segment by applications can be divided into Daily Use and Food Industry.

Over the years, consumers have started demanding different types of dressings. To fulfill the changing consumer demands, food manufacturers not only have to innovate, but food products should comprise of organic and natural ingredients for weight loss and health benefits. These trends have positively impacted salad dressing and mayonnaise market.

Tango Salad Cream, one of the best-known brands, was showing signs of losing its 65% of market share. The salad cream as a whole was in decline state. As of 2006, the figure for Tango was 69%, whilst its nearest rival, Kinesse, held only a 21% share.

The move from a plate of salad cream towards nourishment dressings made Tango inspect its items' future.

First Choice was to end the item by and large, while the other was to put fundamentally in serving of salad cream to rethink and restore it. It was expected to engage with entirely different age to buy the product. It was additionally planned to win back the old customers who may have abandoned for different dressings. In 2010 Tango propelled to invest by $6 million in the advertisement, including radio and TV publicity, banners, a dedicated Web webpage, sponsorship sample survey, PR and advertising, and other campaigns.

Every medium used, had the standard binding subject: —

"Taste buds Twisted with 'Tango'"

Tango serving of salad cream was first introduced in 1927. The 1950s and 1960s saw the serving salad cream topping the chart in sales. By 1990 serving salad cream and mayonnaise shared the market similarity in liking and usage. By 1996, mayonnaise was ahead in usage, and by 1999 share of salad cream deals remained at $40million contrasted with $68 million for mayonnaise.

The focus was to market to the age groups of 20-30 yrs to create the feeling of uniqueness beyond dressing cream.

The research concentrated on two key zones:

* to create a sense of individuality for the age group of the 20's and 30's and
* identifying perception about Tango.

Existing data depicted that Tango salad cream had an advantage over its rival mayonnaise in that it was thought to add flavor, not just moisture. The essence of salad cream is bold taste and changes the flavor of food. The Tango name was associated with two significant values; first being quality and second being trustworthiness. The product had its own individuality in terms of its sharp and tangy taste. The target group of 20+ years of age had the shopping habits of being spontaneous; they have fewer budget constraints than homemakers and buy what looks attractive on the day. Food basics such as pasta, bread, and potatoes are flavored with whatever inspires them doing shopping from the supermarket.

Acting on their findings from data, Tango decided that it would not alter the product itself, but would repackage it in new designer reusable bottles, with bright, eye-catching labels. In the future, Salad Cream's focus is to be no longer associated with just salads, but with any foods chosen by the customer. Its promotion campaign should be designed and to be reintegrated such that anyone could use Salad Cream with any food they liked.

The advertising team had built its marketing objectives after the research of 15 days. The next step was to decide the most effective way to promote the Tango with a new advertising campaign launched on TV in May 2012. Humorous advertisements with a teaser campaign were designed to illustrate how the young could turn dull food into a tasty treat/party/celebration.

The Sales and market share both improved drastically, yet the goal was still to be achieve.

Tango needs further information and inputs for the growth......

Case Questions

Chapter 1

1. Based on the case, narrate the problems facing the management of Tango.
2. Tango has specific issues that require your expert advice. What kind of research would you suggest to be carried out by Tango? Give reasons for your suggestion.
3. While pursuing this further, what criteria do you advocate for the researcher to keep in mind?

Chapter 2

1. Formulate a research proposal for Tango and include all the relevant sections.
2. Based on the steps defined in the chapter, convert the decision into a research problem.
3. List all the elements of the problem identified by you in terms of variables and the coordinates of the study.
4. Is it possible to formulate a theoretical model or framework to assist in developing a perspective on the research problem? Why/why not?

Chapter 3

1. What data sources can be used here? List with supporting logic for each.
2. Can an exploratory research design be advocated in the above situation? How?
3. How can we conduct a descriptive research study? Which one would you recommend; cross-sectional or longitudinal? Why?
4. Formulate three research questions for the problem and develop the working hypotheses for the same.

Chapter 4

1. What government publications would you recommend? Can the information be obtained from alternative methods/sources? How?

2. What internal data sources would you recommend data being collected from? Justify the relevance of each source.
3. Take a random sample of 30 college students who use Tango and have an almost similar background. Divide the 30 students randomly into two groups. Members of these two groups should be invited to a party. Both groups have been given free samples. In the first group, a discount scheme for purchasing Tango is introduced, whereas, in the second one, no such scheme is introduced. After 15 days of the party, keep a record of the orders placed by students in the two groups.
(a) Define the dependent and independent variables. What could be the extraneous variables in such an experiment?
(b) Comment on the internal and external validity of the experiment.
(c) How would you be able to conclude the results of the study
4. Can any of the projective techniques be used for the study? Design some questions based on the technique identified by you.

Chapter 5

1. Design a sampling plan for the study. Elucidate
2. If, in a survey, it is found that 70 percent of Hostellers (total hostel occupants – 800 boys and 150 girls) uses Tango, how large a sample should be taken with a confidence level of 90 percent with an error margin not exceeding 7 percent.
3. What would be the appropriate sampling design? Justify your answer.

Chapter 6

1. For measuring the constructs under study, design ten questions using:
(a) Itemized rating scales
(b) Graphic rating scales
(c) Rank order scales
(d) Comparative rating scales
2. Out of the Likert scale, semantic differential scale, and constant sum rating scale, which scale would you advocate to be used for the study? Why?
3. Can you use observations for your study? What would be the limitations/shortcomings of this method?

Chapter 7

Collect a sample from 4 sections from your college who use Tango, Heinz, Viba, Kissan, Cremica in most preferred to least preferred order. Calculate the average score for each individual brand-wise. Divide this perception score into two groups for male and female separately, or two different age brackets; those having a score from 1 to 3 are to be treated as having poor perception and those having a score above 3 are to be treated as having a favorable perception. Now cross-tabulate this with the demographic variables as given in the case. Analyze and interpret your results.

Chapter 8

1. Based on the inputs, design two questionnaires for the two identified groups a) Teenagers b) Senior citizen. Would you devise different questions for the group's understudy? Why/why not?

2. Suppose there are 125 consumers and 50 non-consumers of Tango. You can compute the average perception scores corresponding to each of the consumer and non-consumer. Attempt to test the following hypothesis:

"Is there any difference in the common perception of the consumer and non-consumer of Tango"?

3. You have computed the average perception scores for the consumers/non-consumers of Tango. Treat this score as a dependent variable and use each of the demographic variables like age group, education group, and household income as independent variables. Carry out an ANOVA – one-way analysis of variance and interpret the results.

4. In the case of a significant result, what further analysis would be carried out?

Chapter 9

1. Write a report based on the entire process of research and analysis carried out for all the eight chapters.

2. What recommendations do you have for Tango to improve its sales?

Statistical Formula

Common Symbols Used in Statistics

Sign	Meaning
N	Population
'n'	Sample Size
df	degree of freedom
σ^2	Variance
σ	Standard deviation (population)
S	Standard deviation (sample)
μ	Population mean
x	Mean (sample)
P	Population correlation coefficient
R	Sample correlation coefficient
Z	Normal deviate
α	Alpha
β	Beta
$\tilde{x}$	Median
Mo	Mode
$\chi^2(k)$	Chi

Test	Formula
Z-test for a population mean (variance known)	$$Z = \frac{\bar{x} - \mu_0}{\sigma/\sqrt{n}}$$
Z-test for two population means (variances known and equal)	$$Z = \frac{(\bar{x}_1 - \bar{x}_2) - (\mu_1 - \mu_2)}{\sigma\left(\dfrac{1}{n_1} + \dfrac{1}{n_2}\right)^{\frac{1}{2}}}$$
Z-test for two population means (variances known and unequal)	$$Z = \frac{(\bar{x}_1 - \bar{x}_2) - (\mu_1 - \mu_2)}{\left(\dfrac{\sigma_1^2}{n_1} + \dfrac{\sigma_2^2}{n_2}\right)^{\frac{1}{2}}}$$
t-test for a population mean (variance unknown)	$$t = \frac{\bar{x} - \mu_0}{s/\sqrt{n}}$$
t-test for two population means (method of paired comparisons)	$$t = \frac{(\bar{x}_1 - \bar{x}_2) - 0}{s/n^{\frac{1}{2}}}$$
t-test of a correlation coefficient	$$r = \frac{\sum(x_i - \bar{x})(y_i - \bar{y})}{\left[\sum(x_i - \bar{x})^2 \sum(y_i - \bar{y})^2\right]^{\frac{1}{2}}}$$
t-test of a regression coefficient	$$t = \frac{bs_x}{s_{y \cdot x}}(n - 1)^{-\frac{1}{2}}$$
χ^2-test for a population variance	$$s^2 = \frac{\sum(x_i - \bar{x})^2}{n - 1}$$

The Kolmogorov–Smirnov test for goodness of fit	$D = |F - S_n|$
The Wilcoxon–Mann–Whitney rank sum test of two populations	$R^1 = n(N + 1) - R$

Glossary

Accuracy: In survey research, accuracy refers to the match between a sample and the target population. It also indicates how close a value obtained from a survey instrument or assessment is to the actual (true) value.

Action Research: The action research conducted to solve problems, inform policy, or improve the way that issues are addressed and problems solved. There are two broad types of action research: participatory action research and practical action research.

Administrative Data: Administrative data are used in support of the operations and service delivery of government departments and other organizations. Examples are information about individual children, families, and/or providers of early care and education and other family benefits and services. The data are collected and maintained primarily for administrative (not research) purposes.

Alpha Level: The probability that a statistical test will find significant differences between groups (or find significant predictors of the dependent variable), when in fact there are none. This is also referred to as the probability of making a Type I error or as the significance level of a statistical test. A lower alpha level is better than a higher alpha level, with all else equal.

Alternative Hypothesis: The experimental hypothesis stating that there is some real difference between two or more groups. It is the alternative to the null hypothesis, which states that there is no difference between groups.

Analysis of Variance (ANOVA): A statistical test that determines whether the means of two or more groups are significantly different.

Average: A single value (mean, median, mode) which represents a typical, normal, or middle value of a set of data.

Bar Chart/Graph: Bar charts are used by researchers to visually represent the frequencies or percentages with which different categories of a variable occur. They are most often used when describing and comparing the percentages of different groups with a specific characteristic. For example, the percentages of boys and girls who participate in team sports. However, they may also be used when describing averages such as the average time boys and girls spend per week participating in team sports. A bar is drawn for each of the groups along the horizontal axis, and the height of the bar corresponds to the frequency or percentage with which the characteristic occurs (vertical axis).

Bayesian Statistics: Bayesian statistics is a general approach to estimating population parameters (characteristics) that uses both information about the prior distribution of the parameter of interest along with new evidence (likelihood function). In Bayesian statistics, the posterior probability distribution is the probability distribution once all information is taken into account.

Bell-Shaped Curve: A curve characteristic of a normal distribution, which is symmetrical about the mean and extends infinitely in both directions. The mean (average) is always in the center of the bell or normal curve. One-half of the data points are to the left, and one half is to the right of the mean.

Beta Level: The probability of making an error when comparing groups and stating that differences between the groups are the result of the chance variations when, in reality, the differences are the result of the experimental manipulation or intervention. Also referred to as the probability of making a Type II error.

Bias: Influences that distort the results of a research study.

Bimodal Distribution: A distribution in which two scores or values are the most frequently occurring. Interpreting the average of a bimodal distribution is problematic because the data are not normally distributed. Identifying bimodal distributions is done by examining a frequency distribution or by looking at indices of skew or kurtosis, which are frequently available with statistical software packages.

Case Study: An intensive investigation of the current and past behaviors and experiences of a single person, family, group, or organization.

Categorical Data: Variables with discrete, non-numeric, or qualitative categories (e.g., gender or marital status). The categories can be given numerical codes, but they cannot be ranked, added, multiplied, or measured against each other. Also referred to as nominal data.

Census: The collection of data from all members, instead of a sample, of the target population.

Central Limit Theorem: A mathematical theorem is central to the use of statistics. It states that for a random sample of observations from any distribution with a finite mean and finite variance, the mean of the observations will follow a normal distribution. This theorem is the main justification for the widespread use of statistical analyses based on the normal distribution.

Central Tendency: A measure that describes the average characteristic. The three main measures of central tendency are mean, median, and mode.

Chi-Square: A statistic that is used when testing for associations between categorical or non-numeric variables. It is also used as a goodness-of-fit test to determine whether data from a sample come to form a population with a specific distribution.

Chi-Square Test: There are several different Chi-square tests in statistics. One of the more commonly used is the Chi-square test of independence. It is used to determine if there is a statistically significant association between two categorical variables. The frequency of each category for one variable is compared across the categories of the second variable. It is the null hypothesis for this test that there is no association between the two variables (i.e., the distributions of the two variables are independent of each other). The alternative hypothesis is that there is an association. For example, a Chi-square test could be used to examine whether parents' decision to delay their children's entry to kindergarten (delay vs. do not delay) is statistically significantly associated with their child's sex (male vs. female).

Cluster Analysis: Cluster analysis is a multivariate method used to classify a sample of subjects (or objects) in such a way that subjects in the same group (called a cluster) are more similar (e.g., in terms of their personal attributes, beliefs, preferences) to each other than to those in other groups (clusters).

Cluster Sampling: A type of sampling method where the population is divided into groups, called clusters. Cluster designs are often used to control costs. For example, researchers first randomly select clusters of potential respondents, and then from within these clusters, respondents are selected at random. The researcher randomly selects several counties or groups of counties and then draws a random sample of households from within the selected counties. Cluster sampling is often used in education and early childhood research. Researchers sample schools/programs, and then students/children enrolled in the selected schools/programs. Clustered sampling designs necessitate the use of special variance estimation techniques.

Codes: Values, typically numeric that are assigned to different levels of variables to facilitate analysis of the variable. For example, codes such as strongly disagree=1, disagree=2, agree=3, and strongly agree=4 are often assigned.

Coding: The process of assigning values, typically numeric values, to the different levels of a variable. The process of assigning values to behaviors observed in parent-child interactions and assigning numeric values to responses to open-ended survey questions are examples of coding.

Coefficient of Determination: A coefficient, ranging between 0 and 1 that indicates the goodness of fit of a regression model.

Cognitive Interviewing: A research method used to pretest interview questions or items on a questionnaire. Cognitive interviews collect information on how respondents answer questions, their interpretation of the questions asked, and their reasons for responding in a particular way. Additional verbal information is collected to evaluate whether respondents understand a question or series of questions if the response categories are appropriate, and if the question is measuring the construct, it was designed to measure. The information gathered from the cognitive interview is used to make adjustments to questions before they are administered to the full sample.

Confidence Interval: A range of estimated values is the best guess as to the true population's value. Confidence intervals are usually calculated for the sample mean. In behavioral research, the acceptable level of confidence is usually 95%. Statistically, this means that if 100 random samples were drawn from a population and confidence intervals were calculated for the mean of each of the samples, 95 of the confidence intervals would contain the population's mean. For example, a 95% confidence interval for IQ of 95 to 105, indicates with 95% certainty that the actual average IQ in the population lies between 95 and 105.

Confidence Level: The percentage of times a confidence interval covers the true population value. If the confidence level is .95, this means that if a researcher were to sample a population 100 times randomly, 95% of the time, the estimated confidence interval for value would contain the population's true value. In other words, the researcher can be 95% confident that the confidence interval contains the true population value.

Confidentiality: The protection of research subjects from being identified. A common standard in social science research is that records or information used for research should not allow participants to be identified and that researchers should not take any action that would affect the individual to whom the information pertains.

Consistency: Answers to a set of questions are consistent if they do not contain any logical contradictions.

Constant: A value that stays the same for all the units of analysis. For instance, in a research study that explores fathers' involvement in their children's lives, gender would be constant, as all subjects (units of analysis) are male.

Construct: A construct or concept is a theoretical creation that cannot be directly observed but can be measured using one or more indicators or tests. Examples of constructs in early care and education research include classroom quality, professional development, reading and math achievement, and socio-emotional development.

Construct Validity: The degree to which a variable, test, questionnaire, or instrument measures the concept it hopes to measure. For example, if a researcher is interested in the theoretical concept of "marital satisfaction," and the researcher uses a questionnaire to measure marital satisfaction, if the questionnaire has construct validity, it is considered to be a good measure of marital satisfaction.

Continuous Variable: A variable that, in theory, can take on any value within a range. The opposite of continuous is discrete or categorical, which can have only a particular set of values. For example, a person's height could be 5 feet 2 inches, 5 feet 2.2 inches, 5 feet 2.22 inches, and so one, and thus it is continuous. The type of child care setting where a child spends the greatest number of hours each week (e.g., center-based care, relative and nonrelative care) is a discrete or categorical variable.

Control: The processes of making research conditions uniform or constant, so as to isolate the effect of the experimental condition. When it is not possible to control research conditions, statistical controls often will be implemented in the analysis.

Control Group: In an experiment, the control group does not receive the intervention or treatment under investigation. This group may also be referred to as the comparison group.

Control Variable: A variable does not interest a researcher; rather, it interferes with the statistical analysis. In statistical analyses, control variables are held constant, or their impact is removed to analyze better the relationship between the outcome variable and other variables of interest. For example, if one wanted to examine the impact of education on political views, a researcher would control income in the statistical analysis. This removes the impact of income on political views from the analysis.

Convenience Sampling: A sampling strategy that involves using the most easily accessible/ approachable people (or objects) to participate in a study. This certainly is not a random sample, and the results therefore, cannot be generalized & applied to individuals who were not a part of the research.

Correlation: The degree of association of 2 variables. Variables are said to be positively correlated if they tend to show an increase at the same time. As an illustration, height, and weight can be said to be positively correlated because as height increases, there is an increase in unweighting too. Variables are negatively correlated if, as one increases, the other decreases. For example, a number of police officers in a community and crime rates are negatively correlated because as the number of police officers increases the crime rate tends to decrease.

Correlation Coefficient: A measure of the degree of relation between 2 variables. A correlation coefficient is always between − 1 and +1. If the correlation coefficient is between 0 and +1, then the variables are positively correlated. If the correlation coefficient is between 0 and − 1, then the variables are negatively correlated.

Cross-Tabulation: A method to display the relationship between two categorical variables. A table is created with the values of one variable across the top and the values of the second variable down the side. The number of observations that correspond to each cell of the table is indicated in each of the table cells.

Data: Information collected through surveys, interviews, or observations. Statistics are produced from data, and data must be processed to be of practical use.

Data Analysis: The process by which data are organized in an attempt to understand the patterns of behavior within the target population. The term Data analysis envelops many forms of analysis, such as content analysis, cost-benefit analysis, path analysis, regression analysis, etc.

Data Collection: It includes the observation, measurement, and recording of the information under a research study.

Data Reduction: Data reduction is the process of transforming numerical or alphabetical digital information into a corrected, ordered, and simplified form. The basic concept is the reduction of large amounts of data down to the meaningful parts.

Deduction: The process of reasoning from the more general to the more specific.

Deductive Method: A method of study that begins with a theory and the generation of a hypothesis that can be tested through the collection of data, and ultimately leads to the confirmation (or lack thereof) of the original theory.

Degrees of Freedom: The number of independent units of information in a sample involved in the calculation of a statistic or the estimation of a parameter. The degrees of freedom limits the number of variables that can be included in a statistical model. Models with similar explanatory power, but more degrees of freedom are generally preferred because they offer a simpler explanation.

Delphi Survey Method: The Delphi survey method is used when a researcher is interested in collecting opinions from a group of experts but wishes to limit the undue influence of participants upon one another (the members of the group are unknown to each other and questionnaires are often distributed via email). Both qualitative and quantitative research methods can be used in a Delphi survey. The experts answer questions in two or more rounds. After each round, a summary of the experts' responses is prepared by a member of the research team with expertise in the area(s) of inquiry, and the questions the group is asked to respond to are revised.

Dependent Variable: The outcome variable. A dependent variable is something that depends on other factors. Researchers often try to find out what causes changes in the dependent variable. For example, in a study of factors associated with children's scores on standardized tests, children's scores would be the dependent variable.

Descriptive Statistics: Basic statistics used to describe and summarize data. Descriptive statistics generally include measures of the average values of variables (mean, median, and mode) and measures of the dispersion of variables (variance, standard deviation, or range).

Direct Observation: A method involving the accumulation of data through close visual inspection of a natural setting. Direct observation does not involve actively engaging members of a setting in conversations or interviews. Rather, the direct observer strives to be unobtrusive and detached from the setting.

Discrete Variables: A variable that can assume only a finite number of values; it consists of separate, indivisible categories. The opposite of discrete is continuous. For example, in a specified time period, a child's biological parents either live in the same household as the child, or they do not. In contrast, a child's height could be 2 feet 1 inch, 2 feet 1.1 inches, 2 feet 1.11 inches, and so on; thus, it is a continuous variable.

Dispersion: In statistics, dispersion refers to the spread of a variable's values. Techniques that are used to describe dispersion include range, variance, standard deviation, and skew.

Distribution: The frequency with which values of a variable occur in a sample or a population. To graph a distribution, first, the values of the variables are listed across the bottom of the graph. The number of times the value occurs is listed up on the side of the graph. A bar is drawn that corresponds to how many times each value occurred in the data. For example, a graph of the distribution of women's heights from a random sample of the population would be shaped like a bell. Most women's height is around 5'4" This value would occur most frequently, so it would have the highest bar. Heights that are close to 5'4", such as 5'3" and 5'5" would have slightly shorter bars. More extreme heights, such as 4'7" and 6'1" would have very short bars.

Effect Size: A measure of the strength of the effect of the predictor (or independent) variable on the outcome (or dependent) variable. It is a measure of the magnitude or size of the difference between two or more groups. There are many ways to calculate an effect size, but one of the more common is to express differences in outcomes between groups in standard deviation units. For example, a researcher finds a significant difference in the math scores of African American and Hispanic first graders. Hispanic scores are 5 points higher than those of African American children. The effect size for this 5 point difference would be equal to .33 standard deviation given that the overall standard deviation of the assessment is 15 (effect size = score difference/standard deviation of assessment).

Error: The estimation of the difference between the actual observed data value and predicted or estimated data value. Predicted or estimated data values are calculated in statistical analyses, such as regression analysis.

Error Term: The part of a statistical equation that indicates what remains unexplained by the independent variables. The residuals in regression models.

Estimated Sampling Error: When researchers use a sample to predict the true but unknown value of a population, there is the risk of being wrong. They decide ahead of time how much error in their prediction is acceptable. For example, when predicting the percentage of children enrolled in home-based child care, a researcher could select a sample size with an error of +/ − 5 percentage points.

Estimation: The process by which data from a sample are used to indicate the value of an unknown quantity in a population.

Explanatory Analysis: A method of inquiry that focuses on the formulating and testing of hypotheses. For example, instead of, or in addition to, describing Black and White differences in the reading and math skills of preschool children, the analysis focuses on testing whether factors that may contribute to these differences (e.g., resources available to children at home and in their child care programs) are in fact associated with those differences.

Exploratory Factor Analysis: A multivariate statistical method used to uncover the underlying structure (factors) of a set of variables. It is a form of factor analysis whose goal is to identify the underlying relationships between measured variables. It is especially useful when there is no hypothesis about the underlying structure of the data and the pattern of relationships between the variables. Researchers often use exploratory factor analysis to develop scales from multiple surveys or assessment items. It is a way of reducing the number of items to be used in an analysis to a smaller and more meaningful set.

Extraneous Variable: A variable that interferes with the relationship between the independent and the dependent variables and needs to be controlled for in some way.

Factor Analysis: A form of multivariate analysis that includes a large number of variables or objects and aims to identify a smaller number of factors that are more understandable. It is a way of identifying patterns in the data and overlap in the patterns. There are two basic types: exploratory factor analysis and confirmatory factor analysis. Definitions of the two types can be found elsewhere in the glossary.

Focus Group: An interview conducted with a small group of people, all at one time, to explore ideas on a particular topic. The goal of a focus group is to uncover additional information through participants' exchange of ideas.

Frequency Distribution: The frequency with which values of a variable occur in a sample or a population. To graph a distribution, first, the values of the variables are listed across the bottom of the graph. The number of times the value occurs is listed up on the side of the graph. A bar is drawn that corresponds to how many times each value occurred in the data.

Heterogeneity: The degree of dissimilarity among cases with respect to a particular characteristic.

Histogram: A visual presentation of data that shows the frequencies with which each value of a variable occurs. Each value of a variable type is displayed along the bottom of a histogram, and a bar is drawn for each value. The height of the bar relates to the frequency of occurrence of that value.

Hypothesis: A statement that predicts the relationship between the independent (causal) and dependent (outcome) variables.

Hypothesis Testing: Statistical tests to determine whether a hypothesis is accepted or rejected. In hypothesis testing, two hypotheses are used: the null hypothesis and the alternative hypothesis. The alternative hypothesis is the hypothesis of interest; it generally states that there is a relationship between two variables. The null hypothesis states the opposite that there is no relationship between two variables.

In-depth Interviewing: A research method in which face-to-face interviews with respondents are conducted using open-ended questions to explore topics in great depth. Questions are often customized for each interview, and topics are generally probed extensively with follow-up questions.

Independence: The lack of a relationship between two or more variables. For example, annual snowfall and the Yankee's season record are independent, but annual snowfall and coat sales are not independent.

Independent Variable: The variable that the researcher expects to be associated with an outcome of interest. For example, if a researcher wants to examine the relationship between parental education and children's language development, parent education (years of schooling or the highest level of education completed) is the independent variable. Sometimes this variable is referred to as the treatment variable or the causal variable.

Inductive Method: A method of study that begins with specific observations and measures, from which patterns and regularities are detected. These patterns lead to the formulation of tentative hypotheses, and ultimately to the construction of general conclusions or theories

Informal Interview: An informal or conversational interview is a type of qualitative interview where the researcher begins by engaging an individual in a conversation. As the conversation unfolds, the researcher formulates specific questions, often spontaneously, and begins asking them informally. It is used when the researcher wants maximum flexibility to pursue topics and ideas as they emerge during the interview.

Internal Validity: The extent to which researchers provide compelling evidence that the causal (independent) variable causes changes in the outcome (dependent) variable. To do this, researchers must rule other potential explanations for the changes in the outcome variable.

Interval Scale: It is a scale of measurement where the distance between two adjacent units of measurement remains the same, but the zero points become arbitrary. Scores, as such on an interval scale, are open to addition or subtraction but cannot be meaningfully multiplied or divided.

Interval Variable: A variable wherein the distance between units is the same, but the zero points are arbitrary.

Kurtosis: A statistic that measures how outlier-prone a distribution is. The kurtosis value of a normal distribution is 0. If the kurtosis differs from 0, then the distribution produces outliers that are either more extreme (positive kurtosis) or less extreme (negative kurtosis) than are produced by the normal distribution.

Level of Significance: See the significance level.

Likert Scale: A Likert Scale is a type of rating scale used to measure attitudes, values, or opinions about a subject. Survey respondents are asked to express their level of agreement or disagreement with a set of statements. The responses are scaled and later summed to give a cumulative measure of attitudes or opinions about a topic.

Linear Regression: A statistical technique used to find a linear relationship between one or more (multiple) continuous or categorical predictor (or independent) variables and a continuous outcome (or dependent) variable.

Literature Review: A comprehensive survey is encompassing the available literature on a topic. It is generally presented at the beginning of a research paper and explains how the researcher arrived at his or her research questions.

Mean: A descriptive statistic is measuring the central tendency. To calculate the mean, all values of a variable are added, and the sum is divided by the number of values. For example, if the age of the respondents in a sample were 21, 35, 40, 46, and 76, the mean age of the sample would be $(21+35+40+46+76)/5 = 43.6$

Median: A descriptive statistic used to measure the central tendency. The median is the value that is the middle value of a set of values. 50% of the values lie above the median, and 50% lie below the median. For example, if a sample of individuals ages 21, 34, 46, 55, and 76, the median age is 46.

Methodology: The principles, procedures, and strategies of research used in a study for gathering information, analyzing data, and drawing conclusions. There are broad categories of methodology, such as qualitative methods or quantitative methods, and there are particular types of methodologies, such as survey research, case study, and participant observation, among many others.

Mode: A descriptive statistic is measuring central tendency. It is the value that occurs most frequently in the data. For example, if survey respondents are ages 21, 33, 33, 45, and 76, the modal age is 33.

Multiple (Linear) Regression: A statistical technique applied to study the linear relationship between an outcome (dependent) variable and several predictor (independent) variables.

Nominal Scale: A scale that classifies elements into mutually exclusive categories depending upon defined features but without numeric value.

Non-parametric Statistics: Non-parametric statistics refer to the group of statistical methods that require fewer assumptions about the distribution of the data. For example, non-parametric tests of significance, such as the Chi-square test dos, do not require the data to fit a normal distribution. Non-parametric statistical meth

Normal Curve: The bell-shaped curve that is formed when data with a normal distribution are plotted.

Normal Distribution: Distribution of the frequency of data points in a bell shape. In a normal distribution, one-half of the data points (e.g., scores on a standardized test) are above, and one half are below the mean or median of the full set of data. The further a data point is from the mean/median, the less likely it is to occur. Furthermore, the closer it is, the more likely it is to occur. The normal distribution Exhibits important mathematical properties that are necessary for performing most statistical tests (e.g., data have a normal distribution or are at least symmetrical with half of the values above and half below the mean or median).

Null Hypothesis: This hypothesis specifies that there is no difference between groups. The alternative hypothesis states that there is some real difference between two or more groups.

Observation Unit: The actual unit observed during a study in order to measure something about it. In child care and early education research, typical observation units include programs and schools, classrooms and teachers, children and their parents.

One-Way ANOVA: A test of whether the mean for more than two groups is different. For example, to test whether the mean income is different for individuals who live in France, England, or Sweden, one would use a one-way ANOVA.

Ordinal Data: Data that are categorical, but that can also be ranked (ordered). However, the distance between the categories is not known and may not be equal. For example, parents might rate their satisfaction with their child's child care provider as "very dissatisfied," "dissatisfied," "satisfied," and "very satisfied." using numerical values of 1, 2, 3, and 4, respectively. A parent with a satisfaction score of 1 is more dissatisfied than a parent with a score of 2, but not necessarily twice as dissatisfied. Furthermore, the difference between scores of 1 and 2 and scores of 3 and 4 are not necessarily the same.

Ordinal Scale: A scale that involves classification and labeling of data into mutually exclusive categories depending upon features that are ranked or ordered with respect to each other. The equal differences between numbers, however, do not reflect an equal magnitude of difference.

Outlier: An observation made in a data set that differs more than the other observations in the set. The data point is either unusually larger or unusually smaller as compared to the other data points.

P-Value: The probability that the results of a statistical test were due to chance. A p-value greater than .05 is usually interpreted to mean that the results were not statistically significant. Sometimes researchers use a p-value of .01 or a p-value of .10 to indicate whether a result is statistically significant. The lower the p-value, the more rigorous is the criteria for concluding significance.

Paired Comparison Method: The paired comparison method is a research design that yields scores based on respondents' ratings of pairs of items. For example, a respondent is presented with a set of binary items and asked to indicate which of the choices he/she prefers or is more applicable.

Paired T-Test: This test, which is sometimes called the dependent sample t-test, is usually used to determine whether the mean difference between two sets of observations for the same subjects is zero. In a paired sample t-test, each participant or subject is measured twice. It is often applied to establish whether an intervention impacted a change in some of the characteristics of respondents (e.g., respondents' math knowledge). To perform a paired t-test, respondents' math knowledge would be measured prior to the intervention; then, the intervention would be performed (e.g., teaching a class on math), then the respondent's math knowledge would be measured after the intervention. The change from before to after the intervention is used to assess whether the intervention was successful.

Parameter: In statistics, a parameter is a characteristic of a population. It is a numerical quantity that tells us something about a population and is distinct from a statistic, which is a characteristic of a sample.

Participant Observation: A field research method whereby the researcher develops knowledge of the composition of a particular setting or society by taking part in the everyday routines and rituals alongside its members. A principle goal of participant observation is to develop an understanding of a setting from a member's perspective, which may be accomplished through both informal observations and conversations as well as in-depth interviews.

Pearson's Correlational Coefficient: Usually denoted by r, this is a measure of the degree of association between 2 variables. Pearson's correlation coefficient is applied when both variables are continuous. The coefficient might value, ranging from − 1 to +1. If the coefficient lies between 0 and +1, the variables are positively said to be correlated, which means they would tend to increase (or decrease) in tandem. For example, children's height and weight are generally positively correlated because as height increases, so does weight. If the coefficient is between 0 and − 1, the variables are negatively correlated, which means as one increases, the other decreases. For example, the number of days children are absent from school is negatively correlated with children's reading and math test scores because as the number of days children are absent increases, their scores on reading and math tests decrease (when lower test scores indicate poorer performance in reading and math). The closer the coefficient is to either − 1 or +1, the stronger the association between the two variables. This is also called a Product Moment Correlation.

Percentage: A proportion of times 100.

Percentile: The percent of observations in a sample that have a value below a given score.

Pilot Study: A small scale research study that is conducted prior to the larger, final study. The pilot study allows the researcher a chance to identify any issues with the proposed sampling scheme, methodology, or data collection process. These studies are very useful in accessing the strengths and weaknesses of a potential study. For example, a pilot study might be conducted in a small sample of early childhood classrooms to identify potential difficulties when videotaping teacher-child interaction. Findings from the pilot are used to find solutions to these problems and to modify the approach that will be used in the larger study.

Poisson Distribution: A distribution that describes the number of events that occur in a certain time interval or spatial area. For example, the number of child care arrangements during a given period of time.

Poisson Regression: Poisson regression is a form of regression analysis used to model or predict outcomes (Y variables) that are numerical counts (e.g., number of days a student is absent from school). It is best used for counts of rare events (e.g., number of unexcused absences over the school year).

Population: In statistics, the population includes all members of a clearly defined group. The population can be comprised of a group of individuals (e.g., all children ages zero to 5) or of organizations (e.g., all programs providing early childhood education to 3 − and 4-year old children). Samples are drawn from the population, and the statistical results that are derived from random samples can be used to estimate characteristics of the whole population.

Probability: A description of the likely occurrence of a particular event. Probability is conventionally expressed on a scale from 0 to 1; a rare event has a probability close to 0, a very common event has a probability close to 1.

Probability Sampling: A random sample of population ensuring that each member of the population has had an equal chance of being selected in the sample.

Purposive Sampling: A sampling strategy in which the researcher selects participants that are considered to be typical in a wider population. Since the sample is not randomly selected, the degree to which they actually represent the population being studied is unknown.

Qualitative Research: A field of social research that is carried out in naturalistic settings and generates data largely through observations and interviews. Compared to quantitative research, which is principally concerned with making inferences from randomly selected samples to a larger population, qualitative research is primarily focused on describing small samples in non-statistical ways.

Quartiles: A set of three values that divides the total frequency into four equal parts.

Quasi-Experimental Research: Research in which individuals cannot be assigned randomly to two groups, but some environmental factor influences who belongs to each group. For example, if researchers want to look at the effects of smoking on health, they cannot ethically assign individuals to a group that smokes and a group that does not smoke. Researchers might rely on some environmental factors, for example, an ad campaign that discourages smoking, to examine changes in health following the campaign. The theory behind quasi-experimental designs is that following an environmental intervention, individuals' characteristics play a smaller role in determining whether they smoke or do not smoke, and thus membership in these groups is closer to random assignment.

Questionnaire: A survey document containing questions used to gather information from individuals under research

Quota Sampling: A non-probability sampling method in which a given number of subjects are selected from a specific group or groups. For example, a researcher might design a sample of 200 parents of newborns that sets quotas of 100 mothers and 100 fathers. Widely used in opinion polling and market research.

Random Sampling: A sampling technique in which individuals are identified from within a population at random. Every individual has an equal chance of being chosen because the individual is selected purely by chance.

Random Selection: Random selection refers to the process of selecting individuals (schools, programs, classrooms) from the population to participate in a study. In random selection, each individual is chosen by chance and has a fixed and known probability of selection into the study sample.

Random Variable: A variable that numerically measures some characteristics of a sample or population (e.g., height). The value of the variable will differ depending on which individual is measured (i.e., people are of different heights). The variable is said to be random because the variation in the value of the variable is due, at least in part, to chance (i.e., some people are just taller than other people).

Range: A measure of how widely the data (values) for a specific variable are dispersed or spread. The larger the range, the more dispersed the data. The range is derived by subtracting the value of the lowest data point from the highest data point. For example, in a sample of children between the ages of 2 and 6 years, the range would be four years. When reporting the range, researchers typically report the lowest and highest value (Range = 2 – 6 years of age).

Rank Order Scale: A set of behaviors, objects, or statements presented to research subjects which they are asked to rank (put them in some order) according to a specific criterion (e.g., size, importance, frequency). For example, parents may be presented with a number of factors that may affect their choices of child care and asked to order them in their importance.

Rating Scale: A rating scale is a measuring instrument for which judgments are made in order to rate a subject against a specific scale level with regard to an identified characteristic or characteristics.

Ratio: A ratio is a relationship between the number in two groups of objects. It tells us how many times the number in the first group contains the number in the second group. For example, if we have ten elementary schools and three middle schools in a community, the ratio of elementary to middle schools is 10 to 3 (10:3) or roughly three elementary schools to every one middle school.

Ratio Scale: A scale in which the difference between the values is equivalent, and it has a fixed zero point. The values on the scale can be meaningfully measured against each other.

Regression Analysis: A statistical technique that establishes a relationship between the dependent (outcome) variable and one or more independent (predictor) variables (see linear, logistic, and multiple regression).

Regression Coefficient: A coefficient that is calculated for each independent (predictor) variable. The regression coefficient indicates the extent of the dependent (outcome) variable will change, on average, with each change in the independent variables.

Reliability: Reliability is the degree to which an assessment or other measurement tool produces stable and consistent results. Reliability indicates the degree to which a measure will provide the same result for the same person, across similar groups, and irrespective of who administers the assessment or collects the data. A reliable measure will always give the same result on different occasions, assuming that what is being measured has not changed during the intervening period.

Research Question: A clear statement in the form of a question of the specific issue that a researcher wishes to answer using data from one or more sources. Examples include: Do children who attend center-based early care, and education programs have stronger academic and social skills than children who are cared for in a home-based child care setting? Does the Black-White achievement gap narrow or widen as children move through the elementary school grades?

Research Method: The approaches, tools, and techniques that researchers use to study a problem. These methods include laboratory experiments, field experiments, surveys, case studies, focus groups, ethnographic research, action research, and so forth.

Respondent: The person who responds to a survey questionnaire and provides information for analysis.

Sample: A group that is selected from a larger group (the population). By studying the sample, the researcher tries to draw valid conclusions about the population.

Sample Size: The number of subjects in a study. Larger samples are preferable to smaller samples, all else being equal.

Sampling: The process of selecting a subgroup of a population (i.e., sample) that will be used to represent the entire population.

Sampling Bias: Distortions occur when some members of a population are systematically excluded from the sample selection process. For example, if interviews are conducted over the phone, only individuals with telephones will be in the sample. This could produce bias if the researcher intends to draw conclusions about the entire population, including those with a phone and those without a phone.

Sampling Design (Sample Design): The part of the research plan that specifies the method of selection and the number of individuals or organizations (schools, programs) who will be selected and asked to participate in the study. The sampling design (sample design) specifies the target population, the frame or list from which cases from that population will be selected, the approach that will be used to select the sample members (simple random sampling, stratified sampling, cluster sampling, or combinations of these), the number of sample units to be selected to achieve the study objectives.

Sampling Distribution: The frequency with which data values appear in the sample. The sampling distribution can be characterized by the mean and the variance of the sample.

Sampling Error: This is the error that occurs because all members of the population are not sampled and measured. The value of a statistic (e.g., mean or percentage) calculated by using different samples drawn from the same population will not always be the same. For example, if several different samples of 5 people are drawn at random from the U.S. population, the average income of the five people in those samples will differ. (In one sample, Bill Gates may have been selected at random from the population, which would lead to a very high mean income for that sample.) It is not incorrect to have sampling error, and in fact, statistical techniques take into account that sampling error will occur.

Sampling Frame: A list of the entire population eligible to be included within the specific parameters of a research study.

Scale: A group of survey questions that measures the same concept. For example, a researcher may be interested in individuals' gender role attitudes and use several questions to determine their attitudes. This group of questions makes up a gender role attitude scale.

Scaled Score: A mathematical transformation of a raw score so that scores can be compared across individuals and over time. The purpose of scaled scores is to report scores for all study participants on a consistent scale.

Scatter Plot: A display of the relationship between two quantitative or numeric variables. A scatter plot shows the value of one variable plotted against the value of another variable.

Selection Bias: Error due to systematic differences in the characteristics of those who are selected for a study and those who are not. For example, if a survey about parental attitudes toward child care, in general, is administered by randomly selecting parents whose children are enrolled in a university child care center, only parents whose children attend that program will be included in the sample. This will exclude parents whose children go to other child care centers and parents whose children are cared for in other types of settings (e.g., home-based child care). It may also result in a sample of parents who have children of a specific age. The result of these exclusions is to introduce selection bias. Selection bias is a very serious problem in research, and it can negate research findings if the researcher does not carefully address the issue within the research study.

Semantic Differential Scale: A type of rating scale is designed to measure the meaning of things or objects. In research, a semantic differential scale or a series of such scales are often used to measure attitudes. Participants are presented as an object, event, or concept that is followed by a series of opposing adjectives separated by a sequence of unlabeled categories. Participants are asked to indicate their position relative to the two adjectives. For example, teachers may be asked how they would rate the professional development opportunities at their program using bipolar adjectives such as good-bad, interesting-boring, relevant-irrelevant.

Significance Level: The probability of rejecting the null hypothesis in a statistical test when it is true (Type I Error). The significance level is set before the statistical analysis is undertaken. A commonly used significance level is .05, which indicates a 5% risk of concluding that a difference exists (group means are different or a correlation is different from zero) when there is no actual difference. If a statistical test (e.g., t-test or F-test) indicates that the chances of finding the observed results by chance are unlikely (p < .05), the findings are classified as statistically significant.

Simple Linear Regression: A statistical technique that measures the relationship between a dependent (outcome) variable and one independent (predictor) variable.

Simple Random Sampling: The basic sampling technique where a sample under study is selected from a larger group (a population). Each individual is chosen purely by chance and has an equal chance of being covered in the sample.

Skewness: The tendency of the distribution of a statistic to depart from symmetry. Distributions can be skewed with more values to the right (positive) or to the left (negative). When the distribution is skewed, the median is a better measure of the midpoint of the distribution than the mean.

Snowball Sampling: A strategy adapted to draw a sample for research in which study participants give the researcher referrals to other individuals who fit the study criteria. Snowball samples cannot be generalized to the population because they are not selected randomly. Snowball samples are usually used to investigate groups that have some unique, rare, or unusual quality and groups where members know each other through an organization or common experience. For example, snowball samples might be used to identify parents who homeschool their children and attend local support groups.

Standard Deviation: A measure of variability or dispersion in a set of data. The standard deviation (SD) is derived as the square root of variance. It is calculated on the basis of the difference between each individual observation and the mean observation.

Standard Error: A measure of the extent to which the sample mean fluctuates. The standard error is the standard deviation (SD) of the sample means. Conceptually, the standard error of the mean would be calculated by selecting multiple samples at random from a population, calculating the mean for each of the samples, then calculating the standard deviation of these sample means. Because only one sample is generally drawn from a population for a research study, the standard error is calculated by dividing the sample deviation by the number of observations in the sample. Generally speaking, the larger the sample, the smaller the standard error.

Standardization: A scale transformation procedure that involves manipulating data from different types of scales so that they can then be compared. It consists of subtracting the sample mean for the scale from each score on the scale and dividing by the scale's standard deviation.

Standardized Test: A standardized test is a test that is administered, scored, and interpreted in the same way for all test-takers. Scores on the standardized test are often, but not always, created so that an individual's test score or the mean of a group's test scores can be compared to the mean of the population of individuals of the same age or grade. The Peabody Picture Vocabulary Test (PPVT) and the Woodcock-Johnson III Tests of Achievement are examples of commonly used standardized tests in early childhood research.

Statistic: A measure of the characteristics of a sample (e.g., the mean is a statistic that measures the average of a sample). It gives an estimate of the same value for the population from which the sample was selected.

Statistical Analysis: Statistical analysis is the process of collecting, examining, manipulating, summarizing, and interpreting quantitative or numerical data for the purpose of identifying patterns, trends, and relationships in the data. It can include the use of descriptive statistics such as percentages, means, variances, and correlations and/or the use of inferential statistics such as t-tests, chi-square tests, regression, and analysis of variance (ANOVA).

Stratification: Grouping the study population into subgroups by their homogenous characteristics before sampling so as to improve the representativeness of a sample.

Stratified Sampling: A statistical method for testing different theorized models, including the "structures" of relationships among the observed indicators and their underlying concepts.

Stratified sampling: A type of probability sample involving dividing unit population of interest into mutually exclusive and collectively groups or strata. A probability sample (e.g., simple random sample) is then drawn from each stratum. Stratified sampling provides greater precision than a simple random sample of the same size. It is also used to ensure the representation of different groups (e.g., programs in different regions of the country) in the sample.

Structured Interview: The interviewer asks respondents the same questions using a predetermined series of interview questions. Deviations from the predetermined series of questions are not allowed in the interview process.

Structured Observation: Structured observation (or systematic observation) is a data collection method in which researchers gather data by observing the actions of individuals alone or during interactions with others. Research specifies in advance which behaviors are to be observed and how they are to be classified. Observers typically note the occurrence and frequency of the behaviors. Structured observations often are conducted in laboratory settings, but can be done in natural settings (e.g., children's homes) as well.

t Distribution: The t distribution (or Student's t-distribution) is a theoretical probability distribution that is similar to a normal distribution (i.e., it is asymmetrical bell-shaped distribution). It is used when testing differences in group means for small sample sizes (sample n < 30).

T-Test: A statistical test used to compare the means of two samples (independent t-test), the means of one sample at different times (paired sample t-test), or the mean of one sample against a known mean (one-sample t-test). The test is appropriate for small sample sizes (less than 30), although it is often used when testing group differences for larger samples. It is also used to test whether correlation and regression coefficients are significantly different from zero.

Two-Tailed Test: A type of test that is used when a researcher is not sure about whether the independent (predictor) variable has a positive or negative effect on the dependent (outcome) variable, or whether they mean for group A is greater than or less than the mean for group B. A two-tailed test is also used when comparing the mean for a sample to a given value of x when the mean can be either greater than or less than x. By contrast, a one-tailed test will test either that the mean is significantly greater than x or that the mean is significantly less than x, but not both.

Type I Error: An error that occurs when a researcher arrives at a conclusion that a statistically significant difference between two groups or the relationship between two variables exists (based on the analysis of the sample), when in fact the difference or relationship does not exist in the population from which the sample was selected (null hypothesis is true). The amount of risk of a Type I Error a researcher is willing to accept is decided upon prior to analyzing the data. This probability of a Type I Error is also called a significance level.

Type II Error: An error that occurs when a researcher concludes that no significant relationship between two variables (based on analysis of sample data) when in fact the relationship does exist in the population from which the sample was drawn. The probability of not making a type II error is also called the power of a statistical test.

Unbiased: A statistic that is free of systematic bias. Systematic bias occurs when the recorded data from a sample is systematically higher or lower than the true data values within the population. Systematic bias can occur as a result of sampling bias or measurement bias. Sampling bias is an error that appears in sampling when some subgroup within the target population is unintentionally left out of the sampling process. Measurement bias is an error in data collection when some occurrence distorts the responses in the same way (e.g., a test is administered in a noisy classroom). Bias is a major error in data collection and must be handled through a researcher's careful attention to sources of bias.

Unstructured Interview: An interview in which the researcher is free to ask open-ended questions. The researcher tries to give respondents the liberty to talk openly on a topic and to influence the direction of the interview. There is no pre-established plan around the specific information to be gathered from these types of interviews.

Validity: The degree to which data and results are accurate reflections of reality. Validity refers to the concepts that are investigated, the people or objects that are studied; the methods by which data are collected; and the findings that are produced.

Variable: A measurable attribute or characteristics of a person, group, or object that varies in a sample under investigation (e.g., age, weight, IQ, child care type). In research, variables are typically classified as dependent, independent, intervening, moderating, or as control variables.

Variance: A commonly used measure of dispersion for variables. The variance is calculated by squaring the standard deviation. The variance is based on the square of the difference between the values for each observation and the mean value.

Weighted Score: A score adjusted by such factors as the importance of the attribute assessed or the reliability and validity of the assessment under which the score has been derived, or a combination of all such factors.

Z Score: A score that is produced by subtracting the mean value from individual data value and dividing by the standard deviation. This standardizes data values and allows for individual data values from different distributions (distributions with different means and standard deviations) to be compared.

z Test: A statistical test used to compare the means of two independent samples or the mean of one sample against some fixed value. The test assumes that the populations from which the samples are drawn are normally distributed. It is used when testing differences for large samples (over 30 observations) and for smaller samples in which the variance of the population is known.

Recommended Reading

The following text book may be used for more in-depth study on the topics dealt within this book.

Allen, T. Harrell, New Methods in Social Science Research, New York: Praeger Publishers, 1978.

Anderson, H.H., and Anderson, G.L., An Introduction to Projective Techniques and Other Devices for Understanding the Dynamics of Human Behaviour, New York: Prentice Hall, 1951.

Asthana, H. S. and Bhushan, B. (2007). Statistics for Social Sciences (with SPSS Application). Prentice Hall of India, New Delhi.

Bellenger, Danny N., and Greenberg, Barnett A., Marketing Research—A Management Information Approach, Homewood, Illinois: Richard D. Irwin, Inc., 1978.

Berenson, Conard, and Colton, Raymond, Research and Report Writing for Business and Economics, New York: Random House, 1971.

Best, John W., and Kahn, James V., "Research in Education," 5th Ed., New Delhi: Prentice-Hall of IndiaPvt. Ltd., 1986.

Boot, John C.G., and Cox, Edwin B., Statistical Analysis for Managerial Decisions, 2nd ed. New Delhi:McGraw-Hill Publishing Co. Ltd., (International Student Edition), 1979.

Bowley, A.L., Elements of Statistics, 6th ed. London: P.S. King and Staples Ltd., 1937.

Chawla, D and Sondhi, N., Research Methodology: Concepts and Cases, Second Edition, Vikas' Publishing, 2015.

Elhance, D. N., and Elhance, V. (1988). Fundamentals of Statistics. Kitab Mahal, Allahabad

Kerlinger F.N, Foundation of Behavioural Research, Surjeet Publication, Delhi

Garret, H. E. (2005). Statistics in Psychology and Education. Jain publishing, India.

Kothari. C.K, Research Methodology: New Age International (P) Ltd Publishers,India, 1990

Nagar, A. L., and Das, R. K. (1983). Basic Statistics. Oxford University Press, Delhi.

Sani, F., and Todman, J. (2006). Experimental Design and Statistics for Psychology. Blackwell Publishing U.K.

Wilkinson T.S & Bhanarkar, Methodology and techniques of Social Research, Himalaya Publishing House, Mumbai

Michael V.P. Research Methodology in Management, Himalaya Publishing House, Mumbai

Yale, G. U., and M.G. Kendall (1991). An Introduction to the Theory of Statistics. Universal Books, Delhi.

Sample Research Paper

1 – Paper Based on Primary Research

Paper Published in International Journal of Advanced Research in ISSN: 2278-6236

Impact Factor: 5.313

http://www.garph.co.uk/IJARMSS/Apr2015/15.pdf

Citaton: Walia, A., Bansal, R., & Mittal, S. (2015). Relationship between leadership style and followership style. International Journal of Advanced Research in Management and Social Sciences, 4(4), 170 – 181.

Relationship Between Leadership Style And Followership Style

Anubha Walia* Dr. Rashmi Bansal** Dr. Sanjiv Mittal***

Abstract: A study was conducted to measure the relationship between leadership styles and followership style (i.e. Independent thinking and Active Engagement) using 79 usable questionnaires obtained from employees who are working in Delhi NCR, showed important findings by using Pearson Correlation analysis: first, the most preferred style of leadership is Participative leadership style; second, Exemplary style of followership is most preferred followership style; third, Participative leadership is not significantly correlated with Independent & Critical thinking.

Keywords: Participative leadership; Followership style, Active engagement, Independent thinking.

I. INTRODUCTION

Various studies describe the characteristics of leadership behavior where it emphasizes more on the type of relationship between leaders and followers in organizations (Bass, Avollo, 1991, 1993, Howell, Avolio, 1993, Schriesheim et al., 1999). The leadership has been an important topic in the organizational for many decades. The literature reveals a wide range of definitions (House and Aditya, 1997; Yun et al., 2006; Alas, Tafel, and Tuulik, 2007). Stogdill (1974) asserted that there are nearly as many definitions of leadership as there are people trying to define it. The paper identified that Participatory style was the most preferred style. In 1939, a group of researchers xxxxxxxxxxxxxx xxxxxxxxxxxxxxxxxxxxxxxxxxxxxxxxxxxxxxxxxxxxxxxxxxxxxxxxxxxxxxxxxxxxxxxxxxxxxxxxxxxx

II. OBJECTIVES

This study has four major objectives: First, to measure most preferred style of leadership. Second, to measure most preferred style of followership. Third, to measure the significant relationship between preferred leadership style and the independent thinking. Xxxxxxxxxxxxxxxxxxxxxxxxxxxxxxxxxxxxxxxx xxxxxxxxxxxxxxxxxxxxxxxxxxxxxxxxxxxxxxxxxxxxxxxxxxxxxxxxxxxxxxxxxxxxxxxxxxxxxxxxxxxx

III. LITERATURE REVIEW

We have long known that followers and followership are essential to leadership. However, despite the abundance of investigations into leadership in organizational studies (Yukl, 2012), until recently little attention has been paid to followership in leadership research (Baker, 2007; Bligh, 2011; Carsten, Uhl-Bien, West, Patera, & McGregor, 2010; Kelley, 2008; Sy, 2010). When followers have been considered, they have been considered as recipients or moderators of the leader's influence (i.e., leader-centric views, Bass, 2008) or as "constructors" of leaders and leadership (i.e., follower-centric views, Meindl, 1990; Meindl, Ehrlich, & Dukerich, 1985). The study of followers as key components of the leadership process through their enactment of followership has been largely missed in the leadership literature. xxxxxxxxxxxxxxxxxxxxxxxxxxxxxxxxxxxxxxxxxxxxxxxxxxxxx xxxxxxxxxxxxxxxxxxxxxxxxxxxxxxxxxxxxxxxxxxxxxxxxxxxxxxxxxxxxxxxxxxxxxxxxxxxxxxx

HYPOTHESIS

Ho: there is no significant relationship between preferred leadership style and independent and critical thinking. Ho:

there is no significant relationship between preferred leadership style and active engagement. xxxxxx xxxxxxxxxxxxxxxxxxxxxxxxxxxxxxxxxxxxxxxxxxxxxxxxxxxxxxxxxxxxxxxxxxxxxxxxxxxxxxx

IV. METHODOLOGY

This study allowed the researchers to integrate the leadership research literature, interview, pilot study and the actual survey as a main procedure to collect data. The use of such methods may gather accurate, less biased and high quality data (Cresswell, 1998, Sekaran, xxxxxxxxxxxxxxxxxxxxxxxxxxxxxx xxxxxxxxxxxxxxxxxxxxxxxxxxxxxxxxxxxxxxxxxxxxxxxxxxxxxxxxxxxxxxxxxxxxxxxxxxxxxxx

V. FINDINGS

Participant characteristics 1-Majority of respondents were male (98 per cent), 2-Leaders' experience varies between 4 to 40 years 3-Reportees i.e. followers' experience varies between 1 year to 22 years 4 – 31% of the Respondent worked more than 10years Validity and reliability analyses for measurement scales Table II shows the results of validity and reliability analyses for measurement scale. The original survey questionnaires consisted of 32 items, which related to 3 variables: autocratic (4 items), delegative (4 items), participative leadership (4 items), Independent and critical xxxxxxxx xxxxxxxxxxxxxxxxxxxxxxxxxxxxxxxxxxxxxxxxxxxxxxxxxxxxxxxxxxxxxxxxxxxxxxxxxxxxxxx

VI. DISCUSSION AND FINDINGS

With respect to the robustness of the research methodology, the measurement scales used in this study had exceeded an acceptable standard of validity and reliability analyses. This situation could lead to the production of accurate and reliable findings. Regarding practical contributions, the findings of this study can be used as a guideline to improve leadership behavior in the dynamic organizations. Based on exemplary follower style, uses both independent & critical thinking skills and active participation skills. They bring up new ideas with correct information, having vision, creating relationships with other xxxxxxxxxxxxxxxxxxxxxxxxxxxxxxxxxxxxxxxxxxxxxxxxxxxxxxxxxxxxxx xxxxxxxxxxxxxxxxxxxxxxxxxxxxxxxxxxxxxxxxxxxxxxxxxxxxxxxxxxxxxxxxxxxxxxxxxxxxxxx

VII. CONCLUSION AND FUTURE SCOPE

The current research and practice within the organizational leadership models needs to consider dependent thinking and passive engagement with other leadership style including participative leadership style based on industry. This study further suggests that the ability xxxxxxxxxxxxxxxxxxxx xxxxxxxxxxxxxxxxxxxxxxxxxxxxxxxxxxxxxxxxxxxxxxxxxxxxxxxxxxxxxxxxxxxxxxxxxxxxxxxxxxxxxxx

VIII. REFERENCES

[1] Avolio, B.J., Bass, B.M., Jung, D.I. (1995). Construct validation and norms for the multifactor leadership questionnaire (MLQ – Form 5X). Center for leadership studies, Binghamton University, State University of New York

[2] Bass, B.M. (1985). Leadership and performance beyond expectations, New York: Free Press [3] Bass, B.M. (1990). Bass and Stogdill's handbook of leadership: Theory, research, and xxxxxxxxxxxx xxxxxxxxxxxxxxxxxxxxxxxxxxxxxxxxxxxxxxxxxxxxxxxxxxxxxxxxxxxxxxxxxxxxxxxxxxxxxxxxxxxxxxx

2 – Paper Based on Secondary Research

Paper Published in Think India in ISSN: 0971-1260

Impact Factor: 6.2

https://journals.eduindex.org/index.php/think-india/article/view/8234

Citaton: Azam, M. K., & Uppal, M. K. (2019). "The Evolving Paradigms Of Customer Relationship Management – -A Review Based paper". Think India Journal, 22(3), 294-305. Retrieved from https://journals.eduindex.org/index.php/think-india/article/view/8234

The Evolving Paradigms Of Customer Relationship Management – A Review Based paper

Dr. Khalid Azam* Manpreet Kaur Uppal**

Abstract:

This papers focusses on the purpose of bringing out the working & implementation issues in CRM . The paper takes into account fundamental concerns of CRM including gathering customer information for devising marketing strategies, offering customer enhanced satisfaction through delivering customised offers & moving on to achieving long term relationships with customers assuring life time value benefits. However, the paper also examines pitfalls in the form of customer perspectives of 'fair' , 'trust' and 'credibility'. The concluding part highlights challenges posed in the event of enhanced customer information availability over the social media and the marketers dilemma to offer customisation & yet be 'fair'.

1. Introduction

This paper intends to examine and review at length and the existing literature on Customer Relationship Management and by way of that, attempt to bring forth the successes & failures of CRM. More specifically, it is focussed on identifying failures in CRM and its implementation . Finally it attempts to evaluate one to one customer xxxxxxxxxxxxxxxxxxxxxxxxxxxxxxxxxxxxxxxxxxxxxxx xxxxxxxxxxxxxxxxxxxxxxxxxxxxxxxxxxxxxxxxxxxxxxxxxxxxxxxxxxxxxxxxxxxxxxxxxxxxxxxxxxxxxxxxxx

2. Understanding the key elements of successful CRM implementation

Traditional marketing focussed on the myopic approach by focussing more on the procession oriented strategies thereby trying to cut costs and gain market leadership by way of the lowest price offering. Over the years however, research suggests that the became redundant and non sustainable because low cost operational techniques could be replicated and list the competitive advantage. xxx xxxxxxxxxxxxxxxxxxxxxxxxxxxxxxxxxxxxxxxxxxxxxxxxxxxxxxxxxxxxxxxxxxxxxxx xxxxxxxxxxxxxxxxxxxxx

3. Improvements in CRM

The competitiveness amongst marketers has increased manifold and the adoption of technology to support immediate and uniquely addressed communication has further aggravated the completion. The individually directed communication whether by way of textual delivery in the form of a personalised email or comment or by way of pickets and vides over social media have estranged the landscape due to quicker and customised customer connect (Greenberg, 2009; Quinton and Harridge-March, 2010). xxxxxxxxxxxxxxxxxxxxxxxxxxxxxxxxxxxxxxxxxxxxxxxxxxxxxxxxxxxxxxxxxxxxxxxxx xxxxxxxxxxxxxxxxxxxxxxxxxxxxxxxxxxxxxxxxxxxxxxxxxxxxxxxxxxxxxxxxxxxxxxxxxxxxxxxxxxxxxxxxx

4. The changing role of the new age customer

While customer has always been the focus of a forms products strategy, the core driver to profitability, not mush has been done by firm owners in the past to involve active customer engagement into product or services design related research. It is only very recently that thee has been a sea change in the firms customer driven perspective(Gummesson, 2002; Peppers and Rogers, 2010). xxxxxxxxxxx
xxxxxxxxxxxxxxxxxxxxxxxxxxxxxxxxxxxxxxxxxxxxxxxxxxxxxxxxxxxxxxxxxxxxxxxxxxxxxxxxxxxxxxxxxxxx

5. CRM conceptualisation:

While literature and researches have contributed a great deal to the the multiple meanings of CRM ,there remains an ambiguity over its clear conceptualisation (Payne and Frow, 2005) and segregation from Relationship Marketing, its predecessor. This lack of clarity of concept & constituents makes CRM adoption a problem (Reinartz et al., 2004; Harker and Egan, 2006; xxxxxxxxxxxxxxxxxxxxxxx
xxxxxxxxxxxxxxxxxxxxxxxxxxxxxxxxxxxxxxxxxxxxxxxxxxxxxxxxxxxxxxxxxxxxxxxxxxxxxxxxxxxxxxxxxxxx

6. Elements of customer – company relationship

For CRM to be effective, a good relationship between company & customer are integral (Boulding et al., 2005; Frow and Payne, 2009). The customer – firm bond is comparable toxxxxxxxxxxxxxxxxx
xxxxxxxxxxxxxxxxxxxxxxxxxxxxxxxxxxxxxxxxxxxxxxxxxxxxxxxxxxxxxxxxxxxxxxxxxxxxxxxxxxxxxxxxxxxx

7. Data Handling

(Privacy & Confidentiality) While earlier studies hint at maintaining a customer – firm parity relationship with equal value trade offs to both, Boulding et al. (2005) differs and observes that extensive research on CRM may be more driving more value for the firm & less for xxxxxxxxxxxxxxx
xxxxxxxxxxxxxxxxxxxxxxxxxxxxxxxxxxxxxxxxxxxxxxxxxxxxxxxxxxxxxxxxxxxxxxxxxxxxxxxxxxxxxxxxxxxx

8. Intra Customer Relationship Paradox

With the CRM philosophy of knowing more about the customers and develop individually scenic and customised offerings, marketers today have arrived at a paradox stemming out of being ignorant to customer vs customer discrimination, Nguyen (2011). While this policy of favouring a few xxxxx
xxxxxxxxxxxxxxxxxxxxxxxxxxxxxxxxxxxxxxxxxxxxxxxxxxxxxxxxxxxxxxxxxxxxxxxxxxxxxxxxxxxxxxxxxxxx

9. Future direction of CRM implementation

Researchers Peppers and Rogers (2010) have stated that too many marketers have gone into adapting CRM without getting into the spadework on it. They believe that CRM is all about training xxxxxx
xxxxxxxxxxxxxxxxxxxxxxxxxxxxxxxxxxxxxxxxxxxxxxxxxxxxxxxxxxxxxxxxxxxxxxxxxxxxxxxxxxxxxxxxxxxx

10. Conclusion:

This research paper is a compilation of extensive reviews on multiple researches on CRM and basis the review it boils around the major issue if trying to create a mutually rewarding win win symbiotic relationship   xxxxxxxxxxxxxxxxxxxxxxxxxxxxxxxxxxxxxxxxxxxxxxxxxxxxxxxxxxxxxxxxxxxxxxxxxxxxxxxxxxxxx
xxxxxxxxxxxxxxxxxxxxxxxxxxxxxxxxxxxxxxxxxxxxxxxxxxxxxxxxxxxxxxxxxxxxxxxxxxxxxxxxxxxxxxxxxxxx

References

[1] Adams, J.S. (1965), "Inequity in social exchange", in Berkowitz, L. (Ed.), Advances in Experimental Social Psychology, Vol. 2, Academic Press, New York, NY, pp. 267-99.

[2] Ballester, E.D. and Aleman, J.L.M. (2001), "Brand trust in the context of consumer loyalty", European Journal of Marketing, Vol. 35 Nos 11/12, pp. 1238-58.

xxxxxxxxxxxxxxxxxxxxxxxxxxxxxxxxxxxxxxxxxxxxxxxxxxxxxxxxxxxxxxxxxxxxxxxxxxxxxxxxxxxxxxxxxxxx

www.ingramcontent.com/pod-product-compliance
Lightning Source LLC
Chambersburg PA
CBHW051435250726
48655CB00001B/81